ELIZABETHAN WINCHESTER

ELIZABETHAN
WINCHESTER

——————————⭐——————————

TOM ATKINSON, M.A.
City Archivist
Winchester

FABER AND FABER
24 Russell Square
London

First published in mcmlxiii
by Faber and Faber Limited
24 Russell Square, London W.C.1
Printed in Great Britain
by Ebenezer Baylis and Son Limited
The Trinity Press, Worcester, and London

© *Tom Atkinson*
1963

'Whoso desireth to discourse in a proper manner concerning Corporated Towns and Communities must take in a great variety of matter, and should be allowed a great deal of Time and Preparation. The subject is extensive and difficult. In England much hath been said by Writers to Puzzle and entangle, little to clear it'.

Madox's Firma Burgi.

Contents

Illustrations

MAP

Foreword

The purpose of this book is to present a picture, as accurate and complete as available material will allow, of the City of Winchester during the reign of Queen Elizabeth I. With the object of ensuring accuracy, the contents have been based upon the authentic and contemporary documents which have survived the passage of time, while legend and conjecture, as far as possible, have been avoided. But the picture can by no means be complete in every detail, for the records of the City have suffered many vicissitudes, chiefly through neglect and removal from place to place. Undoubtedly the collection was at one time large and tolerably well preserved, but many valuable documents have been destroyed by damp, mice and fire, and others have been borrowed and never returned. In 1877, under the provisions of the Royal Commission on Historical Manuscripts, the municipal records of Winchester were examined. They were found in a confused mass, bundled together without care or method, in the large room over the Westgate, where they had been deposited after lying for many years under the roof of the old Guildhall. The Commission's report, after admitting that the examination was merely a cursory one, stated that the records of any great antiquity were not so numerous as might have been expected, nor were they of any marked importance.

At the present time this would not be accepted as a fair statement, for many documents have come to light since the report was published. Amongst these are the more ancient of the thirty-three Charters and Royal Grants (with the exception of that of King John) dating from the year 1155 (Henry II) to the year 1760 (George III), and a complete series of the Books of Ordinances covering the period 1552 to 1835. In addition there are numerous Account Rolls, Subsidy Rolls, Court Rolls and miscellaneous manuscripts relating to the thirteenth and following centuries. Since 1884 provision has been made for the better preservation and systematic arrangement of the City archives. More recently, renewed interest in them has resulted in the examination of neglected bundles of documents and papers brought from the Westgate many years ago, and from these further interesting manuscripts have been recovered. Though there are large gaps in the series of manuscripts, particularly those dating from the medieval period, the Winchester records are of great historical value and deserve greater care and attention than they received before the present century.

With the approach of the Tudor period more documentary evidence becomes available, and the records covering the latter half of the sixteenth century are sufficient to provide glimpses of the numerous and varied activities in which the citizens were engaged during that interesting and important stage of English history.

The various sources from which material has been gleaned are indicated in the footnote references. In planning the arrangement of the material it has been thought advisable to select certain topics which seem to stand out most clearly, and devote a chapter to each one, rather than attempt to compile a year by year commentary on local events covering the whole of the forty-five years of Elizabeth's reign. The first chapter deals with the tarrage roll, and this reveals both topographical and historical data which can give, especially to the reader who is not already acquainted with Winchester, a background for the subjects discussed in subsequent chapters. Following this, consideration is given to local government by means of an account of the work done by the Burgh-mote as a legislative body, and by a summary of the Charters through which the City derived its powers to act as a self-governing community. Then come four chapters dealing with administration, in which it is shown how the ordinances enacted by the Burgh-mote and various Acts of Parliament were put into effect by the Mayor and his 'brethren' and other officers of the City. The duties connected with the various offices are described and examples given of the manner in which the City officers exercised their executive powers and dealt with finance and taxation. The preservation of law and order and the settlement of disputes are matters which seem to follow naturally, since they also were in the hands of the Mayor and his brother officers; therefore, a chapter is devoted to the City Courts, where many cases concerning debt, fraud, assault and breaches of local ordinances came up for judgment. These bring to light many details of the business life and occupations of the inhabitants, together with the regulations governing the marketing of commodities and the associations or incorporations of craftsmen and traders, which are dealt with in the following chapter on Trade. At the City Court of Record there were presented those persons who were charged with failing to observe the ordinances devised to overcome the insanitary conditions which resulted from the congestion of human beings and animals within the walled and confined city; and so a chapter dealing with Health is included, and this reveals some of the duties and obligations of each householder. But there were other duties, dating from earlier times, connected with the defence of the City, and these are described in the next chapter, where there is also a brief account of the royal castle which overlooked Winchester from Norman to Stuart times. The penultimate chapter tells of religious affairs, not because religion became important only in the closing stages of Elizabeth's reign, but because throughout the whole of the reign it played a most vital part in both private and public life. Its treatment at this point should, therefore, provide a review of Elizabethan Winchester from this particular angle. Finally there is a short general summary. By the arrangement of the chapters in the manner thus outlined, it is hoped that a certain degree of continuity has been obtained.

Foreword

The text of the book includes many extracts from the old manuscripts, and in some chapters these are both frequent and lengthy. Their use in this way has been deliberate, for it has been a constant aim to allow those portions of the original documents, which were considered suitable, to speak for themselves. Written in the language of Elizabethan times, not only have they a quaintness which one may find interesting and amusing, but they preserve something of the rich flavour and robust atmosphere which were characteristic of those days. It has been felt that no paraphrase could so adequately convey to the reader the Elizabethan scene.

T.A.

CHAPTER I

The Pattern

What was Winchester like in its physical aspect three or four hundred years ago? What was the impression which the stranger gained in those days when he first looked down on the City, say, from St. Giles' Hill? The answer is to be found in Speed's pictorial map of 1615 which, though somewhat inaccurate in its proportions and considerably lacking in detail, shows the general pattern and lay-out of the City. It gives the picture of the rectangular walled site stretching from the River Itchen, as it had done from Roman times, up the sloping ground to the west for a distance of half a mile, with the castle forming a bastion in the south-west corner. The main feature of the map is the chief thoroughfare, the High Street, reaching, as it does today, from the Eastgate to the Westgate, and thus bisecting the City. From this, to the north and to the south, branch off the other streets which through the centuries have, for the most part, maintained their original courses.

It is true that all manner of ancient relics in the shape of coins, tessellated pavements, burial urns and pottery of many periods have been dug up from time to time, indicating the foundations and sites of former habitations and other buildings, but if the detail of the general pattern of the City is to be filled in with any degree of accuracy then one must search for documentary evidence.

It is in the Winton Domesday Book, compiled between the years 1107 and 1119, that one finds the first attempt to make a survey of Winchester, and this is not complete since the inquiry dealt only with the King's lands within the City, and the ecclesiastical possessions, which were considerable, were excluded. Nevertheless, the actual survey is extremely useful and interesting, and from it much may be learnt concerning the highways and byways of the City and the life and occupations of the inhabitants.

A second survey, however—that taken by order of Bishop Henry of Blois in 1148—is far more helpful, for it is comprehensive and shows that, with one exception, the streets of Norman times were the same both in name and location as in Elizabeth's reign and that the total number of dwellings was about 1,200. If one can assume that there was an average of $4\frac{1}{4}$ persons per house, the population of Winchester at that time would have been 5,100 persons.[1]

Later, when one comes to the fifteenth and sixteenth centuries, and up to the time when Speed produced his map, there is ample written evidence to allow one to follow the general plan of the City, to go through it street by street, not neglecting the lanes and alleys, and to fill in the details of tenements, cottages, inns, churches, gardens and many vacant plots.

It is recorded that in 1575 John White, who together with John Potinger had nine years previously been appointed joint Town Clerk of Winchester, was excused the offices of High Bailiff and Low Bailiff which as a freeman of the City he could be called upon to hold, in consideration 'of hys travayle hereafter to be taken in and aboute the newe makinge of the tarrage for the which he hath noe fee certeyne'.[2] John White's

---

[1] Some difficulty has been experienced in deciding the ratio between the number of households and the total population. J. S. Furley, *City Government*, and J. W. F. Hill, *Tudor and Stewart Lincoln*, adopt 5 as the multiplier, but J. C. Russell, *British Medieval Population*, and J. H. Thomas, *Town Government in the XVIth Century*, use $3\frac{1}{2}$. Recently, J. Z. Titow, *Economic History Review*, XIV, 2, 1961, p. 218, considering that $3\frac{1}{2}$ is too low, suggests that 4.3 would be more accurate. The writer has modified this figure to $4\frac{1}{4}$, the mean between $3\frac{1}{2}$ and 5.

[2] First Book of Ordinances, MS., f. 184, Winchester City Archives.

1. Initial letter 'E' of Queen Elizabeth's Charter of 1587

2. Speed's map of Winchester, 1615

task was one which was undertaken periodically in order to record the 'tarrage'—a Winchester term for terrage, or ground rent, or fee farm rent due to the King as lord of the City—and to make note of alterations since the last review. This was a practice which had gone on for several centuries, but not many of the tarrage rolls have survived. One of the few, and probably the most interesting and revealing, is the roll for 1416. At that time Winchester had fallen on evil days, for Royalty had largely forsaken the City, the Black Death had taken its toll, and the wool staple had been given to the City and then taken away. Consequently, the fee farm rent, then fixed at one hundred marks (£66 13s. 4d.), was difficult to raise.

It is also recorded, in *The Black Book of Winchester*, that in the year 1409, after the King's licence had been obtained, a meeting of the Burgh-mote or the assembly of the freemen of the City was called by the Mayor, Mark le Faire, and it was ordained that all places of void ground within the City should be taken into the King's hands by the Mayor and Bailiffs to the augmentation of the fee farm.[1] When the City officers proceeded to act upon this ordinance it was found that the existing terrier or tarrage roll was faulty. Therefore, in 1416, the Burgh-mote resolved 'that the Maior shall take unto him his peres who pleaseth him together with xii men sworne for our soveraygne lord the kinge and to goe abowt within and without the cittie through the whole libertie and to vewe the defaltes of the Tarrages, and to assesse where they ought to assesse, wheresoever it be, as it was in olde tyme, and now ought to be'. Then a roll of the tarrage was to be written and sealed with the common seal of the City for ever to endure.

Two copies on parchment, one in Latin and one in English, were made and paid for; but the Latin roll has disappeared. There is, however, a Latin paper roll in the possession of

[1] *The Black Book of Winchester*, p. 9. This book, edited by W. H. B. Bird, Wykeham Press, Winchester, 1925, is a printed transcription of a folio volume (Brit. Mus. Add. MS. 6036) written on vellum in various hands, once belonging to the Corporation of Winchester.

Winchester College which appears to have been made at the same time, about 1417, for Hyde Abbey. In the City archives there is a parchment tarrage roll in English which may be the original English copy, for it bears evidence of having been completed before June, 1417. In addition, there are four other tarrage books in English, all copies of the 1416–17 roll, and also a variation, known as the 'purple book' probably made in 1578. One of these four copies is in the British Museum (Additional MSS. 6133) and the other three, now in the City archives, were made in 1604, 1681 and 1700 respectively. In the 1604 copy there are marginal notes which add greatly to its value and interest, for they give the names of the landlords and tenants of the various properties at the time when the copy was made at the end of Elizabeth's reign, together with other matter showing where property had disappeared and new buildings been erected during the period of two hundred years since the original tarrage roll was made.

As one reads this tarrage roll and in imagination accompanies the surveyors as they 'goe abowt within and without the cittie' through the whole liberty, a very clear idea is obtained of what it was like some three hundred and sixty years ago. It must be remembered that when one speaks of the City, or the liberty of the City, there must be excluded almost everything lying adjacent to the walls on the eastern and southern sides, for this district was the Soke and came under the jurisdiction of the Bishop. The College lies outside the city walls and is properly described in the records as the College of St. Mary nigh Winton. Also outside the liberty, but within the walls, was the cathedral and its precincts. On the north and west a very limited area, including the district known as Hyde, was attached to the City, which never seems to have had common fields outside the walls such as were used for pasture and tillage by the citizens of such towns as Oxford and Cambridge. The liberty of the City of Winchester was divided into six aldermanries with an alderman at the head of each; these were the aldermanries of High Street, Jewry Street, Tanner (Lower Brook) Street, Colbrook Street, Gold

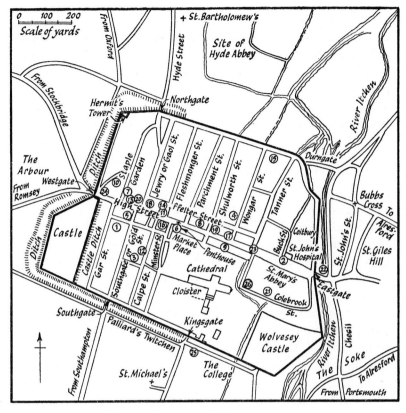

ELIZABETHAN WINCHESTER

(Southgate) Street, and Northgate Street, the last-named comprising the suburbs lying outside Northgate and Westgate.

The surveyors walked through the aldermanries in the order mentioned above, and commenced their task of recording the tarrage at the Westgate. From this point they passed along the inside of the walls in a northerly direction, noting first of all the town pound or pinfold. As far as the Hermit's Tower, at the north-west corner of the walls, there was very little besides gardens, all of which were owned by the City. From the High Street there was a winding lane, four and a half feet wide, which gave access to the site of the former church of St. Paul and to Bridlin Street which was a northern continuation of Staple Garden. This site, which in medieval times was the headquarters of the wool staple, had, in 1604, become a large garden and orchard belonging to the Bailiffs of the City and was apparently untenanted. It is surprising how few tenements were to be found in this north-west quarter of the City. In the High Street itself, on the north side coming down the slope from the Westgate, the property was in the hands of the City, St. John's Hospital and the Dean and Chapter. Below Staple Garden there was a continuous line of tenements, including the fish shambles and the White Horse Inn, with stalls in front, all paying three, four or six pence a year ground rent, until Jewry Street was reached, and in the entry to this street there were three more shops extending to a lane which led back to Staple Garden, and which in those days was a westward continuation of the present St. George's Street.

The next item of note in the tarrage roll concerns the George Inn, placed at the opposite corner of Jewry Street, and owned by the City. It paid twenty pence ground rent and occupied the same site as the New Inn of Mark le Faire, Mayor in 1416, and the same as it did until a very short time ago. Lower down the High Street as far as Fleshmonger (St. Peter's) Street were more tenements with stalls, most of which were owned by the Dean and Chapter, together with the liberty or manor of Godbegot at the corner of Flesh-

monger Street. This property previously held courts of its
own under the Steward of St. Swithun's Priory (the Cathedral), with juries composed of tenants of the liberty, while
claiming to be altogether free of the jurisdiction of the Mayor
of the City. It must have been galling to the City officers to
have an independent sanctuary in the centre of the busiest
street and for the sergeants of the Mayor and Bailiffs to find
themselves helpless when evil-doers eluded their clutches by
slipping into the jurisdiction of the Prior. During the twelfth
and thirteenth centuries controversy arose on several occasions
regarding the apprehension and trial of malefactors who tried
to take refuge in the precincts of Godbegot. The small enclave
which then measured, as it does today, 132 feet by 148 feet,
was originally given by King Ethelred to his wife, Queen
Emma, who at her death in 1052 bequeathed it to the Priory
of St. Swithun. At the Reformation it passed into the hands
of the new body, the Dean and Chapter, and at the same time
lost its original privileges, much to the satisfaction of the
Mayor and Commonalty.

In the entry to Fleshmonger Street and opposite to Godbegot there was a large house newly built, on the site of four
small cottages, by John White, former Town Clerk and
Mayor, the same who in 1575 was charged with the revision
of the tarrage. He also owned the Inn of the Chequer with its
cellar, three shops and a stall, a little further down the High
Street. Next door to this was another inn, that of the Tabard,
which had a porch, three shops and a stall, and paid the same
ground rent as the Chequer, namely, twelve pence a year.
It is interesting to note that in the whole of the City there
were no more than twenty-eight buildings described as
shops, and these were all in the vicinity of the High Street.
At the same time the roll records that practically every tenement in that street had a stall for which ground rent was
paid, showing that the general practice was for the tenement
to be both dwelling house and business premises, and for the
stall to be used for the display of wares on the side fronting
the street.

The Pattern

At the corner of Parchment Street there resided Anthony Bird, a prominent citizen and cloth merchant, and beyond that as the tarrage proceeded down the High Street was the church of St. Mary Kalender, once the finest parish church in the City, but by 1604 in ruins. After two more tenements with stalls there was the inn of the King's Head (formerly the Star, says the tarrage roll) at the corner of Shulworth (Upper Brook) Street. Continuing from here were many cottages with stalls as far as the Bell Inn at the corner of Wongar (Middle Brook) Street, and in the entry to this street came, on the one side, a 'plott of grownde sometime Ode Church' (also known as the church of St. Mary of Wolde), paying a rent of eighteen pence, and on the other side the site of the church of St. George with some cottages, all owned by the City. Between Wongar Street and Tanner (Lower Brook) Street the property, chiefly of the cottage type, was mainly in the hands of the City or St. John's Hospital.

The surveyors, having completed half the tarrage of the aldermanry of the High Street, which comprised the High Street itself together with the entries to the side streets as far as the back streets running parallel to the High Street, crossed over to the south side, and after passing property belonging to Charles Newbolt (Mayor in 1588 and 1600) they went through the church of St. Maurice to Temple Ditch which divided the cathedral close from the City. This led to St. Thomas's Gate (Market Street) a very busy and congested locality judging by the number of tenements, cottages, shops and stalls it contained. Returning to the High Street, there were tenements under the Pentice (or penthouse) 'which is called now in theschequer of our soveraigne lord the kinge the Draperie, which sometimes was called the minte'. Here the rents were very high, several paying as much as twenty shillings a year, and the tenants were all very prominent citizens. The last house but one at the west end of the Pentice was called 'Hell', and here lived William Symonds, a former mayor and a cloth merchant, whose brother, Peter, left money to found Christ's Hospital in Winchester. Near the church of

St. Lawrence and the City Cross, was a void plot, no more than five feet by eight feet eight inches, called 'Bole Hall of the French', a name which has baffled local historians, and next to it a tenement with a stall and five posts called 'Heaven'. The next street was Minster Street, at the entrance to which was 'the common Towne pump' and a tenement belonging to the City called the old hall, that is, the old Guildhall, paying no less than twenty-six shillings and eightpence in ground rent. Proceeding westwards up the High Street, one found the 'Inne called the Hart' and at the next corner, leading into Calpe (St. Thomas's) Street, an enclosed garden on which later was built a new guildhall. A little further along came St. Nicholas's Lane (Hammond's Passage), leading from the High Street to St. Clement's Street, the latter getting its name from the church of St. Clement in Gold (Southgate) Street, and then there was Gar (Trafalgar) Street, which had little else but gardens, in one of which once stood the church of St. Andrew.

Having completed their task in the aldermanry of the High Street, the surveyors went to the aldermanry of Jewry Street, which extended from St. George's Street to the walls on the north side of the City, and from Bridlin Street (Staple Garden) eastwards to Shulworth (Upper Brook) Street. What strikes one most is that the tarrage roll shows a marked absence of houses north of St. George's Street. Nearly all the district stretching two hundred yards within the walls consisted of gardens, with but a few cottages scattered here and there. On the west side of Jewry Street stood the 'Gaole howse' with gardens reaching into Staple Garden, and at the Northgate was 'a stayre within the gate' for which the parishioners of the church upon the gate paid twopence in rent. On the east side of the same street and to the north of St. George's Street there were only four tenements and four cottages until the storehouse, formerly called 'Redhatt', at the junction of the latter street with Fleshmonger Street, was reached. On the west side of this street, now called St. Peter's Street, were ten cottages, seven of them being tenanted by Launcelot Thorpe, who had

succeeded John White as Town Clerk. On the opposite side
a large garden extended from the north walls half-way along
the street, then came a 'common privye' and two cottages.
Parchment Street presented a similar picture, the portion
nearer the High Street having a few dwellings while the area
under the walls consisted of orchards and gardens. Turning
into Shulworth (Upper Brook) Street from St. George's
Street there were, at this corner, the ruins of St. Ruell's
Church and beyond this seven tenements, and then no fewer
than eleven large gardens in a row stretching away to the
north walls.

The east side of Shulworth (Upper Brook) Street came
within the aldermanry of Tanner (Lower Brook) Street and
was the next to be tarraged. It was more thickly populated,
for on its east side it had twelve houses, but there were several
gardens at the northern end. In Wongar (Middle Brook)
Street, on the west side at the corner of St. George's Street,
stood a tenement 'next to the Maiden Chamber'. This was the
midden chamber or public latrine which had been in existence
for a considerable time, for it was recorded in 1362 that John
de Byketoun removed two of the 'foramina' (apertures) to
provide for enlargement of his own premises, and a few years
later a monk of St. Swithun's Priory appeared at the City
Court charged with having taken away a seat from the place
'to the damage of those living near'. Through the streets of
this aldermanry, which comprised the district now known as
'the Brooks', there flowed open streams which probably carried away the soil from the latrines. The surveyors were now
in a fairly populous locality, for they found twenty-two
houses on the west side of Wongar (Middle Brook) Street
with a large garden under the north walls, and on the other
side twenty-nine dwellings and another seven in Silver Hill,
the eastern continuation of St. George's Street. Going into
Tanner (Lower Brook) Street was the large house, formerly
three tenements, occupied by Sir Walter Sands, captain of the
City militia. Houses occupied the whole of the west side of
the street from Silver Hill to the north walls, all paying three-

pence or fourpence as ground rent. Some way along this street was a lane called Butler's (Cossack) Lane leading back to Wongar (Middle Brook) Street, and to the north of this towards the walls a large open space on which formerly stood the church and convent of the Franciscan or Grey Friars, dissolved in 1539 and later handed over to Winchester College. At the north end of Tanner Street and in the north-east corner of the City, the roll notes 'a little lane lyinge under the towne wall leading from Durngate to the waterside'. Returning along the street on the east side were many tenements which had been re-erected on the site of smaller cottages. The older property belonged to St. John's Hospital, the newer to the City. At the south end Sir Walter Sands had another large house opposite the one he owned on the west side of the street. This had taken the place of three smaller houses and two cottages, and for the ground rent Sir Walter paid three shillings.

The aldermanry of Colbrook Street included the whole of the east end of the City, with Buck Street (Busket Lane) on the north side of the High Street and Colbrook Street on the south side. The survey started at Newbridge which crossed the stream entering High Street from Tanner (Lower Brook) Street. Here, opposite the present Guildhall, were twenty small cottages before one reached Buck Street (Busket Lane), where there were more cottages and the land called Coitbury, in which formerly stood two fulling mills. Towards Eastgate there was St. John's Hospital, supposed to have been founded, following a conjecture of Leland, in A.D. 932 by St. Brinstan, Bishop of Winchester. But according to a manuscript of John Trussell, an alderman and twice Mayor of the City, written about 1640, the Hospital was founded or re-founded about 1275 by John le Devinishe, a citizen, by licence from Edward I, for the relief of sick and lame soldiers, poor pilgrims and necessitous wayfaring men. At the suppression of such houses in Henry VIII's reign the bare house with a few beds was granted to the City to be employed as the place of election of the mayor and other officers, and for the holding of the assemblies of the freemen. It was further endowed in 1554 by Ralph Lamb for the support of six poor widows of citizens, the whole being under the patronage and direction of the Mayor for the time being. Nearer still to the Eastgate was the site of the former church and convent of the Dominicans or Black Friars, which like the property of the Grey Friars had passed into the hands of Winchester College. This part of the High Street, which today is spacious and is known as the Broadway, was in Elizabeth's time quite narrow. The centre of the present roadway was open water by the side of which on the south were several tenements and the remains of the charnel chapel of the Holy Trinity, founded by Roger Inkpenn in 1318, and beyond was St. Mary Litten, or the graveyard of St. Mary's Abbey of Benedictine nuns. This property covered much of the ground enclosed by High Street and the western part of Colbrook Street. The Abbey, sometimes referred to as Nunnaminster, was founded by Alfred and his queen, Alswitha, and was one of the most ancient and considerable of the religious establishments in Winchester. It had been suppressed in 1540, and according to the tarrage roll it yielded no rent. Then, as now, many small houses clustered round the south side of the Abbey grounds, very few paying more than twopence a year as tarrage.

The Bishop's castle, Wolvesey, and the cathedral close interposed a solid barrier between the survey of Colbrook Street and the next aldermanry, that of Gold (Southgate) Street, the tarrage for which started at Kingsgate. The survey proceeded under the City wall along what is now St. Swithun's Street to Motte's Corner, the old name for the junction with the present Symond's Street. A marginal note in the tarrage roll records that in this street preparations were being made to erect the new hospital founded by Peter Symonds. Beyond this, at the corner of the lane now called Minster Lane was the High School, where according to tradition William of Wykeham, founder of Winchester College, received his education. A further note in the roll states that this lane was formerly a procession way leading to the west door of the cathedral. Leaving this spot, then known as Richmond Corner, very little tarraging of importance was done until one reached the north end of Calpe (St. Thomas's) Street where it was joined by St. Clement's Street. Calpe Street, on its east side, had both tenements and cottages, the roll making a clear distinction between the two types of dwelling. It is noticeable that whereas the tenement paid fourpence or more, the smaller dwelling rarely paid more than one penny. On the west side there were gardens from the south walls as far as the lane now called St. Thomas's Passage. Then came another garden 'nigh the church late St. Peeters'. Here the scribe made a double error, for the church in question was formerly St. Petroc's; and his next entry, 'now the church of St. Thomas Thappostle' should read 'the church of St. Thomas the Martyr'. The survey of Gold (Southgate) Street revealed the general decay of the City, for on the east or lower side there were only three houses, the remaining space being taken up with gardens, all of them large as shown by the comparatively high rents ranging from tenpence to three shillings and fourpence. The west side of the same street had a few cottages and gardens, behind which was a large open space called Bewmonds, which belonged to the Bailiffs of the City, stretching westwards up to the Castle. Here the citizens played bowls and practised archery. There was a lane leading to it from Gar (Trafalgar) Street, and at this point the surveyors completed their task within the walls of the City.

The sixth and last aldermanry to be surveyed was that of Northgate Street, lying outside the walls on the north-west of the City. The tarrage roll notes that on the south side of Sarum (Romsey) Road there was the water ditch of the Castle which was fed by the water coming from the high ground to the west of the City. Further up this road as far as the burial ground of the former church of St. James, there was nothing but crofts and gardens, the only signs of buildings being 'three cottages now a barn, and three tenements now a croft'. From the roll it is quite clear that on the opposite side of Romsey Road, the Harbor (now Oram's Arbour), which is enrolled as City property, extended as far as Romsey Road itself, for the last tarrage in that road in 1416 was 'a crofte in the corner upon Barditch nigh the Chappell of St. James'. The course taken by the Barditch is not at all clear, however, but it probably ran from Romsey Road in a sweeping curve along the present site of Clifton Road to Northgate. Returning down the north side of Romsey Road the tarrage was taken on the west of the road leading from the Westgate to Fulflood, that is, approximately along what is today Upper High Street and St. Paul's Hill. To the west was the Harbor (or Erberye), covering at least twice its present area, tenanted by Edward Cole who was three times Mayor of the City, and enlarged by the gift of five crofts from William Burton, a wealthy citizen who died in 1603. Coming back along the same road to the Westgate, there was an acre of arable land on the south side of the former church of St. Anastasius, which must have stood very near where the present church of St. Paul stands. After this there was nothing but gardens, one with a pigeon cote, where once was to be found the church of St. Leonard, but whose actual site the tarrage roll queries.

Sussex Street, called 'the street ledinge from the Westgate unto the church of the Vale', was taken next. The west side was practically a continuation of the Harbor, consisting of crofts, one being called Hawkehaye, the Domus Havoc of the earlier Norman survey, where the King had kept his hawks. The east side of this street was on the ditch of the City which ran from Westgate to Hermit's Tower. Here again gardens and crofts had taken the place of former dwellings, and one of these was called Picked Croft, probably the 'Parrok' of Norman times. The City Road of modern times did not exist, this area being part of Barditch. At Northgate a bridge crossed the ditch which continued eastwards outside the north walls. The tarrage was taken outside the gate along a street leading to Hyde as far as a great stone lying in a meadow towards Abbots Barton, which marked the northward limit of the liberty of the City. First, across the bridge outside Northgate, and on the east side of the street, was the Swan, and then a continuous row of tenements and cottages paying three or four pence a year. Most of this property was owned by Thomas Clarke, who lived in the Elizabethan mansion built, in the middle of the sixteenth century by the Bethell family, on the site of the suppressed Hyde Abbey. Beyond this near St. Bartholomew's churchyard were the ruins of nine cottages which had been tarraged at one penny each and had belonged to Hyde Abbey. But the Abbot had altered the doors of the cottages so that they could be approached only through the Abbey gateway, and therefore the City could get no rent for them until the doors to the King's highway were opened up again. A good deal of space in the tarrage roll is devoted to Hyde Street, Worthy Lane and 'the road which leadeth towardes Oxforde' (Andover Road). In this district, outside the walls, there were two interesting and ancient landmarks, namely, 'a Crosse which standeth in the Kinges highe waye betweene the Churche of St. Maryes in the Vale and the gallowes upon Barditche nigh the way leadinge to Whitchurche'. From the tarrage roll it would appear that the cross in the King's highway (Andover Road) stood near the west end of Worthy Lane, that the Church of St. Mary in the Vale was near to the spot where the present Eagle Hotel stands, while the gallows were on the site of the present railway goods siding in Andover Road, through which there formerly ran in a southerly direction an ancient way known as Gallows Lane. And it was at this point that the surveyors, as in previous years, completed their tarrage in 1604.

A detailed analysis of the tarrages made in 1416 and 1604 respectively reveals some very interesting facts. Within the City walls in 1416 there were 275 cottages and 363 tenements, and in the aldermanry of Northgate Street (Hyde), outside the walls, 66 cottages and 21 tenements, showing in all a total of 725 occupied dwellings within the liberty of the City. If one takes an average of $4\frac{1}{4}$ persons per house, thereby using the ratio adopted earlier in this chapter, this gives the population of the six aldermanries as 3,081, of whom 370 were living in the north-west suburbs.[1] But in the fourteenth and fifteenth centuries there were religious houses within the liberty of the city, such as St. Swithun's Priory, St. Mary's Abbey, Hyde Abbey, and several Friaries, which are not included in the tarrage roll but whose inhabitants should be included in the total population. It is difficult to estimate exactly the total number of persons domiciled in these religious houses, but there is a certain amount of helpful information available. For example, St. Mary's Abbey had at its dissolution, in 1540, 26 professed nuns and 50 other residents, including chaplains, household officers and servants, together with 26 children. It is also known that the number of monks at St. Swithun's was 35 and at Hyde Abbey 21.[2] If it is assumed that in each of these two establishments the number of lay persons was on the same scale as at St. Mary's Abbey, and if additional allowance is made for the Friaries, then the total is in the region of 350. This, together with the estimated population of the aldermanries, namely, 3,081, gives a total of 3,431 for the whole city and liberty. In the absence of definite census returns it is impossible to check this computation, but it is interesting to note that it is somewhat higher than an estimate based on the poll-tax return of 1377. According to that estimate, Winchester, with a population of 2,700, ranked as the twenty-ninth town in this kingdom, and Southampton, with 2,160, as the thirty-fourth. London had 44,770, and York and Bristol, second and third, had 13,590 and 11,904 respectively.[3]

It should be noted that in estimating the population of Winchester in 1416 on the basis of the tarrage roll, no account has been taken of the parishes of St. John, St. Peter Chesil, St. Michael and St. Swithun upon Kingsgate, all of which were in the Soke, and outside the liberty of the City. If it is assumed that the Soke had a population equal to that of the

[1] See note 1, p. 16.
[2] Dugdale's *Monasticon*.
[3] C. Creighton, *History of Epidemics in Britain*, Vol. I, p. 201.

Northgate Street aldermanry, namely, 370, and this does not appear unreasonable, then the population of greater Winchester in 1416 was in the region of 3,800.

This may seem a low figure when one considers the important rôle which Winchester had played in the past, but an explanation is forthcoming in the petition sent by the citizens to Henry VI in 1439, for in this they complained that through pestilence and the withdrawal of trade, eleven streets, seventeen parish churches and nine hundred and eighty-seven messuages in the City had fallen into ruins during the preceding fifty years. This statement also helps to explain the very large number of garden plots, numbering no fewer than one hundred and forty-four, which had formerly been the sites of cottages, and the large uninhabited areas adjacent to and within the walls of the City, as plainly shown in the tarrage roll. The figures mentioned in the petition, and repeated in letters patent of Henry VI of the same date, are startling, yet there is probably very little exaggeration. The list of ruined churches as supplied to the King is still extant, and from this and from the frequent references to ruined churches in the tarrage roll the figure of 17 as regards such churches can be taken as correct. Neither is the number of decayed houses, 987, impossible. It asks one to believe that the population of Winchester had declined by just over a half, that is, by about 4,000, since the late twelfth or early thirteenth century when the City had reached the peak of its fame and prosperity. If the period of fifty years, during which it was claimed the decay had taken place, is taken as a loose estimate and is extended to include the time of the Black Death, the figures can indeed become credible. There is, for example, a striking contrast between the survey of 1148 and that of 1416 in the matter of the suburb outside Westgate, which in Norman times was fairly thickly populated, and there is no doubt that the area within the walls, provided the vacant plots had been built upon, was capable of holding a population twice as large as that which has been estimated for 1416. But of the 11 streets which had disappeared it is difficult to speak with certainty, for as far as can be ascertained from the survey of 1148 only one main street, namely, Alwaren Street, running parallel to and east of Jewry Street, had disappeared by 1416. It may be, of course, that some of the smaller and narrower streets, of which there is no definite record, became enclosed within the increasing number of gardens and orchards as cottages fell into decay. In any case, it is unlikely that the Mayor and his brethren would petition the King and quote these figures unless they could show proof of their accuracy.

During the period of nearly two hundred years which elapsed between the compilation of the tarrage roll of 1416 and its revision in 1604, the number of changes which had taken place, according to the marginal notes of the roll, was remarkably small. The general street plan had not altered at all, and as far as one can gather, with the exception of the disappearance of Alwaren Street, it was very much the same as in Norman times. But by 1604, more dwelling houses had decayed, though not at the same alarming rate as in the fourteenth century. The 725 habitations noted in 1416 had now become 647. The number of occupied tenements within the walls was 370, including 6 inns, as against 363 in 1416, while in the Northgate Street aldermanry outside the walls there were now 20 tenements, one less than before. It was the cottages and smaller houses which had been disappearing. The roll gives information concerning the rebuilding of tenements, often on a large scale, and there are several cases of a large new tenement taking the place of three or more old cottages. There were 50 fewer cottages in the City, and 14 fewer in the suburbs than in 1416, and the number of gardens, orchards and void places had now increased from 144 to 212. In the north-east corner of the City there was even a meadow within the walls and, quite near to it, at the north end of Parchment Street, two gardens had been transformed into four ponds. It is apparent that the gradual depopulation of the City, previously noted, had continued. There were now, at the end of Elizabeth's reign, 647 dwellings within the liberty

3. Seal of Queen Elizabeth attached to the Charter granted to
Winchester in 1587

GVIL.MARCHIO.WINTON.THES.ANGL

5. William Paulet (1485–1572) Marquis of Winchester, Lord High Treasurer of England (from a portrait in the Guildhall, Winchester).

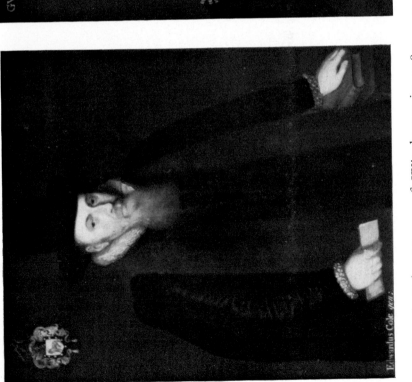

Erasmus Cole fecit.

4. Edward Cole, Mayor of Winchester in 1587, 1598 and 1612 (from a portrait in the Guildhall, Winchester).

of the City, and this number, if one uses the same ratio as previously, would give a population of 2,750. But since the monasteries and religious houses had been uninhabited and in a process of decay for over sixty years, no addition can be made to this total on their account. It only remains, therefore, to add the residents of the four parishes in the Soke, as in the former estimate, and one comes to the conclusion, by the method of reckoning which has been used, that in 1604 the population of greater Winchester was approximately 3,120, which shows a decrease of about fifteen per cent since 1416.

The object of the tarrage roll, as has already been said, was to record the amount which each property should pay towards the fee farm rent of the City. In 1416 the amount due to be paid into the Exchequer by the Bailiffs of the City was 100 marks (£66 13s. 4d.), but long before Elizabeth's reign some relief had been obtained by the grant of the ulnage of cloth for the county of Southampton, and this brought in 40 marks per annum. The City had, therefore, to raise 60 marks (£40) to meet its obligations, and of this amount 50 marks was paid to William Paulet annually, as it had been since 1551, when he was created Marquis of Winchester. From the tarrage roll it appears that the total sum collected as ground rent, in both 1416 and 1604, was £27 and that there were very few cases of any alteration in the amounts paid by individual properties in the interval between the two surveys.

Where a garden took the place of a tenement, or a new tenement had been built on the site of two or three former cottages, the amount of the ground rent remained the same. There was, therefore, a deficit of about £13 which had to be found from other sources, and it is clear from the Chamberlains' rolls, which give account of the City's annual income and expenditure, that this deficit was met by an allocation from general income.

CHAPTER II

The Burgh-Mote

Whatever its constitution may have been in earlier times the Burgh-mote had become, at the time when Elizabeth came to the throne, a meeting of the freemen of the City at which local legislation was enacted. Decisions were embodied in ordinances which were duly enrolled in Books of Ordinances. These are still in existence and contain much information concerning the municipal affairs of the City of Winchester. The First Book of Ordinances, for example, which covers the latter half of the sixteenth century, contains all the enactments of the Burgh-mote for that period, and besides showing the efforts to regulate trade, ameliorate social conditions and make smooth the working of local government, it gives details of streets, houses and other properties, and thus supplements the information given in the tarrage roll described in the preceding chapter.

In this book one reads that 'at a common convocation of the citizens of the Cytie of Winchester it was ordained', etc., and again, that 'it is ordayned and established by the Mayor and bayliffs and the whole Comynaltie of the Cytie aforesaide', etc. These phrases suggest that the 'commonalty' included all citizens and it is difficult to say whether or not this interpretation was at one time correct. But there is ample evidence to show that long before Elizabeth's reign only a limited number of the citizens had the right to attend and vote in the assembly, and these were the freemen, that is, those who had been admitted to the Merchant Gild.

In the *Black Book of Winchester*, which includes, amongst

other matters, some of the recorded proceedings of the Burgh-mote from the reign of Henry IV to that of Henry VIII, the names of those present at the assembly are often given and at times they number no more than twenty. The First Book of Ordinances, which contains those ordinances of the *Black Book* which were thought worthy of retention together with all those passed between 1552 and 1609, shows that the attendance was sometimes as low as forty but occasionally rose to seventy. The average attendance throughout Elizabeth's reign was approximately sixty, and there is a tendency for the numbers attending each assembly to increase towards the end of the century.

There are numerous entries, always in Latin, in the records showing that on a given date certain individuals had been "sworn" into the Merchant Gild of the City. For example,

'xxvi° Die Octobris Anno domini, 1565.

Willelmus Symonds
Ricardus Harvye
Willelmus Colyns
Johannes Valoer
} Jurati sunt die et anno predicto in Guildam Mercatoriam civitatis.'[1]

At the next meeting of the Burgh-mote in April, 1566, the names of the above four new freemen are found at the end of the list of those present; and so throughout the whole of the First Book of Ordinances, which covers a period of fifty-seven years, it is found that new members appear at the Burgh-mote next following their admission to the Merchant Gild.

The origin of the Merchant Gild is obscure. The oldest of the royal charters possessed by Winchester, namely, that granted by Henry II in 1155, or 1158, gives privileges to the Gild, but it is not unsafe to believe that the Merchant Gild was in existence before the Norman Conquest in the reign of Edward the Confessor, 1042–66. John Trussell, a local attorney and twice Mayor of the City, writing in the time of Charles I, states that the Gild was founded in the time of Athelstan, 925–40. Originally, no doubt, it consisted of those

[1] 1st Bk. Ord., f. 142.

men who had successfully terminated their period of apprenticeship to some trade or 'mistery', and who were, by virtue
thereof, master craftsmen. Each of these had the status of a
merchant which had been acquired by membership of the Gild.

According to the Ancient Usages of the City of Winchester, which were drawn up about 1275, candidates for
admission to the Gild were accepted at a formal meeting;
they had to be presented by the craft or 'mistery' to which
they belonged, and the craft was bound to make inquiry as
to who were suitable and of good report to be recruited into
the Gild. The property qualification was considerable, being
four pounds in chattels, and this together with the fee payable
on entry excluded anyone below the status of a master of his
craft. The entry fee varied from time to time and over a long
period it was fixed at half a mark (6s. 8d.). It appears from
the Chamberlains' rolls, however, that in Elizabeth's reign
the fee was one and a half marks (£1) paid in six annual
instalments following the candidate's admission.

The history of the Merchant Gild in its relation to municipal government is very complex. In some towns the two
merged, and the power of regulation of trade passed, together
with the gild's other functions and properties into the hands
of the corporation. As far as Winchester is concerned it is
sufficient to note that in the sixteenth century admission to the
Gild was the one and only means of becoming a freeman and
being admitted to the franchise of the City, and the 'liberty'
of the City was therefore confined to a small oligarchy, whose
statutes, agreed upon in the Burgh-mote, regulated the
government of the City.[1]

In the course of time exceptions to the regulations governing the admission of freemen were made. In 1489, during the
mayoralty of Richard Bull, it had been 'agreid that the
Mayor of the Cytie for the tyme beinge shall make one
ffranches man of his own Gyfte without a Common assemble'.
This practice continued until 1574, when it was 'agreed that

[1] The identification of the Merchant Gild with the Commonalty of
the City is discussed by J. S. Furley, *City Government*, Chap. VI.

no mayor hereafter shall make any franches man within this Cytie but with thassent of the more part of his bretherne, and that one Acte made in the tyme of Richarde Bull mayor concernynge the makinge of ffranches men be from henceforth voyed and of none effect'.[1] Later, in 1584, it was ordained that 'noe person or persons shall from henceforth be made free of the Guilde of marchantes of this citie but by the assente of the Maior bayliffes and Commonaltie of this Citie in the open assemble anie usage custome or ordinaunce whatsoever hertofore made had or used to the contrary notwithstandinge'.[2] And later still, in 1595, a further ordinance stated that 'it shalbe henceforth lawfull at the tyme of the eleccion of the Maior for the Maior and the more parte of the fower and twentie to call and admitt into the fredome anie person inhabitinge within the Cittie'.[3]

Mention of the Mayor's 'bretherne' and of the 'fower and twentie' calls for some explanation. In all towns there were privileged citizens, possessing influence or authority, who were known as jurats, capital portmen, etc. In Winchester such persons were called collectively the 'Twenty-four'. They were prominent citizens, members of the Merchant Gild, and their chief duty was to act in an advisory capacity, helping the Mayor 'in saving and sustaining the franchise'. The mayor's 'brethren', or 'peers' as they were sometimes called, consisted of former mayors and, after 1587, the Recorder of the City. The Mayor called upon them for advice and assistance in exercising his executive powers, and on rare occasions when more serious matters were under consideration he also called the 'Twenty-four' into consultation.

Eventually, the custom of presentation by the craft to which a candidate belonged, when he sought admission to the Merchant Gild, fell into disuse. In Elizabeth's reign candidates were not necessarily citizens engaged in trade or commerce. In 1571, Thomas Michelborne was elected as one of the City's representatives in the third parliament of Elizabeth and at the same time the Burgh-mote agreed that he

[1] 1st Bk. Ord., f. 178.   [2] Idem, f. 231.   [3] Idem, f. 284.

should be admitted to the Merchant Gild without paying any entrance fee, and further that he should not be burdened, against his will, with any manner of office in the City.[1] They also granted him the lease of a house and other property in Parchment Street, from which fact it can be concluded that he was a newcomer to Winchester. At the same assembly, William Bethell, who had inherited the Elizabethan mansion built by his father on the Hyde Abbey estate, was admitted to the Gild and to the Twenty-four, and excused the office of the mayoralty for seven years. In the following years there were many instances of election to membership of the Gild of Merchants of eminent persons from outside the City, as in the case in 1582 of Thomas Fleming, who had shortly before become Recorder of Winchester and was later to become Lord Chief Justice of England, and in 1592 of Sir Edward Stafford, who was a member of parliament for the City in the following year.[2, 3]

In earlier times, no doubt, membership of the Merchant Gild was an honour much sought after, but later it seems that citizens were not so eager to avail themselves of whatever privileges membership bestowed. It is possible that the duties involved, particularly those of jury service, outweighed any advantages gained. As early as 1507, it is recorded that every man who was presented to enter the Gild and would not do so should be fined 6s. 8d.[4] In 1593, the penalty was raised to £1, and two years later one reads 'that whereas divers of the inhabitantes of the Cittie which are by Mr. Maior and the more parte of the xxiiii[tie] thought meete to be of the fredome of the Cittie doe refuse or contemne the same in regarde of the smaleness of the penaltie heretofore imposed, it is agreed therefore that the penaltie formerlie agreed upon shalbe encreased to the some of five poundes for everie refusall once in everie year.'[5, 6]

On admission to the Gild candidates took 'the othe to

---

[1] Idem, f. 163.   [2] Idem, f. 224.   [3] Idem, f. 270.
[4] Idem, f. 7.   [5] Idem, f. 273.   [6] Idem, f. 284.

swere men to be ffree, knelinge on their kneys', as follows:
'I shalbe hole man and trew to the kinge of Englande and his
heyres and successors and to the Citie of Winchester and I
shall beare all charges and offices and paye all talages of that
Citie to me isett with all my powre. And I shall never plede
anie freeman of that Citie in no temporall court but in the
court of the same Citie unlesse that court faile me of right
without lycens of the Mayor for the tyme beinge. And I
shalbe obedient to the Mayor bayliffs and all other officers and
mynisters of that Citie lawfull. Ne no man kever ne favor under
my ffranches and all manner statutes and usages of that Citie
whereof I shall have knowledge I shall do and kepe well and
treulye to my poure so helpe me god and by this book'.[1, 2, 3]

Following admission, the new freeman was expected to
attend regularly. From time to time it was found necessary to
reaffirm previous ordinances dealing with slackness in this
matter. An order of 1581 states that 'whereas remisse negligence and greate slackness hath of late tyme been founde in
the freemen of this Citie in comminge to the assembles without remorse of conscience regard of dewtie or consideracion
of the common utilitie of this Citie to the great decaye and
utter subversion of good order, for remedie whereof it is nowe
agreed that any freeman or franchised man of this Citie which
after reasonable warninge to hym or at his dwellinge house
geven by the space of three dayse next before any common
assemble to bee holden within this Citie (he beinge then or at
any tyme within the same three daise at home and not having
lawfull licence to be absent or not havinge reasonable excuse
to be allowed by Mr. Mayor) shall make defalte and not
appeare at the same assemble shall lose and forfeite for every
such defalte iis'.[4]

Not only was regular attendance required but it was also
decreed that every freeman of the City should have and
should wear at every assembly and every gaol delivery and
Burgh-mote 'a decente goune' upon pain of forfeiture for

---

[1] Idem, f. 95.   [2] Isett = established.
[3] Kever = cover, screen.   [4] 1st Bk. Ord., f. 216.

every offence of 5s.[1] One duty which was probably rather unpopular among freemen, especially those of advancing years, was the annual riding of the bounds of the City for which the following provision was made: 'It is agreed that everie freeman of this Citie being under the xxiiii^tie shall yerelie at the usuall tymes accompanie the bayliffes of the Citie beinge on horsebacke in ridinge the lymittes and liberties of the Citie uppon payne that everie such freeman makinge defalte without a lawfull excuse to be allowed by Mr. Maior and the more parte of his brethern shall forfayte iis. vid.'[2]

As a general rule the Burgh-mote met twice yearly. The first meeting, at which the mayor, bailiffs and other officers were elected, was usually held in the latter half of September of each year at St. John's House or Hospital, while the second, at the Guildhall or rarely at St. John's House, was held between Easter and Whitsuntide, with occasional deferments to a date between Whitsuntide and Midsummer Day. The following extract from the First Book of Ordinances shows the method of recording the proceedings and the kind of business which was transacted:[3]

'Civitas Wintonie.

At a common assemble holden at the house of the hospitall of St. John the xvi^th of Aprill in the fiveth yere of the raigne of our Soveraigne Ladye Elizabeth by the grace of god etc., Thomas Colye then beinge maior Stephane Ashton and Edmonde Bedham bayliffes it was enacted and ordeyned as folowethe,

Mr. Thomas Colye mayor	Thomas Byrde
Mr. Thomas Bathe	John Bedham
Mr. William Lawrens	John Edwardes
Mr. Roberte Hodson	Roberte Dodson—infirmus
Mr. Edmonde ffoster—	Christofer Genyns
habuerit veniam	

---

[1] Idem, f. 201.   [2] Idem, f. 255.   [3] Idem, f. 135.

Mr. John Edmonde

Mr. Richard Bethell

Mr. Roberte Bethell

Mr. Giles White

Mr. Richarde Burton

Mr. John Skinner

Mr. William Lane

Mr. Herman Bilson

Roberte Samwell

William Brexstone

Harry Geste

William Hall

George Browne

Anthony Williamson

Stevin Asheton

John Potinger

John Griffithe

James Waterson

John Hibbarde

Edmonde Bedham

William Badger

Water Jonson—infirmus

Stephan knighte

John Aderlie

William Sturte

William Baylie

Roberte Greye

Thomas Hodson

William Walis

Launcelot Jonson

Richarde Alison

Anthony Byrde

Thomas Thorpe

Thomas Eridge

Nicholas Barsdale

William Pavior

Thomas Brode

Richard Byrde

Richarde Barfote

George Dalamye

Richarde Lambe

John White

Stevine Browne

Richard bethell Junior

John Luke

Thomas Aderlye

John Winall senior

Edmunde Draper

John Simons

ffirst it is agreide by the whole assemble that William Badger thelder shalbe frelye during his liffe discharged of all manner of offices with whome the sayde William is nowe chargeable or hereafter maye be charged by vertue of his ffredome of the sayde Cytie thoffice of the mayraltie and all other offices which the mayors hathe bene accustomed to beare after the office of the mayraltie onelye excepted And it is leikewise agreide that the saide William shall not be frome hensforthe chargeable with the sayd office of the mayraltie untill such tyme that the sayde William shall discontinewe his trade of attorneyshippe at the common lawe

And that he maye lawfullye pleade at barre within the Cytie as he dide before the makinge of this ordinance Anye other actes or ordinances hertofore made or hereafter to be made to the contrarye notwithstandinge.

Item that it shalbe lawfull to the mayor and the more parte of the xxiiii^{tie} before the daye of the election of the mayor nowe next cominge to devise an ordinance for infranchesinge of free mens sonnes and suche as be and shalbe covenaunt servantes with freemen by indenture within the Cytie and the same ordinance so devised shall stande and be in full strengthe and effecte as if it had byn devised and agreide uppon by this whole assemble.

Item that Leonarde Howston have the tenement he dwellithe in with thapputtenances from mychaelmas nexte for xx^{ti} yeres yeldinge yerelie xiiiis. Provided that he muste make upp a newe pale abowghte the grounde within iii yeres after the commencemente of the lease or else this graunte shalbe voyde.

Item to thentente to avoyde the great disorder of standinge saltfishemongers at the highe crosse it is agreide that from hensforthe it shalbe lawfull for everye fissher to stande at his owne dore if he like or els at suche place as uppon a view shalbe thowght good and in none other place And that all suche as water there saltfishe and throe there water oute of there dores shall throwe twisse so myche cleane water after the same fishewater uppon payne of everye fissher offendinge to the contrarye to forfette for everie tyme iiis. iiiid., the one halfe to the bayliffes and the other to the finder if it be dewlye proved by two witnesses or any other lawfull prouffe.

Item that Richarde browninge have the reversion of the house and gardin that Hewe browne holdethe in St. Thomas parrishe after the yerys grauntyd to John Netterbe expyred for xxi^{ti} yeldinge yerlie xvis. Provided alwaye that the saide hewghe browne and his wiffe shall not be putte oute of the same after the yerys endide so longe as they wyll inhabite there and paye suche rente as shalbe assigned by Mr. Mayor and the more parte of the xxiiii^{ti}.

It is agreid that the Cytie shall and maye chaunge grounde for grounde in the herber with John Edmonde.[1]

Item that the lycence that Anthony Williamson hathe under seale for sellinge wyne be resumed and he discharged of sellinge of wyne.

Item that John Cooke have a gardin lyenge in partchement streate nigh to the towne wall frome the feaste of thannunciation laste for xxi[ti] yeres yeldinge yerlie iis. vid.

Item that no occupier or artificer other than clothiers and suche as do clothe makinge and workinge uppon that arte onlye do appirtayne beinge no franches man shall frome hensforthe occupie or sett upp there occupations mysteryes or craftes within the Cytie before theye hathe compounded with the mayor for the tyme beinge and his bretherne uppon payne of iiis. iiiid. for everie weke occupienge to the contrarye to be levied by distresse and the profitts thereof comynge shalbe thre partes therof to the bayliffes for the tyme beinge and the sayde bayliffes shall gather the same so compounded fee. Provided alwayes that common victuallers maye come in the daies accustomed this ordinance notwithstandinge payenge to the bayliffes as theye hathe bene accustomed hertofore.

Item that no person frome hensforthe laye anye ded dogge ratte or horse or anye other ded carreyne in anye strete or highe waye of the Cytie nether shall lay any such ded carreyne in anye other place excepte he burye the same sufficientlye fforthewith uppon payne of vis. viiid. for everye tyme if he maye be deulye convicte therof by two wytnesses or other wayes.

Item it is agreide that the acte made for pavinge before mennys howses in the tyme of Mr. John Edmonde mayor shalbe understood as folowethe, that is to saye that the tennente beinge bounde to repayre his tenemente shall also pave before his howse and otherwise the owner of the lande shall pave it.

Item that Richarde Birde have the gardine which he nowe holdethe nigh the Westgate from michaelmas nexte during so

[1] Herber = the arbour, now Orams Arbour.

manye yerys as are nowe to come in the howse he dwellithe under the penthouse yeldinge yerlye iis.'

There is nothing in the above record of the proceedings of the Burgh-mote, when it met in April, 1563, to suggest that they were otherwise than orderly, dignified and business-like. But they were not always so, for during the six months following the accession of Queen Elizabeth there were several outbursts of heated argument and recrimination within 'the councell howse'. At the very first meeting of the Burgh-mote after Elizabeth came to the throne, when Mr. William Goodwin was Mayor, it was agreed that 'Mr. John Edmonde one of thaldermen for divers sclaunderous words and mysdemeanours by hym spoken and done against Mr. William Lawrens sometyme Mayor' (and a member of parliament for the City) 'be committed to warde at Mr. Mayors pleasure and also to paye' twenty shillings.[1] The 'same daye and yere it was agreid that Mr. Thomas Colye, one of the twenty-four, for divers unseemlye wordes by him spoken to Mr. Hodson, one of thaldermen of the Cytie, for his ponishment shall amende one pane of glass windowe in the councell howse and ii quarelles in two other panes'.[2]

Seven days later, Mr. John Edmonde was released from his imprisonment but it was ordained 'that he shall make a barge of lead of ii handes breadithe in the myddle of the glasse windowe in the councell howse all the length of the same wyndowe'.[3] Shortly afterwards, Mr. Richard Burton, a magistrate, 'for dyverse unfittinge woordes spokyn by him to Wylliam Brexstone, one of the twenty-four', was ordered to 'paye according to an ordinance thereof made' twenty shillings, and 'Wylliam Brexstone was expellyd the councell howse for that he revealyd the secrettes spoken in the same howse unto strangers'. For his readmission he paid 'for the makinge of a cubborde for the recordes of the Citie which is nowe fastened in the councell howse, fourteen shillings'.[4]

[1] Idem, f. 121. [2] Quarelles = squares of glass set diagonally.
[3] Idem, f. 121. [4] Idem, f. 122.

The above-mentioned misdemeanours took place during the mayoralty of William Goodwin in 1559. No sooner had Goodwin, however, completed his year of office than he himself was charged before the newly-elected Mayor, Richard Burton (the same who had been fined for using divers unfitting words some months previously), in that he committed 'dyverse and sondrye enormyties and mysdemeanours in the tyme of his mayraltie, sowndinge and tendinge to the slaunder of the office of the mayraltie and the disworship of the cytie, that is to saye, for that he oftentymes dyd ryde out of the Cytye to Hampton' (Southampton) 'and to other townes within the shire without a servant waightinge uppon him, beinge desyred the contrarye by dyverse of his brethern, And also for that he commaunded George Browne, one of the twenty-four, to the Westgate, the gate beinge shutt uppon him contrary to an ordinance made in the tyme of Mr. Giles Whyte being mayor, when he shulde have commaundyd him to St. John's Howse, And also for that openlye in the chequer betweene the gate he drewe his dagar at one of the Sergeants contrary to the quenys peace'.[1]

The record of these incidents goes on to say that 'forasmiche as the reformacion and correction of such enormyties and mysdemeanours appertaynethe to the mayor for the tyme beinge and others that hathe byn mayors of the Cytie accordinge to an olde auncient custome of the sayd Cytie It is agreid and adiudged by Mr. Burton nowe mayor and the more parte of such as hathe byn mayors that the sayd Mr. William Goodwin shall at his proper costs and charges glaise the windowe on the west part of the chymney in the hall of thospytall of St. Johns Howse contayninge two lights with new glasse And also shall new make the stone worke of other ii wyndows of the same hall'.[2]

There was possibly more than a little spite and malice shown both within and without the council chamber during the early days of Elizabeth's reign, and such a state of affairs cannot really cause a great deal of surprise when one

[1] Idem, f. 123.   [2] Idem, f. 124.

remembers that the country had become 'ragged and torn with misgovernment', and that religious differences had caused widespread bitterness and strife; but there was undoubtedly more than a compensating display of authority and a strong determination on the part of the majority of the freemen that the dignity of the City should be upheld.

CHAPTER III

The Charters

Every community in the country had, from early times, its own customs which it continued to enjoy until it encountered external interference and the consequent danger of losing its powers, however small they were, of managing its own affairs. The safeguard against such loss was an appeal to the Crown for the grant of a charter which would guarantee the enjoyment of the privileges already possessed. In the First Book of Ordinances and other records of the City of Winchester there is the constantly recurring phrase 'according to the custom of the City'—evidence that rights were based on local custom. There thus grew up a tendency for each town or borough to conduct its business in its own way under the protection of the Crown, and with very little attempt on the part of the latter to enforce uniformity throughout the country. Therefore, what was the law in one town was not necessarily the law in another, and it was not until a much later date that legal procedure was uniform in this country.[1] In Tudor times, for example, the procedure at Winchester for the recovery of property was different from that of other towns, and the privilege of being sued for debt only in his own town, if the debt had been incurred there, could be claimed by a Winchester merchant, although he might have dealt with a merchant from another town whose charter had not secured for its burgesses the same privilege.

[1] J. S. Furley, *City Government*, p. 27.

What was true of law was also true of administration, for each town had its own method. Winchester had its own particular way, in the case of food, of safeguarding its citizens against short measure, light weight and exorbitant prices, and of drawing the offenders upon hurdles through the streets. In general, a person's civic rights and responsibilities depended almost entirely upon local custom and not upon a common and uniform right. In truth, it was an age of infinite variety created by the terms of the individual charter which the particular town had gained. But it should be noted, however, that a certain amount of uniformity gradually crept in, for there were occasions when a new charter was granted to a town declaring that it should have the same privileges as those already enjoyed by some other town. Thus a Winchester charter became the model for that of other towns, such as Portsmouth, Taunton, Marlborough, Wilton and Wallingford. The charter granted to Andover in 1175 stated that the burgesses 'shall be quit of toll and passage and customs throughout the whole of the land as the burgesses of Winchester are quit who are of the Merchant Gild'.[1]

Winchester possesses a collection of charters and royal grants, thirty-three in number, dating from the reign of Henry II to that of George III. A close study of these, up to that granted by Queen Elizabeth in 1587, which is the twenty-seventh of the series, reveals the gradual growth of the liberty and independence of the City until it had become very near to being a self-governing community.[2] During the preceding four hundred years the citizens had gained for themselves many rights and privileges of prime importance, and the earnestness with which they regarded these and the zeal with which they were prepared to defend them are well exemplified by the following extract from the *Black Book*:[3]

[1] Idem.

[2] The main provisions contained in the Winchester Charters are given in *City of Winchester, Calendar of Charters*, compiled by J. A. Herbert, 1915.

[3] *Black Book*, p. 34; 1st Bk. Ord. f. 3.

'ffirst to the honor of almighti god our holye mother the chirche and of our soveraigne lorde the kinge and to the releiffe of the Cittie There is a provision and consideration made which beginnethe in this wyse: Before this tyme the hole cominaltie hathe by there corporall othe made with one hart one mynde and one assent bownde them selfs by all there goods and catalls movable and unmoveable whereso ever thei be that if it chaunce onye of them (which god forbede) to againe say any article towchinge the charter usage or custome of the libertie of the Cytie or the common proffytt of the same by cowncell or helpe pryvilye or openlye in tyme to come when he shalbe therof convicted he shall geve ten marks to the common affayres of the Citie which shalbe employed to suppli the common necessities when nede shall require. And if he be not of habilitie to redeme the trespas with the payment of ten marks he shalbe expellyd frome the feloshipe and the libertye nother for any redemption shalbe reconsiled except he be by a common consent. And if it chaunce ony man so beinge reconsiled to offend againe he shall by no means be admitted in to the company and felowshipe againe. Iff any person or ony persons be grevid by any man by occasion of this provision all and singular of the hole cominaltie shall sustayne the coste and charge and shall kepe him harmles to thuttermost of ther poures'.

In 1561 Elizabeth had confirmed the letters patent of Philip and Mary and those of Henry VIII, but it was not until 1587 that she granted the charter which defined a new constitution for the City. This did not necessarily mean the granting of new rights and privileges; it was more in the nature of a re-statement of what were, at the time, considered to be rights possessed by Winchester resulting from previous grants, usage and local customs. This charter was given by the Queen to the City 'at the humble petition of our faithful and well-beloved counsellor, Sir Francis Walsingham', who had in 1582, five years prior to the granting of the charter, been made by the Mayor, Bailiffs and Commonalty the first High Steward of the City, 'for the better direction defence and

D

mayntenaunce of this Cittie and the rightes liberties and privileges of the same'.

The charter, like most of its kind, is extremely wordy and repetitious, so much so that a complete translation of its seven thousand five hundred words would hardly fail to weary the reader. It will, of course, be necessary to summarize its contents and to accentuate to some degree the main clauses; in addition, there may be a reasonable excuse for quoting the preamble in full in order to show the phraseology then used in such documents and possibly to stimulate an interest in this particular royal grant.

'Elizabeth, by the grace of God, Queen of England and Ireland, Defender of the Faith, etc., To all to whom these present Letters shall come, Greeting. Whereas our City of Winchester in our County of Southampton is an ancient town having for rule and government thereof a Mayor, six Aldermen, two Bailiffs, two Coroners, two Constables and other public officers of the citizens and inhabitants of the same City by which Mayor, Aldermen, Bailiffs, Coroners, Constables and other officers aforesaid our City of Winchester and the citizens and inhabitants of the same City time out of mind of man have been governed, And whereas there have been anciently divers lands, tenements, hereditaments, jurisdictions, liberties and privileges given and granted to the citizens and inhabitants of the said City, sometimes by the name of the Mayor and Citizens, sometimes by the name of the Mayor, Bailiffs and Commonalty of Winchester, as by several Letters Patent, as well ours as of divers of our progenitors sometimes Kings of England, more fully manifest and may appear, And whereas also the said Mayor, Bailiffs and Commonalty and Citizens of our said City have peaceably had, holden and enjoyed divers jurisdictions, liberties, franchises, freedoms, customs, privileges, injunctions and exemptions by prescription and from time whereof the memory of man is not to the contrary, And whereas divers debates, questions and ambiguities have before this time been moved and arisen and doth daily grow and arise as well upon the force and validity

of the said Letters patent, by reason of the verity of the name
and incorporation aforesaid and by reason of divers other
defects in the said Letters Patent, as also upon the validity and
force of the prescriptions and usage aforesaid, whereupon
many and grievous inconveniences have often times happened not only to the citizens and inhabitants of our said City
but also unto very many other of our faithful subjects
contracting and bargaining with them, Know ye that we,
desiring that all such like debates, ambiguities and inconveniences should hereafter be altogether taken away and
considering that our said City of Winchester amongst other
ancient cities of our realm of England was anciently chosen
and is most famous both for the celebration of the coronations
and sepultures and for the preservation of other famous
monuments of our progenitors, and now is fallen into great
ruin, decay and poverty, and chiefly desiring the amendment
of the state and profit of the same City and that from henceforth a certain, sure, undoubted order and manner in our said
City of, in and concerning the keeping of our peace and the
rule and government of our people there may continually be
had, and that the same City for ever hereafter may be and
may remain a City of peace and quietness to the fear and
terror of the evil and for the reward and comfort of the good,
and also that our peace and other works of justice may be
kept there and done without any delay, and hoping that the
said citizens and inhabitants of the said City and their successors may by our grant and of our princely bounty enjoy more
ample liberties and privileges that then they will receive
and acknowledge themselves bounden more especially and
earnestly to bestow their service towards our heirs and
successors, and also that on the humble petition of our faithful
and well beloved counsellor, Sir Francis Walsingham, knight,
our principal Secretary and High Steward of our said City, of
our special grace have willed, ordained, constituted and
granted and by these presents do for us, our heirs and successors, will, ordain, constitute and grant and declare that our
said City of Winchester shall be and remain for ever hereafter

a free City of itself and that the citizens and inhabitants in the City aforesaid from henceforth for ever shall be in deed and in name one body politic and incorporate by the name of the Mayor, Bailiffs and Commonalty of the City of Winchester, and by the same name they shall have perpetual succession and shall be for ever hereafter persons able and in law capable to have, acquire, receive, hold and possess lands, tenements, liberties, privileges, jurisdictions, franchises, hereditaments, goods and chattels of what kind, nature or quality soever they shall be to them and their successors in fee and perpetuity, and also to give, grant, let and assign the same lands, tenements, hereditaments, goods and chattels, and for the doing and executing all and singular other matters and things by the name aforesaid, and that by the name of Mayor, Bailiffs and Commonalty of the City of Winchester aforesaid they may and shall be able to implead and be impleaded to answer and to be answered, to defend and to be defended, in any courts or places whatsoever of us or our heirs and successors in all and singular actions, suits, plaints, causes, matters and demands whatsoever of what kind, nature, condition, or quality so ever they be in the same manner and form as other liege people of this our realm of England being persons able and in law capable, and by the same name possess lands, tenements, and hereditaments and likewise shall and may be able to have, acquire, receive, possess, give, grant and demise goods and chattels, and they the said Mayor, Bailiffs and Commonalty of the City aforesaid may for ever have a Common Seal to serve for the doing, making and executing of their demises, grants and all other causes and business of them and their successors whatsoever.'

The charter goes on to declare that there shall be one Mayor, one Recorder, six Aldermen, two Bailiffs, two Coroners and two Constables, all chosen from the elder, circumspect, better and more honest sort of citizens, and that there shall also be a body of persons to be known as the Twenty-four, as in the past, consisting of twenty-four of the better, discreet and more honest men of the City, to assist and help the Mayor. The present mayor, Edward Cole, who had been elected in September, 1587, was to remain in office until noon of the feast day of St. Michael the Archangel next coming, when another person was to be chosen and sworn to the same office according to the ordinances, statutes and ancient customs of the City. There then appears the name of Thomas Fleming, the Recorder, whose previous appointment to that office is duly confirmed, and he is to have a deputy to be known as the Town Clerk. Following this there are the names of the six Aldermen who are appointed for life 'provided they behave themselves in the office aforesaid', and next come the names of the Twenty-four, with the reminder that any one of them might be deposed, if he should at any time misbehave or betray the trust reposed in him, and his place taken by another to be chosen by the Mayor and Aldermen.

The Mayor, Recorder and Aldermen were to be Justices of the Peace, sitting at the Quarter Sessions within the City to hear and determine all manner of murders, felonies, misprisions, riots, routs, oppressions, extortions, forestalling, regrating, trespasses and all other things whatsoever arising in Winchester. All fines, issues, redemptions and amerciaments arising from the cases brought before the Justices were to be handed over to the Mayor and Bailiffs for the benefit of the City. The Burgh-mote was to be kept twice a year at the same time as two of the Quarter Sessions in the manner and form as had hitherto been accustomed. In addition there was to be a Court of Record held in the Guildhall every Wednesday and Friday before the Mayor, Recorder (or more often his deputy) and the Bailiffs to hear all pleas, plaints and actions, and the City was again to have the use of all fines and profits of the court. It was also stipulated that the Mayor was to be Escheator for the Crown, taking charge of all property lapsing to the Crown when the owner died intestate without heirs. Linked with these clauses was the warning that the Justices of the Peace for the County of Southampton should not 'in any wise intermeddle with the said city or liberties

53

thereof, nor exercise any jurisdiction or authority concerning any causes, matters or things whatsoever arising or appertaining to the said city'.

Markets were to be held each Wednesday and Saturday, and three fairs annually, 'one to be holden on the feast-day of St. Edward and on the eve and morrow of the same day; another on Monday and Tuesday in the first week of Lent; and a third on the feast-day of St. Swithun and on the eve and morrow of the same; together with a court of Pyepowder to be held there during the time of the said fairs'.

All the inhabitants of the City were to be acquitted and discharged from the suit of the county and hundred courts which came within the jurisdiction of the sheriff of the county, and they were also to be free, as they had been in the past, throughout the country from a number of tolls, such as lastage or the custom paid for wares, including fish, hides, corn, wool, which were sold by a measure known as a last, passage or payment for passage especially over water, pontage, or bridge toll, piccage or payment to the owner of the soil for breaking ground to erect booths, etc., stallage or toll for erecting a stall, murage or tax exacted for repairing the walls of a town. The Mayor was to be appointed clerk of the markets and the City was granted the assizes of bread, wine and other victuals, and all weights and measures. Authority was given for the creation of corporations or companies of the various trades and occupations in the City and for the drawing up of regulations for such bodies. Also, in order to stimulate trade and commerce, particularly in the cloth industry, permission was granted to manufacture broadcloths and kerseys.

Lastly, all former rights and privileges, including those granted by the late King and Queen, Philip and Mary, were confirmed to the City, particularly the guardianship of the Hospital of St. John the Baptist; and there is a proviso, at the very end of the charter, that 'by this our present grant the reverend father in God, Thomas, lord bishop of Winchester, nor his successors, bishops of Winchester, nor the cathedral church, nor any tenement, officer or minister of the said bishop of Winchester, may be damnified, molested or troubled or in any way wronged under colour or pretence of this charter'.

In the above summary of this charter of 1587 one sees the basic rights and privileges upon which municipal government in Winchester was, for the future, to be founded. Procedures, which previously had arisen from local and ancient customs, now obtained royal sanction; doubts and uncertainties concerning previous royal grants were now clarified; there was to be an end to all quibbling regarding the respective jurisdictions of the City and the County of Southampton. The power, dignity and prestige of the Mayor and his officers were considerably enhanced, the City was enabled to accumulate and dispose of property, and there was more than a pious hope that decay and poverty, which had been prevalent for at least two centuries, would be overcome. But what is planned in theory does not always materialize in practice, and in succeeding chapters an attempt will be made to expand and explain in much greater detail many of the items mentioned above and to show how the day to day life of the citizens was carried on within the framework of this constitution.

CHAPTER IV

The Mayoralty

Previous to the Norman Conquest, Winchester appears to have been governed by a provost or portreeve, and it was not until the early part of the thirteenth century that, as far as one can gather, the leading citizen was known as the Mayor. The exact date at which the title of the holder of the office was changed from provost to mayor is not known and, through lack of documentary evidence, probably never will be known. But it has been a matter of considerable local interest and the subject of a controversy which seems to have embraced the further question as to which of the two important medieval cities, London and Winchester, had the first mayor. It was the assumption that in the year 1184 Winchester had its first mayor that led the leading citizens to celebrate in 1884 the seven hundredth anniversary of the founding of the mayoralty. They did this although it was pointed out publicly at the time by a well-known local antiquary, who had undertaken a great deal of research in the matter, that there was no sound evidence to support the assumption.[1] When, however, one examines the evidence which is available, it seems that Winchester, unlike London which obtained by charter from King John in 1215 the right to elect a mayor annually, never secured such a royal grant, and therefore the title of mayor in this City most likely arose

---

[1] Baigent papers, Winchester City Archives.

out of ancient usage about the end of the twelfth or the beginning of the thirteenth century.

Dr. J. Milner in his *History of Winchester* gives a list of the mayors of Winchester from A.D. 1184 which he claimed to have copied from an old catalogue, extant in 1799, at St. John's House. But it can now be shown from the more ancient records which have survived that this list, as far as the twelfth, thirteenth and fourteenth centuries are concerned, is largely fictitious.

From the early part of the fourteenth century the mayor was elected annually, and there is no difficulty in ascertaining, from the City records, the names of those who held this office, together with the dates of their election. The actual date of the election varied from time to time, but it was always held in the month of September. In King Henry VIII's reign, in 1517, it was held five days before Michaelmas Day, and if the latter fell on a Sunday then the election took place four days previously. But in 1560, in order to avoid all doubt whether Michaelmas Day should be counted as one of the aforesaid five days, it was ordained that the election from henceforth should take place yearly on the Tuesday following Holy Rood Day (September 14th).[1] In 1575, a further amendment was made to the effect that the day of the election of the mayor should be yearly on the Monday next after Holy Rood Day provided that the Monday was not a 'fish day', or fast day; if it were a fish day then the election was to be held on the Tuesday following.[2]

On the day of election the citizens gathered in St. John's House to elect a mayor, bailiffs, chamberlains and other officers according to ancient custom. During the reign of Elizabeth the procedure for the election of the mayor was that laid down by ordinance in King Henry VIII's reign, in 1520, when 'the Right Reverende ffather in god Richard' Fox, 'Bisshope of Winchester, singuler good Lorde to the saide Cytie', had acted as mediator in divers divisions, debates and variances which had arisen concerning the nomination of the

[1] 1st Bk. Ord., f. 126.   [2] Idem, f. 181.

57

mayor.[1] In accordance with this ordinance, all those who had been mayors of the City and who were present at the assembly should name two able persons of the Twenty-four who, in their opinion, were the most fit and able to fill the office of the mayoralty for the following year. The two names, in writing, were handed to the present Mayor, who struck out the name of one of them as he thought advisable and then added the name of the person who had been unsuccessful in the previous year's election. If there was an equal division of opinion among the former mayors in choosing the names of the two to be put up to the Mayor, then the senior of the ex-mayors was to have the casting vote. When all this had been done, the voting for the new mayor went forward 'in manner and forme as hathe been used and accustomed'.

Attached to this ordinance dealing with the order for the election of the mayor, there is 'Master Maiors othe', which runs as follows:

'Ye shall swere that ye shall well and lawfullye serve our soveraigne lorde the kinge in thoffice of the Mairaltie in the Citie of Winchester and the same Citie saffelye and surely kepe to the use of our soveraigne lorde the kinge of England and his heyres kings of Englande and the proffyt of the kinge shall do in every case in that to youe belongithe, And the right of the kinge and every thinge to his crowne belonginge in the foresayd Citie lawfully shall kepe, And ye shall not assent to the decrease nother to the conceilment of the righte of the francheses of the kinge and by that youe may save the right of the kinge be it of the crowne or in lands or in rents or in ffrancheses or in sutes or in conceilments withdrawn ye shall put to your payne to repell, And if that youe can not so doo ye shall showe it to the kinge or to them of his councell which youe do intende will showe it to the kinge, And that lawfullye and rightfullye ye shall intreate the people of your baylywike and right shall mynister to every person aswell to strangers as to pryvies and to poore as to riche in that to youe belongithe to doo, And that nor for hatred nor for riches

[1] Idem. f. 93.

nor for gifts nor for promys nor for love right ye shall not fayle to doo to no man nor no mannys right disturbe nor nothinge ye shall take by the which the kinge may lose or by the whiche the right maye be disturbed, And that ye shall well kepe and surelye put thassize uppon brede and drinke and upon all other manner of victualls and measures within the same Citie made and done, And that ye shall yelde and do due execution uppon the defawts of the same which shalbe founde before youe, And that in every thinge which belongithe to the maior of the sayd Citie to do well and lawfullye as god youe helpe and all Saynts and by the contents of that booke.'[1]

Under the title 'Another Othe of Mr. Mayor', there appears a declaration which was in all probability the response given by the mayor when the oath of office was administered:

'I shall observe and kepe all statutes and usages of our Cytie and all ordinances confirmed of our predecessors made before this tyme ne none office discharge ne mynister ne offycer chaunge ne none make newe without thassent of the xxiiii[tl] of the Cytie but by my poure treulye put them in execution so god helpe me at the holydome.'[2]

Following the annual election, the newly appointed Mayor was called upon to entertain at his own expense the retiring mayor, bailiffs and commonalty to dinner at St. John's House upon pain of forfeiture of five pounds to be deducted out of his fee. This fee, payable to the mayor to enable him to meet the expenses of his office, was fixed throughout Elizabeth's reign at twenty pounds per annum; ten pounds to be paid to him at the time of his election at the September Burgh-mote, and the remaining ten pounds within fourteen days after the finishing of the audit of the city accounts following his term of office.[3] But should the Mayor do or leave undone anything contrary to an Act of Parliament made for the rating and certifying of the rates of the wages of servants and artificers, or contrary to a proclamation prohibiting the eating of flesh in the time of Lent and other fasting days, or contrary to any ordinance of the City which the Mayor was in duty bound to

[1] Idem, f. 94.   [2] Idem, f. 94.   [3] Idem, f. 183.

put into execution, then the auditors, of whom there were eight elected annually to scrutinize the Chamberlains' accounts, were empowered to deduct the whole or part of his fee.[1]

This proviso, formulated undoubtedly to prevent any dereliction of duty on the part of the Mayor, was put into effect on more than one occasion. For example, there is a note in the Chamberlains' account roll for the financial year 1566–67 stating that the remainder of the fee, to wit, ten pounds, due to William Hall, late Mayor, would not be paid because he did not seem to the auditors to be worthy to receive it for various reasons. Firstly, because contrary to the Mayor's oath he had allowed Joan Bethell, widow, to erect two 'bulks', that is, stout frameworks on which goods could be displayed for sale, outside her house on the south side of St. Lawrence's Church, and thus encroach on the Queen's ground, and he had not taken action to have them removed contrary to the advice of his brethren; secondly, because he had not carried out an ordinance for the repairing of the streets; thirdly, because he rode to London, Southampton, and divers other well-known places during his mayoralty without an attendant or servant contrary to the custom of the city; fourthly, because he uttered in the general assembly certain scandalous and defamatory words against William Lawrence, Recorder of the City, and other aldermen contrary to the form of divers ordinances.

However, in this particular case, when the decision of the auditors to disallow the second moiety of the fee became known to the succeeding mayor and the former mayors they immediately met to consider the situation. They came to the conclusion that although the auditors had acted within their powers there were mitigating circumstances, and they pointed out to the auditors that the former mayor, William Hall, had been put to considerable expense in providing a dinner for Her Majesty's Clerk of the Market and his attendants and in providing a further two dinners for Her Majesty's Com-

[1] Idem, f. 174.

missioners for Taxation, and that he had committed the above-mentioned offences, not deliberately and in open defiance of the ordinances, but through lack of wider experience for he had previously held no other office in the City. They expressed their confidence in him there and then, and for the future, and backed this up with a warrant addressed to the auditors authorizing them to pay the remainder of the fee.

There was another civic function, known as St. John's Supper, which was held at St. John's House annually on the Sunday following the feast of the Nativity of St. John the Baptist, that is, the Sunday following the twenty-fourth of June. It was the custom on this occasion for the magistrates to pay twelve pence, other members of the Twenty-four ten pence, and the remainder of the freemen eight pence each, whether they were present or not.[1] Also the Mayor for the time being had to provide a capon at the same supper and the alderman of the High Street another capon. The origin of this supper is uncertain as the evidence concerning it is somewhat scanty. There are, however, three references which throw a little light on the matter. In the *Black Book*, under the date 1546, there is the ordinance which sets out the graduated scale of payments already quoted above. Also in the *Black Book* there is a note made in 1539 to the effect that the supper was no longer to be held, and therefore it seems that it was in abeyance until its revival in 1546 with a new arrangement as regards payments. The date 1539 is significant, for this was the year of the dissolution of the religious houses, and uncertainty as to the future of St. John's House may have prompted the decision to hold no more suppers for the time being. Also, there is among the records a small roll which gives a list of fifty-four freemen each of whom paid twelve pence for the supper in 1536, and who collectively are named as the Fraternity of St. John's. From the roll it appears that this supper was also attended by the Mayor's Chaplain, who was Warden of St. John's House, and by the Abbess of St. Mary's Nunnery. From this evidence one is tempted to

[1] Idem, f. 15.

conjecture that the supper had, on the one hand, some religious connection and further, that this was an occasion when the freemen met, not as members of the municipal corporation, but as members of the anciently founded Merchant Gild which in course of time had become known as the Fraternity of St. John's.

In 1562 it was decided by the assembly of freemen that the supper should not be held as was customary on the Sunday following the feast of St. John the Baptist, but on the next Sunday, because of the visit to the City of the Justices of Assize who, together with the Sheriff of the County, would require the use of the 'vessell' of the City for their repast, and also because victuals could not be obtained so conveniently on that day when large numbers of people from the countryside usually flocked into the City.[1] The 'vessell' referred to above comprised the City plate and utensils used on festive occasions, concerning which there was a regulation that every time the Mayor and Bailiffs used them they should pay threepence, and strangers sixpence.[2] Two years later, in 1564, 'for diverse consideracions and specially for avoydinge the daunger of the plage nowe remayninge (which god of his mercye ceasse)', it was decided that the supper should not be held that year.[3] In 1587 there was some difficulty in balancing the accounts of this annual event. It is not stated whether this was due to faulty book-keeping, or to non-payment of fees particularly by absent brethren, or to the provision of too sumptuous a repast on which the expenditure exceeded the income. But the assembly decided that the arrears on this particular supper should be discharged by some means or other at the discretion of the Mayor and his brethren.[4]

The upholding of the dignity of the mayor's office was constantly under review, and there are recurring ordinances dealing with the mayor's place of residence, in front of which bull-baiting was not allowed to take place, with the mayor's profession or occupation, with his robe of office and even with

[1] Idem, f. 131.   [2] Idem, f. 14.   [3] Idem, f. 138.
[4] Idem, f. 254.

his wife's gown. In 1536, in the reign of Henry VIII, it had been declared that no mayor during his term of office should dwell in an inn or hostelry, nor should he have any ale or beer drawn or tapped within his house on account of the dishonour which might ensue.[1] But a difficulty arose in 1573 when Stephen Ashton, who combined the occupations of inn-keeper and fishmonger, was elected mayor. It was surmounted by agreeing that during his mayoralty it would be lawful for him to live in the east part of his house provided he did not use it as an inn, but his wife and servants could use the remainder of the house as an inn as in time past. In order that the Mayor should not be unduly incommoded it was also agreed that it would be lawful for him to receive into the east part of his house any man of honour or justice of the peace, together with their attendants, and provide them with food and lodging. Such were the conditions imposed on Mr. Stephen Ashton in his capacity as inn-keeper, but as a fish-monger he was not allowed to sell any fish openly in the streets, neither was it lawful for him to ride to the sea for fish, and if it should be necessary for him to ride out of the City he was to have a man accompanying him. Although the assembly were prepared to allow him to buy fish in the open market for the use of his own house and gave him leave to provide lodging for those who brought it from the coast, they forbade him to buy fish either in the open market or secretly in order to sell it to others.[2]

The wearing of slovenly or unconventional dress by mayor, ex-mayor or alderman was regarded with disfavour. An ordinance 'againste goinge in jerkyns and coates' states that aldermen and former mayors of the City were not to come into the High Street or into the common market, unless they were riding out of the town or going shooting, without a gown or cloak. They were allowed, however, to walk before their doors or shops without gown or cloak provided they were attending to their customary business affairs.[3] With regard to ceremonial occasions, provision was made that the

[1] Idem, f. 12.   [2] Idem, f. 174.   [3] Idem, f. 148.

mayor elect was to have his scarlet gown ready to wear on the first Burgh-mote day, and all former mayors were to wear their scarlet gowns on the following days: the first Burgh-mote day, Christmas Day, St. Stephen's Day, the day of Epiphany, Easter Day and the Monday following, Ascension Day, the second Burgh-mote day, Whitsunday and the Monday following, Trinity Sunday, Corpus Christi Day and All Hallows Day.[1]

In 1579 an attempt was made to revive an ancient custom by passing an ordinance to the effect that the Mayor should, immediately after his election, provide for his wife a scarlet gown, according to the ancient order of the City, and that she should wear it on all occasions when the Mayor wore scarlet.[2] If any man failed to provide his wife with such a gown when he became Mayor, he lost ten pounds which was deducted from his fee, and if the wife failed to wear it on the specified occasions the Mayor was fined six shillings and eightpence. In the following year this ordinance was amended to include the wives of all former mayors, and these were to wear scarlet gowns on all festival days and other accustomed times when the Mayor wore his scarlet gown, the penalty for non-compliance remaining the same.[3] But twelve months later, it appears that Mr. Edward White, then Mayor, 'for certeyne reasonable speciall causes by hym alleaged', but not specified in the records, could not conform with the ordinance in so short a time, that is, before the first Burgh-mote after his election.[4] He was therefore excused until the following Easter by which time he had to provide the necessary gown. The two succeeding mayors, William Hodson and Anthony Bird, found themselves in a similar predicament and each was excused until the following Easter. The second of these mayors, Anthony Bird, however, called a special meeting of the assembly in the February preceding the Easter of 1583, and finally put an end to the business of providing the mayor's wife with a scarlet gown with the following

[1] Idem, f. 129. [2] Idem, f. 200. [3] Idem, f. 204.
[4] Idem. f. 216.

6. Master Mayor's oath (First Book of Ordinances, f. 94).

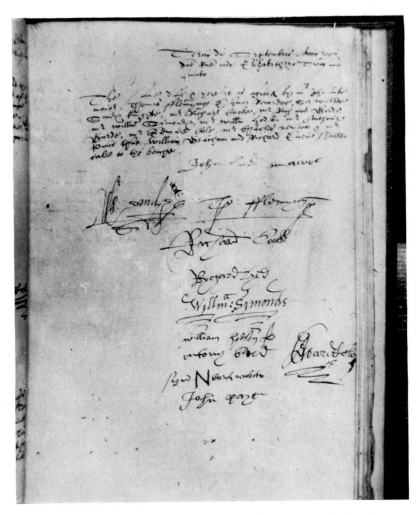

7. Signatures of the Mayor and his Brethren, 1593. (John Luke, maior, Walter Sandys, Thomas fflemynge, Richard Cooke, Rychard Byrd, William Symonds, William Hodson, Antony Burd, Edward Cole, signed N Carolus Newbote, John Payce.)

ordinance: 'It is agreed that all ordinaunces heretofore made for the providinge, havinge and wearinge of skarlet gownes for women nowe beinge the mayors wiffe and which shalbe hereafter the wiffe of any mayor and all paynes and penalties therein conteyned shalbe repelled and from henceforth utterlie voyde.'[1]

The question of seniority among former mayors became a matter of dispute in 1572 when it became necessary to frame an ordinance for the special purpose of avoiding doubts and ambiguities which might arise through the challenging of places by former mayors. This ordinance stated that according to the ancient custom of the City the practice was that any person who had been mayor twice should have seniority over one who had been mayor once only, even though the latter had held the mayoralty in point of time before the one who had held that office twice, 'and so the oftener mayor the more auncient'.[2]

It is possible that such questions of precedence had a greater significance in Elizabeth's time when, for example, every member of the Twenty-four, as well as every other freeman, was required every Sunday and on all principal feasts, 'in tyme of processions and sermons', to meet the Mayor at the High Cross of the City, being the most public and convenient place, and accompany him to the Cathedral Church and remain with him until he returned to his house. Without a reasonable excuse which would satisfy the Mayor and the Justices of the Peace, any person who failed to attend at such times was fined fourpence, and this was doubled if he were of the Twenty-four. The offender, however, could avoid the fine by spending a day and a night in prison, if he so decided.[3]

Nowadays one is quite familiar with the rôle played by the mayor of a municipality and with the duties which he is expected to undertake as chairman of the council or as the spokesman for his fellow-townsmen as occasion demands. He is, or should be, the dignified and respected leader of a

[1] Idem, f. 226.   [2] Idem, f. 172.   [3] Idem, f. 276.

particular community, within the bounds set by statute. But in Elizabethan times, judging by the records which have survived, he was more than this. He had the Twenty-four, whose advice he could seek according to ancient custom, but they had no power to over-rule him; he was subject only to the ordinances enacted by the Burgh-mote and to local custom and usage; otherwise he was an autocrat. Should the mayor transgress the ordinances and customs of the City, the matter was usually rectified during the mayoralty of his successor when either a fine was inflicted or a deduction made from the balance of the fee then due to him, as has already been shown.

It had long been a regulation of the City that every one of the Twenty-four should remain silent and hold his peace at the command of the Mayor under pain of a penalty of three shillings and fourpence, and that every citizen should present himself before the Mayor when summoned to do so.[1,2] The Mayor could order any owner of land or property to pave the street in front of his land or premises; moreover, he had the power to mitigate and diminish the penalty inflicted on an offender against any regulation or ordinance.[3] It was the Mayor who fixed the price of bread and other commodities.[4] These and many other examples which could be quoted show the enormous power which was vested in him. All executive business was in his hands, and things are recorded as being done by the Mayor or on his orders. With the exception of those authorized by the Burgh-mote, payments from the City funds were made through the Chamberlains by order of the Mayor, and receipts from all sources were, by his orders and in his presence, placed in the City coffers. Quite frequently when the Burgh-mote failed to come to a definite decision on a particular matter, they agreed that action should be taken 'at the discretion of Mr. Mayor', who usually consulted 'the more parte of his bretherne'.

Towards the end of the sixteenth century the powers

[1] Idem, f. 7.   [2] Idem, f. 8.   [3] Idem, f. 11.
[4] Idem, f. 13.

of the Twenty-four seem to have diminished, for they were called into consultation with far less frequency than formerly.

The important advisory body by this time consisted of the former mayors together with the Recorder of the City, and membership of the Twenty-four seems to have become little more than a stepping stone to the mayoralty or to the magistrates' bench. The records of the day to day management of the City's affairs show by the signatures subscribed thereto that the Mayor was attended by the Recorder or his deputy and a few former mayors, often numbering no more than four but occasionally as many as ten, and it was this select group which settled the numerous problems confronting the Mayor. The latter, however, was the predominant figure and there were numerous occasions when he took action on his own initiative. In 1593, when the plague was raging in the City, there was disagreement among the brethren concerning a preventive measure to be taken. Instead of giving a casting vote, the Mayor called another meeting attended only by those whose opinions coincided with his own and thereby secured a unanimous decision.[1]

The Mayor and his brethren met quite frequently. There was rarely more than the space of a week between their meetings and, at times, it was necessary to meet on three or four consecutive days. The matters which came before them show an infinite variety.[2] They admitted poor men and women to St. John's Hospital, made allowances for the clothing and the instruction of poor children who were to be apprenticed to a trade, decided on the nature and cost of New Year and other gifts, such as a gallon of sack or claret, or a sugar loaf, to the Marquis of Winchester and other notable persons, examined the accounts of the Chamberlains and other collectors of money, and made preliminary inquiries into cases of felony before committal to the sessions. Though much of their business was of a routine nature, there were times when

[1] Proceedings of the Corporation, Book A, MS., City Archives.
[2] These matters are dealt with more fully in Chapter VI.

weightier and more important matters claimed their attention. In 1591 they had to make all the necessary arrangements for the contemplated visit of the Queen; on another occasion it was reported to them that the Sheriff of the County had taken a distress of the goods of William Hodson, an alderman and former mayor, on account of money not previously paid by him on behalf of the City to the Exchequer, and they thereupon decided how they could best help their colleague; in 1595 the Mayor and burgesses of Southampton procured letters from the Queen's Council indicating that Winchester was to share with Southampton the cost of supplying a ship and a hoy, and to meet this situation the Mayor and two of his brethren immediately set out to interview the Marquis of Winchester, the Lord High Admiral and Lord Mountjoy, then High Steward of the City, and seek their advice.

The extremely wide powers with which the Mayor of Winchester was at this time invested ensured that he was not only a great personality, but also that he was kept extraordinarily busy throughout his term of office. He certainly held no sinecure, and it was perhaps as a recompense for his twelve months of concentrated effort that the holder of the mayoralty was excused from holding that office again during the following five years, except when his successor happened to die in office, in which case the former mayor was then recalled to serve for the uncompleted term. Such a case occurred in 1580 when the Mayor, Edward White, died and his predecessor, Richard Cooke, resumed the office. Of this event the following is a translation of the entry (in Latin) in the First Book of Ordinances: 'Richard Cooke, gentleman, who in the preceding year performed the office of the mayoralty of this city, was recalled of his own choice to the same office by virtue of a certain ordinance of the aforesaid city on account of the untimely death, which intervened, of Edward White, lately Mayor of the same city, whose year of office from the date of his election was not completed, and whose soul may Jesus the Redeemer graciously receive.' To which entry the scribe has added:

'Urbs infelici hoc duplex caput induit Anno
dum Cochus nitidum revocatus depulit Album.'

which may be translated:

'Two heads in this sad year the city took;
Neat White departed, it recovered Cooke.'[1]

For some citizens, as in modern times, the honour of being
Mayor was worth striving for, while possibly for the others
the great responsibility and onerous duties outweighed any
honour which the mayoralty might confer. Every member
of the Twenty-four was eligible for election to this office, and
it would seem that there were occasions when citizens
attempted either to seek or avoid nomination, even by
bribery, for in 1575 it was agreed in the general assembly that
no freeman of the City should receive or give any money or
other reward, or any promise of any money or reward, to
have his name either put forward or left out, or the name of
any other person put forward or left out, in the election of
the mayor. The fact that a person convicted of giving or
offering such a bribe was fined ten pounds, an extremely large
amount in those days, acted no doubt as a strong deterrent.
Certain offices, such as those of the Bailiffs, could be avoided
on payment of a substantial fee, but a freeman of the City
could be discharged from holding the office of Mayor only
by swearing a solemn oath, in the presence of the assembled
freemen and immediately after his election, that he was unable to carry out such a duty. The only case throughout
Elizabeth's reign of a person availing himself of this ancient
custom happened in 1584, when Christopher Genens, having
been elected to the office of the mayoralty, corporally testi-
fied and swore upon his solemn oath in manner and form
following, namely: 'I, Christopher Genens doo here corpor-
allie take my othe in this assemble that I am not of abilitie to
beare and susteyne the office of the maioraltie of this citie for
this yere to come without daunger of my utter undoinge.'[2]

During the forty-five years which covered Elizabeth's

[1] 1st Bk. Ord., f. 216.   [2] Idem, f. 234.

reign, the office of Mayor of Winchester was occupied by twenty men. Of these Richard Cooke was Mayor four times, including the uncompleted portion of Edward White's tenure in 1580. It was not at all uncommon for a man to be Mayor two or three times during his life-time, but always with a gap of five or more years between each occasion. Thus, William Badger was elected Mayor in 1572, 1586 and 1597; William Symonds in 1575, 1585 and 1596, and William Hodson in 1581, 1590 and 1602. The election of these three men, each on three occasions, points to their being persons of outstanding ability and character, but as far as available evidence shows they were outmatched by Edward Cole, who was Mayor in 1587, 1598 and again in 1612 in James I's reign. His rise to a position of importance in the City was quite unique. On September 12th, 1578, Edward Cole was admitted to the Merchant Gild, thereby becoming a freeman of the City; three days later at the meeting of the Burgh-mote he had the office of Bailiff of the Commons (Low Bailiff) freely forgiven him, and at the same time he was made a member of the Twenty-four and then elected Bailiff of the Twenty-four (High Bailiff). Why this man was advanced so rapidly to high office is not clear; it might have been that he had influential family connections, or he might have been sponsored by the Bishop of Winchester for whom he acted as principal registrar.[1] But whatever the cause, his election to office was fortunate for the City, for he spared no efforts throughout his life in furthering its interests. He was excused the office of mayor between the years 1579 and 1584, but was elected to it in 1587, when the City received its very important charter, and as has already been mentioned on two subsequent occasions. In 1601 he was elected one of the burgesses to Elizabeth's tenth and last parliament.

[1] Edward Cole was the son of John Cole of Sudbury, Suffolk, who was the great-grandson of Sir John Cole, a Devonshire knight, who fought at Agincourt, 1415. (See *Genealogy of the family of Cole of County of Devon, etc.*, by James Edwin Cole, pub. John Russell Smith, London, 1867.)

The Mayoralty

At the time that Edward Cole relinquished the high bailiwick in 1579 an ordinance was passed declaring that if he or his wife, Christian, should at any time engage in any trade or occupation which entailed buying and selling they would not be required to pay the usual fees for so doing. A little later, the mill outside Eastgate and the fulling mills at Coitbury were leased to Edward Cole, but there is no record of his having engaged in trade or commerce.[1] He was a lawyer who became a very wealthy and prosperous citizen, as the formerly ornate, but now dilapidated, memorial in the north aisle of the cathedral testifies. During the thirty years from the time of his first mayoralty in 1587 to his death in 1617, he figured prominently in all municipal affairs and particularly in the various law-suits in which the City was engaged. He took the initiative in promoting a bill in the Court of Chancery concerning the revenues from lands which Peter Symonds, a native of Winchester and a merchant of London, left to the City of Winchester for the purpose of founding a hospital; he was constantly journeying to London to further this particular case, which lasted for over five years, and also the cases against Alresford and Bishops Waltham who had each set up markets in their respective towns to the detriment of Winchester traders. That he was greatly trusted by his fellows is shown by the fact that when the City coffers were burgled in 1589, all City funds were placed in his hands until a more satisfactory coffer could be provided in the council house. An amusing incident happened after his election as Mayor for the second time in 1598. It is recorded that 'Mr. William Badger, mayor, Mr. Recorder and the residew of the mayors brethrene beinge assembled in the guyldhall attendinge the cominge of Mr. Edward Cole, maior electe, to take his othe, did send Thomas Bedham and William Budde, the chamberlains, to Mr. Cole to declare unto him they were assembled to attende his comynge to the guyldhall to receyve his othe, which Thomas and William returninge declared to the sayde

[1] Coitbury; these mills were situated on a branch of the River Itchen alongside Buck Street, now Busket Lane.

Maior and Recorder that they went thither and requested to speake with Mr. Cole but yt was answered he was asleepe and so they could not speake with him'.

But Edward Cole was no sluggard, for from the written pages of the records there emerges no figure more clearly and sharply defined as a worthy champion and sustainer of the City's liberties and privileges. He was a man of action, vigorous and determined. During his terms of office royal proclamations, such as the one dealing with the monopoly in starch which was very unpopular, were put into effect immediately; letters from the diocesan ecclesiastical commissioners concerning recusants and seminary priests were acted upon with promptitude; more than once, he personally organized and joined in searches through the City, including the gaol, for offenders against the law. One is tempted to conclude that he was of a calibre beyond that of his colleagues. This may be true, but it should not imply that the other mayors of this period were lacking in public spirit and devotion to their duties. In fact, there is evidence to the contrary. For example, six of them jointly, including Edward Cole, did not hesitate to stand bound for the repayment of a loan of two hundred and eighty pounds, which must have been equivalent to more than twelve thousand pounds in modern currency, to meet the legal charges of the suit concerning Peter Symonds's will. There is, however, insufficient evidence to allow one to form an estimate of the successive mayors who came from various walks of life, some being of independent means and connected with county families, while others were members of the legal profession or prosperous tradesmen. The scholarly signatures of some of these stand out in sharp contrast to the 'X' of William Lane, a butcher, and the 'N' of Charles Newbolt, a builder, but unlettered though a few of the mayors might have been, this deficiency was counterbalanced by their zeal for the welfare of the City.

CHAPTER V

City Officers

THE BAILIFFS

Next in importance to the Mayor came the Bailiffs, who were named with him in the address of all documents and the recorded proceedings of the Burgh-mote. Thus, in 1586 a writ and proclamation by the Queen's Majesty concerning the sentence against Mary, Queen of Scots, was addressed 'to the Mayor and Bailiffs' of her city of Winchester, and minutes of every meeting of the Burgh-mote were dated by the phrase 'Mr. A. B. then being mayor, C.D. and E.F. bailiffs'. The Bailiffs were also magistrates, sitting on the Bench in the Town Court and at times deputizing for him.

Before Winchester had its first Mayor at the beginning of the thirteenth century, it was governed by Provost and Bailiffs who represented the King's authority in the city. After the creation of the office of Mayor both these titles continued in use for a time. It seems probable that originally there were always provosts and at times there might have been bailiffs as well, and that in time the two names were used indifferently for the same office. By 1300, as far as Winchester is concerned, the title of provost had disappeared, and bailiffs was the term used for the officers who, acting under the Mayor, enforced regulations which had royal authority.

The two Bailiffs were elected annually at the same time as the Mayor at the September Burgh-mote, and in a somewhat similar manner. From a thirteenth-century record it appears that at that time they were chosen by the citizens, whose choice was limited by their having to take two out of the four nominees submitted by the Mayor and the Twenty-four; but by Elizabeth's reign the procedure was slightly different. There was now a distinction, not previously apparent, between these two officers, for one is called the Bailiff of the Twenty-four or High Bailiff, while the other is referred to as the Bailiff of the Commons or Low Bailiff. The nominators of the former were all those who had previously been mayor and who were present at the assembly, and it was their duty to bring forward the names of two able men from among the members of the Twenty-four of whom one was then elected High Bailiff by the assembly of freemen. In the case of the Bailiff of the Commons or Low Bailiff, it had been the rule since 1564 that the Twenty-four should nominate two freemen for the office and that the already elected High Bailiff should then choose one of them at his pleasure.[1] It is obvious from the ordinances of the Burgh-mote that occasionally freemen were nominated for the High Bailiwick though at the time they were not members of the Twenty-four; but whenever such a freeman was elected to that office he was automatically made a member of that select body.

Formerly the duties of the Bailiffs had been described in a single phrase, namely, 'loyally to keep the provosty and to do justice to all the Commons'; but in Tudor times this was expanded considerably, and the oath taken upon election to office was in the following form:

'Ye shall well truely and lawfullye serve the kinge in the office of bayliwyke in the Cytie of Winchester frome the feast of Mychaelmas next comynge by one hole yere unto the sayd feaste of mychaelmas frome thens next folowinge tyll the howre of twelve at none. The same Cytie under the Mayor surelye and saffelye to kepe unto the use of our soveraigne lorde the kinge of England and of his heyres kings of Englande and all things profitable to the kinge belonginge and appertaininge to thoffyce of bayliwyke there ye shall do

[1] 1st Bk. Ord., f. 140.

that to youe appendithe the rights of the kinge and all that to
the crowne beleithe or belongithe lawfullye to kepe and
warde. And that common right ye do mynister to every man
aswell to straungers as to pryvies, to poore as to riche, in that
to youe belongithe for to do. And also the foresayd Cytie
lawfulle and treulye to charge and discharge and acquite in
thende of the yere in all that in youe is that to the bayliwyke
of the sayd Citie belongithe to do ye shall do well and treulye
and lawfullye. And treulye to enter or see to be entryd all
manner of attachments and arrests so god youe helpe and by
that booke.'[1]

The office of Bailiff had undoubtedly been instituted in the
first place to ensure that the King's interests would be safeguarded, and therefore the Bailiffs were in reality the King's
officers although they were by now elected by the citizens.
Formerly their main duty had been to see to the payment and
collection of the rents, fines and dues which belonged to the
King and to hand them over to the Exchequer. But later,
although they were still responsible for the collection of all
such items of revenue, they paid over to the Exchequer only
the fixed sum, which from the year 1264 onwards was one
hundred marks or £66 13s. 4d., at which the City by charter
had made composition for them. Thus, butchers who threw
'intrayles or other vile things' in the river to the annoyance
of their neighbours forfeited 'to the use of the Bayliffs' three
shillings and fourpence, while inhabitants who failed 'to make
clene their strets and carrye awaye their duste and soyle
before their houses everye Saturdaye wekelie' forfeited for
every time fourpence 'to the Bayliffs'. Dyers standing in the
market to receive cloth for dyeing paid to the Bailiffs ten
shillings annually, and artificers who were not freemen had
to pay a fee of three shillings and fourpence to the Bailiffs
before setting up their occupation or craft within the City.
The Bailiffs also received and recorded ground rents, particularly of gardens and open spaces, and the rents of certain
properties such as the fulling mills in Coitbury and the houses

[1] Idem, f. 94; also *Black Book*, p. 108.

comprising the Pentice, for these had all been the King's property before the City acquired any in its own right. The Pentice, sometimes called the 'penthouse', on the south side of the High Street, had consisted, since the fourteenth century, of tenements built on a site formerly known as the 'Drapery', and before that as the 'Mint'; it was on this site that William the Conqueror had built his palace. There were other duties which devolved upon the Bailiffs; when property was transferred they made the necessary alterations in their tarrage rolls, when a tenant died they took possession of the land or tenement until the heir established his claim, and it was only by their assent that a tenant could be ejected for arrears of rent or that distress could be taken for rent.

At the end of their term of office the Bailiffs were allowed twelve months in which to balance their accounts and make the necessary payment to the Exchequer. When this period had elapsed they were called upon, on the day of the election of the Mayor, to present their acquittance or quietus est, on pain of a fine of forty shillings unless they could allege reasonable excuse. There have survived for Elizabeth's reign eight rolls, each of which shows the amounts paid by the Bailiffs of Winchester to the Exchequer for the fee farm and other rents, and each one also takes account of the annual payment, which commenced in 1551, of fifty marks ($£33$ 6s. 8d.) to the Marquis of Winchester. It is obvious that the task of these officers must have proved both burdensome and unpopular, for besides acting as tax gatherers they had to be constantly on the alert to detect cases of fraud and evasion, and moreover, as far as can be ascertained, they received no financial remuneration for their work. In carrying out their duties, especially in connection with property, they were always in danger of infringing an individual's rights and liberties and thereby of being sued in court. It seems that they received little sympathy on such occasions for in 1594 William Beacham, the Mayor, granted to William Symonds, a former mayor, and one of his brethren, licence 'to sue and make defense in anie and whatsoever courte against Thomas

Bethin and William Budde, late bailiffs of the Citie, for and concerninge certaine goods of the saide William Symonds distrained by them for such quitrents as are behinde and dewe owte of the tenemente of the saide William Symonds under the Penthowse of the Citie'.

It is not surprising therefore to find that citizens were sometimes prepared to pay a heavy penalty, six pounds or more in the case of the High Bailiff and four or five pounds in the case of the Low Bailiff, for exemption from holding these offices. But the office of Bailiff was a stepping stone to that of Mayor, and all the Elizabethan Mayors of Winchester had previously held one of the two bailiwicks, and sometimes both, with but four exceptions. A bailiwick was assuredly a hard but good training ground for one who aspired to the higher office of the mayoralty and wished to fill it with dignity and distinction. In 1562 William Hall was discharged of both bailiwicks and also of the constableships on payment of six pounds, and later became Mayor in 1566 and 1576. William Bethell, a wealthy cloth merchant, whose mansion had been built on the site of the former Hyde Abbey, outside Northgate, was, in 1573, made a freeman, one of the Twenty-four and a magistrate, without any payment, and became Mayor in 1578. Richard Cooke who, as already mentioned, was four times Mayor, was in 1576 freely without any consideration of payment released from holding the offices of Bailiff, but for his discharge from other offices he had to pay three pounds six shillings and eightpence. The above three men settled in or returned to the City as persons already of standing and substance, and it may have been thought that it was to the advantage of the City that they should be invited to take part in municipal affairs without the usual apprenticeship. The fourth exception was the case of John White who was Mayor in 1583. He had previously acted as Chamberlain on four occasions and as joint Town Clerk. In 1576 it was decided that he should have 'thoffices of the Baylywykes clerely forgeven hym in consyderation of hys travayle hereafter to be taken in and aboute the newe makinge of the tarrage and any other bookes and wrytinges for the Cytie upon and for which he hath noe fee certeyne'.[1] Of the other freemen, numbering a dozen or so, who sought exemption from the bailiwicks by payment of a fine, not a single one ever became mayor.

THE CHAMBERLAINS

These officers, of whom there were usually two, are first mentioned in the Winchester records in 1367; they received the various funds, except those collected by the Bailiffs, and handed them over to the Mayor. Disbursements from the City coffers were originally made by the Mayor, but as his duties increased the Chamberlains gradually took over these payments which they made 'on the precept of the Mayor'. They thus became the financial officers or treasurers of the City, but they had no concern with the external payments to the Exchequer, which were undertaken by the Bailiffs, nor with the collection of those rents, fines and dues by which the latter met their obligations. The Chamberlains' duties consisted in gathering in the monies due, as the records say, 'to the use of the Chamber of the City', making payments ordered by the Mayor or the Burgh-mote, and in presenting their accounts for audit at the end of their year of office. In Tudor times, when these officers were elected at the same time as the Mayor, they are referred to as 'Chamberlains and Collectors', but there is no doubt that the actual collection of dues was done by minor officials.

In spite of a careful examination of the ordinances of the Burgh-mote, it is difficult to place exactly the dividing line between those dues which naturally accrue 'to the use of the Chamber' and would therefore be paid to the Chamberlains, and those which would be 'to the use of the Bailiffs'. In 1558 when John Edmonde, an alderman, contravened an old ordinance by slandering the Mayor, he was fined twenty shillings which was to be paid 'to the proffyt of the Cytie',

[1] 1st Bk. Ord., f. 188.

and not to the Bailiffs.[1] Richard Byrde had 'the bayliwicke of the commons forgevin him so he paye for the same to the chamberlayne' four pounds.[2] Steven Asheton, for allowing a butcher to sell 'bulls fleshe unbaighted contrary to the form of a proclamacion of the cytie' had to pay five pence 'to the use of the chamber'.[3] These fines apparently came into the hands of the Chamberlains because they were levied for offences committed contrary to the regulations made by the Mayor or the Burgh-mote.

On the other hand, Sir Harry Seymour was given 'licens to buylde a chymney two foote into the streete yeldinge to the bayliffes yerelie one penny'.[4] In this case there was encroachment on the King's highway of which the Bailiffs were the custodians, and they therefore exacted a ground rent of one penny a year. It was the Bailiffs who, as already shown, collected the market dues and punished fraudulent dealing, and so it is found that any outside butcher who came to the City to sell any veal 'that shalbe blowen or otherwise unlawfullie stuffed' forfeited twelve pence, sixpence of which went to the Bailiffs and sixpence to the poor people.[5]

For reasons which are not at all clear, however, the fines inflicted were occasionally divided between the Bailiffs and the Chamberlains. If an inn-keeper allowed any person (strangers and travelling men only excepted) to drink, eat or play within their premises during the time of divine service, he was fined three shillings and fourpence, half of which went to the Bailiffs and half to the Chamberlains.[6] Also, if a person sold salt butter without licence he forfeited the butter or its value to the Bailiffs and paid twenty shillings to the Chamberlains. Even in the case of rents there is division of payment. John Adderley leased a garden at Northgate for forty years for an annual rent of four shillings, and it would seem customary that he should pay this sum to the Bailiffs; but they received one shilling and sixpence only, the remainder going to the Chamberlains.[7] In the case of Harry

---

[1] Idem, f. 121.   [2] Idem, f. 141.   [3] Idem f. 134.
[4] Idem, f. 147.   [5] Idem, f. 149.   [6] Idem, f. 133.   [7] Idem, f. 128.

Crocker who built 'a lytill newe house' for which he paid annually eightpence to the Bailiffs and eightpence to the Chamberlains, it may be that the former sum represented the ground rent, but the reason for the payment to the Chamberlains remains obscure.[1]

There were certain rents with which the Chamberlains alone had to deal. These were connected with the lands and properties in Winchester and in the County of Southampton which had been granted to the City in 1554 by King Philip and Queen Mary, and were known as 'the suppressed lands', being part of the monasteries, nunneries and religious houses which had been dissolved by Henry VIII. For the collection of these rents and for their pains in the oversight of the reparations to the properties from which the rents were derived, the Chamberlains received an extra ten shillings a year above their accustomed fee, which was somewhere in the region of three pounds per annum.

Of their other duties the repairing of city property and buying of stores for that purpose were probably the most important. In the sixteenth century when the City, by virtue of the privileges granted in various charters, had acquired a considerable amount of property both inside and outside the walls, it had been found necessary to have its own stores and a staff of its own to cope with the building and repairing operations.[2] The renovation of dilapidated houses became so urgent at the beginning of Elizabeth's reign that the Chamberlains who were due to retire from office in September were required to continue until Christmas, and thus overlap their successors' term of office, to enable the new Chamberlains to become fully acquainted with all the work in hand.

To the new Chamberlains there had to be handed over, within fifteen days of their assuming office, an inventory of 'all the vessell and all other implements in their custodie'.[3] From this it is gathered that these officers were also responsible for all the movable property of the City, most probably kept in the Guildhall and in St. John's Hospital, including the

[1] Idem, f. 141.   [2] Idem, f. 110.   [3] Idem, f. 13.

plate, vessels and utensils required for civic functions. Like the Bailiffs, they had to render a financial account covering their period of office, but in their case it had to be presented by 'the ffeast of thannunciacion of our Ladie the virgin' (Lady Day) 'next ensuinge uppon payne of imprisonment there to remayne untill they have satisfied the same'. But the ultimate responsibility rested upon the Mayor who, if there was any failure or default in presenting these accounts, had a compensating amount deducted from his annual fee.

There is no record of any person seeking to avoid this office; this was probably due to the fact that it carried some financial remuneration. On the other hand, there are many instances where a Chamberlain remained in office for a number of years. John Potinger was sole Chamberlain from 1563 to 1566, and again from 1577 to 1579; from the latter date he was one of two Chamberlains and at the same time he was joint Town Clerk until his death in 1584. John White was joint Chamberlain with George Browne in 1567 and 1568, with John Potinger in 1581 and 1582, and again in the same office in 1599 and 1600; previously he had acted as one of the Town Clerks and he had been Mayor in 1583 and 1593. There are several other cases of former mayors acting as Chamberlains; for example, Anthony Birde was Mayor in 1582 and then became Chamberlain eight years later, and William Lane, who was Mayor in 1563 and 1570, held the office of Chamberlain in 1586 and the two succeeding years. There was therefore no loss of dignity when a former mayor became a chamberlain, but it is noticeable that there is no case of a former mayor being elected a bailiff, nor of any person occupying the same bailiwick on more than one occasion.

THE ALDERMEN

Elizabeth's charter of 1587 states that 'for times out of mind' Winchester had six Aldermen to assist with the government of the City, and from Henry VI's charter of 1442 it is learnt that the citizens were given power to elect four Aldermen who should have the powers of Justices of the Peace for enforcing the Statute of Labourers. But at what point between the granting of these two charters the number of Aldermen was increased from four to six is not certain. There is no doubt, however, that the six Aldermen were in charge of the six street-wards into which the City was divided: High Street, Jewry Street, Tanner (Lower Brook) Street, Colebrook Street, Gold (Southgate) Street, and Northgate (Hyde) Street, each ward taking its name from its principal street.[1] Recorded references to these aldermanries show that they existed long before Elizabeth's time.

The Aldermen of these street-wards had several different duties to perform. At one time they had been responsible for the collection of the murage rate for the repair of the walls and gates of the City, but in the sixteenth century their main duties were, firstly, to act under the authority of the Bailiffs and supervise the transfer of property from one tenant to another and 'view' property when disputes arose concerning repairs and other matters; secondly, to act as police in keeping peace and good order in their respective aldermanries, bringing to the City Court all cases of nuisance and breach of the ordinances; and thirdly, if Justices, to sit on the bench at the City Quarter Sessions. Thus it is found that every Alderman or his deputy had to make a weekly inspection of the streets within his aldermanry and see that they were kept clean, and that the indenture made by a master and his apprentice had to be brought by the Alderman for enrolling into the City Court before the Mayor and at least one other Alderman.[2, 3] Of their police duties in connection with which they reported offenders by 'presentment' to the Court, more will be said later when dealing with the procedure of that Court.

THE CORONERS

Winchester had also 'for times out of mind' elected two Coroners, but it is very strange that although the duties of

[1] Idem, f. 151.   [2] Idem, f. 227.   [3] Idem, f. 153.

such officers are known generally, very little reference is to be found either to them or to their activities in the City. At the end of the thirteenth century, they were elected annually to do duty both in the City and the Soke, and in both places they acted on behalf of the King and his Justices.[1] They saw that appropriate cases were passed on to the Crown Courts by the Mayor and Bailiffs, and they made inquiry into cases of treasure trove. In the fourteenth-century records there is little said of Coroners beyond two cases, one where they inquired with the Bailiffs whether a certain person was guilty of felony, and the other where the selection of a particular jury was challenged and the Coroners were ordered to summon a new jury.[2] Elizabeth's charter confirms the City's right to elect these two officers, and from the lists of officers appointed at the time of the election of successive mayors it is found that the practice continued up to the nineteenth century.

THE CONSTABLES

Likewise, so Elizabeth's charter of 1587 says, there were to be two Constables elected by the City. In Edward I's time the Constables supervised watch and ward in the City, and later, in the fourteenth century, they had power to summon offenders before them and fine them if they neglected the summons.[3] The six Aldermen of the street-wards were responsible for peace and order in their aldermanries, but since there were only two Constables for the whole of the City, it seems that they occupied a higher position than the Aldermen whose duties were confined to their own wards. This view is further strengthened by the fact that the names of the Constables appear before those of the Aldermen in the lists of City officers, and that the fine for avoiding election to a

[1] *The Ancient Usages of Winchester*, transcribed and translated from the Anglo-French version preserved in Winchester College, Clarendon Press, 1927. There are two versions in English (XVth century) in the City archives.

[2] J. S. Furley, *Town Life in the XIV century*, Wykeham Press, p. 46.

[3] Idem, p. 58.

Constable-ship ranked next to that for exemption from the office of Bailiff.

In Elizabethan times one of the Constables was known as the High Constable and this office was regarded as one of some distinction.[1] In 1582, Thomas Thorpe, an arrow-maker, living in the High Street, was elected High Constable and on that account was discharged of the office of High Bailiff, which was the office ranking next to that of the Mayor. The Constables were executive officers who were assisted in their duties by the Aldermen; no doubt the latter drew attention to the more serious offences committed within their street-wards. The Constables were also required to investigate the activities of all suspicious persons entering the City, and if necessary bring them before the Mayor and his brethren for examination. They had the power to search for and arrest all malefactors and bring them to justice, while the safe keeping of prisoners in the gaol and elsewhere was in their hands. In times of plague, which were fairly frequent, the Constables saw to the carrying out of the measures devised to segregate those suffering from the infection and to prevent the spread of the sickness. With regard to the less serious offences their watchdogs were the beadles, six in number, one for each street-ward. They were uniformed and salaried officials who were constantly on the look-out for breaches of the City ordinances. If any person permitted his hogs or weanling pigs to wander in the streets he paid for every hog of or above one year old, two shillings, and for every hog and pig under that age, one shilling, one half of the fine going to the Bailiffs and the other half to the beadle.

THE SERGEANTS

The duty of carrying out the decisions of the City Court fell upon the Sergeants, of whom there were usually three, but sometimes four, and who were generally referred to as Sergeants of the mace. They were officers of the Mayor and

[1] 1st Bk. Ord., f. 220.

Bailiffs under whose orders they acted. As part of their task they summoned juries and defendants to the Court and collected the fines inflicted. In cases where debt was proved, it was they and not the creditor who collected the debt or distrained goods of equal value and rendered account to the Bailiffs. At least one Sergeant got into difficulty with his accounts. When John Stoner, the 'City Sergeant', died in 1592 he owed the City fifteen pounds, but in regard of the poverty and mean estate wherein he died, five pounds of this amount were clearly forgiven him and the remaining ten pounds were to be repaid at the rate of ten shillings annually, presumably by his heirs, provided sufficient security was forthcoming.[1]

At one time the Sergeants were more closely associated with the Bailiffs to whom they handed over the sums of money and the goods which they had collected; at the same time the Bailiffs were required to provide the Sergeants with their distinguishing uniform. But later, it is quite clear from repeated references to the Mayor's Sergeant and to the Sergeants of the High Bailiff and the Low Bailiff that each of these major officers had his own Sergeant, that of the Mayor being the senior. In 1584 when an ordinance was passed forbidding the keeping of pigs within one hundred yards of the High Street, it was also decided that if the Bailiffs should fail to exact the penalty for infringement of this regulation, then it would be lawful for the Mayor to appoint a special Sergeant to levy by distress the appropriate penalty.[2] Again, it was agreed that it should be lawful for the Mayor, with the assent of two of his brethren, to appoint by process under the Mayor's seal a special Sergeant for the apprehension and arrest of any person who could not be arrested by the other Sergeants.[3]

It is evident that the Sergeants, and particularly the Mayor's Sergeant, were prominent features in the everyday life of the City, dressed in their livery gowns of three and half yards of broad Kentish cloth, costing at least seven shillings a yard.[4]

[1] Idem, f. 270.   [2] Idem, f. 230.   [3] Idem, f. 234.   [4] Idem, f. 175.

They were men of position and of good family, often the sons and younger brothers of prominent freemen, and it was necessary for them to provide security for the proper discharge of their duties. By ordinance they were forbidden to keep an inn or ale-house, and it was essential, if they wished to retain their posts, that they should be circumspect not only in conduct but also in speech, for 'whatsoever Sergeant of this Cittie shall utter or disclose anie secret talke used or uttered at the maiors table or at anie of the bayliffes tables or owte of the councell howse (not beinge against her Maiestie, her heires or successors, neither againste the lawe) shall be expelled from his office uppon proofe made of the offense'.[1]

THE RECORDER

In *The Black Book of Winchester* there appears, along with the oath taken by the Mayor, that sworn by the Recorder of the City, as follows:

'Ye shall be hole and treu to the kinge of Englande and to his heyres kings of the same lande. Ye shall see that treu records and due processe be made betwene partie and partie and treu judgments in there sutes be gevin, and treulye and indifferentlye to mynister the common right after the common lawe of this lande of England to every person that here shall sue, aswell to poore as to riche. And also treu councell to geve unto the mayor and the xxiiii[ti] for the Cytie of Winchester and there counsell well and treulye to kepe as one of the xxiiii[ti] And not to absent youe at any tyme where youe sholde geve your attendaunce and maye attend uppon warning without cause reasonable uppon payne of your besant at every tyme that you ffawten so god youe helpe by that booke.'[2, 3, 4]

This oath, dating from 1471, was in use until the granting of Elizabeth's charter in 1587. It shows the duties of the Recorder to be threefold; firstly, he has to see that true

[1] Idem, f. 248.   [2] Idem, f. 94.   [3] Besant = two shillings.
[4] ffawten = default.

records of the proceedings of the Court are kept; secondly, he is the general legal adviser to the City and in that capacity he attends the Court; also he sees that a true judgment is given in all cases and he advises the Mayor and the Twenty-four, of which he is a member, upon points of law; and thirdly, he has to minister truly and indifferently the common right after the common law to every person. From the last of these duties it appears that the Recorder shared in the decisions given by the Mayor and Bailiffs, but although this may be so he was in no way comparable with the modern Recorder who is a judicial officer holding the City Quarter Sessions.

It was not until 1587 that, under the terms of Elizabeth's charter, the office of Recorder for the City of Winchester was officially recognized, though for many years prior to that date there had been an officer whose primary duty was the keeping of records. He is most frequently referred to as 'the clerk', and it is not until the beginning of the fifteenth century that there is any mention of his undertaking legal duties, or indeed, any mention of an officer called 'recorder'. In 1400 there was a deputy-clerk who was forbidden to plead in the City Court; from this it has been inferred that the Clerk was by this time a person with legal qualifications who could act as advocate in the Court, and that a deputy-clerk was appointed to attend to the routine work such as record-keeping.[1] Shortly afterwards mention is made of a Recorder, and by the time of Henry V (1413–22), the old office of Clerk had obviously been divided between a Recorder or Clerk, both titles being used, who acted as legal adviser of the City, and a deputy-clerk who was concerned with purely clerical work. Two examples of persons holding the major office can be quoted. John Bye, referred to both as Recorder and Clerk, was a lawyer employed by the City, who accompanied the Mayor to London on legal business, conducted negotiations with Cardinal Beaufort, Bishop of Winchester, and acted as City attorney.[2] Later he became a freeman of the City and

[1] J. S. Furley, *City Government*, p. 50.   [2] Idem.

was elected Mayor in 1428.[1] Also Richard Wallop, who was not a citizen, but most probably a London lawyer, was employed as counsel by the City, receiving an annual fee of twenty shillings and a furred gown as 'livery'. Although on one occasion he is referred to as a Justice of the Peace at the County Sessions, he is never called Recorder of Winchester.

Although, as already stated, it was not until 1587 that the office of Recorder was first mentioned by charter, the Burgh-mote assembling five years earlier in 1582 had decided that Thomas Fleming should have the office of City Recorder for life, and that for his counsel in the City's affairs and for the execution of that office he should be paid an annual fee of four pounds.[2] This sum seems a small remuneration for such an important post, but there were added to it various emoluments arising from business transacted in the Court as, for example, those coming from the taking and enrolling of recognisances for each of which the Mayor took four shillings, the Recorder four shillings, the writer thereof three shillings and fourpence, and the Mayor's Sergeant, for the wax, eight-pence.[3] It will be noted that the appointment of Thomas Fleming was for his lifetime, and this suggests that the office was now permanent whereas in the past various persons had been employed as occasion demanded and frequent changes had been made.

Henceforth, Thomas Fleming's name appears immediately after that of the Mayor at all assemblies, as he is now a freeman of the City, a member of the Twenty-four, a magistrate, and he is excused all the other offices which a freeman might be called upon to hold. In order of precedence he comes before the Bailiffs and Aldermen, and ranks next to the Mayor as a Justice in the City Court of Sessions. Like the Recorders of many other boroughs Thomas Fleming entered parliament, sitting as one of the burgesses for Winchester in the three parliaments between 1584 and 1593, and representing the County of Southampton in 1597 and the Borough of Southampton in 1601.

[1] 1st Bk. Ord., f. 4.　　　[2] Idem, f. 224.　　　[3] Idem, f. 259.

Thomas Fleming was a native of Newport, Isle of Wight, who had entered Lincoln's Inn in 1567 and been called to the bar in 1574. It has been said that the country gentleman and his cousin, the lawyer, captured the House of Commons during Elizabeth's reign.[1] Fleming was one of that numerous band, and it was at Westminster that he was afforded the opportunity of displaying his outstanding ability. He rose to great eminence in the legal profession, for after leaving Winchester in 1593 he was called to the degree of sergeant-at-law and became Recorder of London in the following year. In 1595 he was appointed Solicitor-General and retained that office on the accession of James I, who bestowed a knighthood upon him in 1603. A year later he was Chief Baron of the Exchequer, and in 1605 he helped to try the conspirators in the Gunpowder treason. In 1607 Fleming was advanced to the Chief Justiceship of the King's Bench, and in 1610 he deputized for the Lord Chancellor during the latter's illness.

In spite of his elevation to such high rank, he retained his interest in the City of Winchester for which his son, also named Thomas and the eldest of fifteen children, sat as member of parliament in 1601. The elder Fleming found time to attend the meetings of the Burgh-mote in the City, and there are records of his attendance at most of the meetings up to the time of his death in 1610. There can be no doubt that Winchester owed him a deep debt of gratitude for the services which he rendered on her behalf, for whatever prestige and prosperity the City enjoyed during the later years of Elizabeth's reign they were in large measure due to his influence. He was succeeded as Recorder of Winchester by John Moore, who continued in that office for many years and like his predecessor became one of the members of parliament for the City.

THE TOWN CLERK

This officer was the successor of the deputy-clerk mentioned

[1] J. E. Neale, *Elizabethan House of Commons*, p. 147.

in earlier records who dealt with the clerical side of the City's affairs, leaving the Clerk, later called the Recorder, free to carry out his duties as a lawyer. In 1476, in Edward IV's reign, 'it was ordayned and established that the towne clerke that then was and that in tyme to come shulde be shulde have yerelie one gowne of the lyverie of the Bayliffs of Winchester or tenne shillings in readie monye at theleccion of the same clerke for his labors and attendance and speciallie for the extracts of the Courts yerelie there holden to be wrytton'.[1] In 1554 it was agreed that 'the towne clerke have for his paines leckewise for markinge the bookes of the chamberlains iiis. iiiid. yerelie out of the chamber of the citie above his accustomid ffee'.[2] These two extracts show clearly the nature of the work undertaken by the Town Clerk, but it is possible that the holder of the office may have had some legal qualification or training, for in 1557 it was agreed that 'the towne clerke may pleade at barr when councell shall lacke in the Cytie'.[3] This was at variance with previous practice and was a complete reversal of the ordinance of 1400, which forbade the deputy-clerk to plead in the City Court; but it may be that the provision was made to meet any special case arising through the absence of counsel and thus to avoid delay, which was all too common in those days.

Up to 1566 all references to the Town Clerk are in the singular, but in that year it was declared that 'John Potinger and John White shalbe towne clerkes ioyntlie and severallye duringe their naturall lyves and the longest lyver of them and shall have all benefyttes, profittes, casualties, fees, stypends, advantages, lyveryes and commodities to the same apperteynynge and belonginge'.[4] No mention is made of the total amount of their emoluments, though four years previously it had been decided that the Town Clerk should have in augmentation of his fee for his good service heretofore done and hereafter to be done six shillings and eightpence yearly.[5] From the list of sources from which their income might be

[1] 1st Bk. Ord., f. 6. [2] Idem, f. 103. [3] Idem, f. 115.
[4] Idem, f. 150. [5] Idem, f. 134.

derived, as shown above, it is more than probable that there was very little City business from which they did not reap some reward. Moreover, it is known that these two men held the office of Chamberlain from time to time while they were still acting as Town Clerks, and thus received remuneration from still another source. It is to be noted, however, that many of the fees which they exacted, as in the case of the enrolment of the indentures of apprentices, were not paid by the City but by the individual citizen.

John Potinger continued in office until his death in 1584. He had been joined as Town Clerk in 1583 by Anthony Dawley, owing to the election of John White as Mayor, which office the latter again held in 1593. Anthony Dawley continued alone as Town Clerk until 1597, when John White returned and held the post jointly with Lancelot Thorpe, who in turn became Mayor in 1615 and 1623 in James I's reign. It may seem strange in modern times that a Town Clerk should be elected to the mayoralty, but it is to be remembered that the holder of the former office in Elizabeth's time was not only a freeman, but also a member of the Twenty-four. He was therefore eligible for election as Mayor, and having invariably acted as Chamberlain as well as Town Clerk he was more conversant with the affairs of the City than most of the other citizens and consequently was a most suitable candidate for the position.

OTHER OFFICERS

There were many other officers, either permanent or temporary, playing minor parts in the story of City life. The annual audit of the Chamberlains' accounts was an important occasion which called for the appointment of no less than eight auditors, four from the Twenty-four and four from the Commons, as the remainder of the freemen were called. At the same time three of the Twenty-four were elected to act as 'cofferers' who held the keys and were responsible for the strong box, or treasure chest, lying in the Guildhall. For the regulation of trade and commerce there were searchers and sealers of woollen cloth, the registrar, searchers and sealers of leather, the flesh tasters and the ale tasters, the registrar for horses and beasts sold in the High Street, together with a registrar for hay and a hay-ward or herdsman. At each of the four City gates, north, south, east, west, and at Kingsgate, there were permanent keepers; in each of the six aldermanries there was a beadle; from time to time there were minstrels appointed to enliven the citizens. These, together with all the other minor officials, were elected annually by a special panel of twelve freemen summoned for that purpose.

There remain other offices of a somewhat different category to those already mentioned to which persons were elected by the citizens of Winchester, namely, that of High Steward of the City, and those of the two members of parliament for the City.

The High Steward

In May, 1582, the Burgh-mote decided that for the better direction, defence and maintenance of the City and the rights, liberties and privileges of the same there should be from henceforth elected, chosen and made one High Steward, who should be known and called by that name, and who, for the execution of that office, should have an annuity or yearly fee of six pounds thirteen shillings and fourpence.[1] At the same meeting it was also agreed that the Right Honorable Sir Francis Walsingham, Knight, Chief Secretary to the Queen's Majesty and one of Her Majesty's Privy Council, should have the office of the High Stewardship for life and should have the yearly fee paid in advance. It was Sir Francis who, five years later in 1587, was instrumental in securing for the City its most important charter, and he may have had some influence in persuading the City to appoint its first permanent Recorder, Thomas Fleming, for this occurred in the September of 1582. Winchester was undoubtedly fortunate in securing so powerful a friend at Court, but it was an advan-

[1] Idem, f. 221.

tage which was shared by other communities for Walsingham held also, among his many offices, the Recordership of Colchester and the High Stewardship of Ipswich.

He was succeeded in 1592 as High Steward of Winchester by Thomas Sackville, poet and statesman, who had been created Lord Buckhurst in 1567 and who had been employed as a diplomatist in France and in the Low Countries.[1] Like Walsingham he had been High Steward of Ipswich, and Bristol had also bestowed a similar honour upon him. It was he who, in 1586, was given the unenviable task of announcing her death sentence to Mary, Queen of Scots. He held the High Stewardship of the City for a short time only, giving way for reasons not recorded, in 1593, to Sir Thomas Heneage, a trusted and favourite servant of Queen Elizabeth, who was also High Steward of Salisbury.[2] He was a Privy Councillor and Chancellor of the Duchy of Lancaster, and from 1553 until his death in 1595 sat in every parliament as member for various constituencies. As one of the select body of courtiers who surrounded the Queen, he was a close friend of the famous Earl of Leicester and of Sir Philip Sidney.

The next High Steward was Charles Blount, Lord Mount-joy, afterwards Earl of Devonshire, who took office in 1595 at a time when he was Captain of the town and island of Portsmouth and also High Steward of the same town.[3] He was a distinguished soldier who took part in the Earl of Essex's expedition to the Azores in 1597, and put down Tyrone's rebellion in Ireland for which he was made Lord Lieutenant of that country. He died in 1606 and the High Stewardship of Winchester then passed again to Lord Buckhurst, who had previously relinquished the office in 1593 and who was now Earl of Dorset and Lord Treasurer of England.[4]

The original ordinance of 1582 makes it clear that the person appointed High Steward was expected to look after the general interests of the City, to give his help in preserving its rights and in furthering its prosperity, and particularly to use his influence in the defence of those privileges which had

[1] Idem, f. 269.   [2] Idem f. 272.   [3] Idem, f. 286.   [4] Idem, f. 312.

been gained through the previous centuries. It is noticeable that each of Winchester's High Stewards was closely connected with Elizabeth's Court and could therefore easily approach the Queen and place before her any petition or request made by the City. The citizens had undoubtedly learnt that it was extremely wise to have a friend at Court, but they were not alone in this respect. Throughout Elizabeth's reign there was a tendency for members of the Court and the chief statesmen to collect High Stewardships and it was not at all uncommon for great noblemen, such as the Earl of Leicester, the Earl of Bedford and the Earl of Essex, to act in this capacity for several boroughs at the same time. It has been suggested that it was probably the prestige and sense of power, in a time of scheming factions, that made election to these offices so attractive, but the fees attached to them, comparatively small though they may have been, were possibly an added attraction.[1] The annual fee varied as a rule according to the size of the town; Plymouth paid ten pounds, while Nottingham paid four pounds. At Winchester and at Salisbury the fee was ten marks or six pounds thirteen shillings and fourpence. There is no evidence that the High Steward had any part or place in local government at Winchester, though he may, as at the present time, have attended in his official capacity the more important functions which took place there. It is, however, well known that the High Stewards wielded a widespread influence throughout the country in parliamentary elections and there were very few boroughs which did not come under their sway in this respect.

THE MEMBERS OF PARLIAMENT

The first parliament in England to which burgesses from each city were summoned was that called at Westminster in 1265 by Simon de Montfort after he had defeated Henry III at Lewes in the previous year. In 1283 Winchester, along with

[1] Neale, p. 209.

other cities, sent two of the wiser citizens, chosen by the citizens from among themselves, to a national council at Shrewsbury for the discussion of affairs arising from the difficulties of the Welsh War.[1] Later, with the issue of the writs of the Model Parliament of 1295 the normal representation of Winchester by two burgesses was begun and continued until the second Reform Act of 1867 reduced the representation to one member. Up to the nineteenth century the electors were the Mayor, Recorder, Aldermen, Bailiffs and freemen of the City, and the election took place at an assembly of the Burgh-mote.

During the reign of Queen Elizabeth there were ten parliaments and these, together with the names of Winchester's representatives, may be summarized as follows:

Dates of Sessions	*Winchester members*
1. 25 Jan.–8 May, 1559	William Lawrens, former Mayor
	Robert Bethell, former Mayor
2. 12 Jan.–April, 1563	William Lawrens, former Mayor
3 Sept., 1566–2 Jan., 1567	Thomas Michelborne
3. 2 April–29 May, 1571	Richard Birde, former Mayor
	Thomas Michelborne
4. 8 May–30 June, 1572	Thomas Michelborne
8 Feb.–15 March, 1576	John Caplin
11 Jan.–18 March, 1581	
5. 23 Nov., 1584–	John Woolley
29 March, 1585	Thomas Fleming, Recorder
6. 29 Oct., 1586–	John Woolley
23 March, 1587	Thomas Fleming, Recorder
7. 4 Feb.–29 March, 1589	John Woolley
	Thomas Fleming, Recorder
8. 19 Feb.–10 April, 1593	Sir Edward Stafford
	Thomas Fleming, Recorder
9. 24 Oct., 1597–9 Feb., 1598	William Badger, former Mayor
	John Moore, Recorder
10. 27 Oct.–19 Dec., 1601	Edward Cole, former Mayor
	Thomas Fleming, jun., son of former Recorder

[1] *Victoria County History of Hampshire*, Vol. V, p. 25.

This list shows that Winchester was represented in parliament during the Elizabethan period by twelve individuals. Five of these were former mayors, two were recorders and one was the son of a former recorder. The other four were strangers or 'foreigners', as non-residents were called, who came to the City for the express purpose of being elected as burgesses in parliament. It will perhaps be advisable, in the first place, to give a brief account of each one of these.

Thomas Michelborne was a member of a well-known and rather numerous family settled round Westmeston in Sussex. He had been admitted to Gray's Inn in 1551 and later came to Winchester to practise as a lawyer. In 1560 he married Alice, daughter of William Lawrens, who was himself a lawyer and a very prominent citizen, having been Mayor on three occasions and one of the burgesses in parliament for some years. It was, without doubt, due to his father-in-law's influence that Thomas Michelborne was elected to accompany him to Westminster in 1563.

John Caplin was a citizen of Southampton where he was Sheriff in 1550 and Mayor in 1552, and it is possible that he was a relative of Steven Caplin, a freeman of Winchester, who was Low Bailiff in 1552, Chamberlain in 1555, and died in 1558. The election of John Caplin as a member for Winchester was the outcome of a letter written by Robert Horne, Bishop of Winchester, to 'the worshipful my loving frendes the Mayor and his Brethren' from his house in Southwark in 1572, reminding them of the coming parliament and of the order for choosing burgesses. He frankly desires 'their goodwills unto him as to nominate and appoint for their city and incorporation' his friend John Caplin of Southampton, who, he says, is 'your own countryman and well known to the more part of you, who can, I am assured, do that city and country such service in that calling as is required to be done, and also will ease you of such trouble and charge as usually you have been at in that behalf; so that therein you shall further yourselves and also pleasure me; which your doing, to requite you shall find me both mindful and ready, as knoweth the Almighty unto whose protection I do commend you, and so bid you farewell.'[1]

John Woolley (or Wolley) was Secretary to the Queen's Majesty for the Latin and also a member of the Privy Council. He took his part, from 1572 until his death in 1596, in every parliament, where at all times he was a staunch supporter of royal prerogatives. It is extremely probable that it was through the influence of Sir Francis Walsingham, High Steward of the City, that he was elected one of the members for Winchester in 1587 and 1589.

Sir Edward Stafford, whose mother was mistress of the robes to Queen Elizabeth, was employed by the Queen on several diplomatic missions, and from 1583 to 1590 was resident ambassador in France. On his return he was knighted, and his election to the parliament of 1593 as a member for Winchester was possibly the result of something more than a hint from Court circles.

It has been claimed that in the fourteenth century the Winchester citizens in parliament were not held in much esteem, and that election to the mayoralty carried far greater honour than did election to parliament.[2] In support of this it can be shown that at that particular period Winchester was never represented in parliament by anyone who had held more than a minor office at home. The City's members had a rather unhappy time, for they were of little account at West-minster and were subject to abuse and complaint when they returned to Winchester on account of the concessions or grants of money to which they had agreed in parliament. But in Tudor times the situation had altered, for by now the burgess members were invariably prominent citizens who had held the office of mayor, possibly on more than one occasion, and been successful in trade and commerce or in the legal profession. Of the five former mayors who were returned to parliament in Elizabeth's reign, two, Robert Bethell and Richard Birde, were wealthy cloth merchants,

[1] Misc. MSS., City archives.   [2] Furley, *Town Life*, etc., p. 43.

and the other three, William Lawrens, William Badger and Edward Cole, were prominent lawyers.

At this time many cities and boroughs started the practice of returning Recorders as one of their members. Winchester was no exception, for after his appointment as Recorder in 1582 Thomas Fleming became one of the City's members in the next three parliaments, and was followed by his successor in the recordership, John Moore. But this was not the only innovation, for it was in this reign that Winchester for the first time in its history took for its parliamentary representatives persons of prominence from outside its boundaries, a change which was at variance with the ancient custom and with the law that members of parliament should be elected by the citizens from among the citizens themselves. The first of these outsiders, Thomas Michelborne, sat in the parliament of 1563–67 although he was not a citizen; but when he was elected for the next parliament in 1571 he was at the same time admitted to the Merchant Gild, thereby becoming a freeman of the City, and was granted the lease of a tenement, garden and stable in Parchment Street. He was thus fully qualified, being a resident citizen, to sit as a member for the city.[1, 2] His colleague in the next parliament, 1572–81, was John Caplin of Southampton, who as far as the records show was never a freeman nor a resident within the City. As regards John Woolley and Sir Edward Stafford who were returned as members at later dates, they were both admitted to citizenship by being sworn into the Merchant Gild prior to their respective elections, but there is no evidence of their ever becoming residents.

By adopting these changes in the type of representative sent to Westminster, the City of Winchester was by no means unique; in fact, the action was in conformity with a practice which became widespread in Elizabeth's reign. During the sixteenth century the number of members in the House of Commons increased from 296 in 1520 to 462 in 1601.[3] Henry VIII had granted 31 new seats and Elizabeth en-

---

[1] 1st Bk. Ord., f. 134.   [2] Idem, f. 163.   [3] Neale, p. 140.

franchised 31 parliamentary boroughs sending 62 new members, including the neighbouring Hampshire towns of Andover, Christchurch, Lymington and Stockbridge. This increase in membership did not arise as one might suspect from a desire and design on the part of the Crown to pack parliament with royal nominees and government supporters. The initiative in petitioning for the granting of enfranchisement was local and not central, coming from the townsfolk themselves who were supported either by the lord and owner of the borough or by some influential patron attached to the Court, such as Sir Francis Walsingham, the Earl of Leicester or the Earl of Essex. Consequently the member for such a borough was often the nominee of the nobleman upon whose support it relied. For example, Christchurch, which was enfranchised in 1571, was in 1584 prepared to allow the Earl of Huntingdon to nominate one of the burgesses for parliament.[1] Again, in the same year, the Earl of Leicester wrote to the Borough of Andover, 'Being Steward of your town, I make bold heartily to pray you that you would give me the nomination of one of your burgesses . . . and if, minding to avoid the charges of allowance for the other burgess, you mean to name any that is not of your town, you will bestow the nomination of the other burgess also on me, I will thank you for it.' As a postscript the Earl added, 'If you will send me your election return with a blank, I will put in the names.'

It has been computed that in the later years of the sixteenth century, when the law whereby borough members had to be chosen from the more discreet and suitable of the resident citizens or burgesses was rarely observed, between 50 and 60 only out of the 462 members were merchants or borough officials.[2] The majority numbering about 400 could be classified as country gentlemen or lawyers. It can thus be seen to what extent the influence of High Stewards and borough patrons had grown. Although there were instances of towns refusing to accede to the wishes of their patrons, many had been quite ready, chiefly on the grounds of avoiding expense,

[1] Neale, p. 144. [2] Idem, p. 147.

to allow both their representatives to be nominated by such people. Others had compromised by allowing one, but very few indeed had managed to preserve complete independence. Winchester never allowed both its members to be nominated by a patron, and it was only in the middle part of the period under review, that is, from 1572 to 1593, that one member was chosen from outside the City. At both the beginning and the end of the reign they were bona-fide and resident citizens who were elected to take their seats in the Commons.

The payment of members of parliament introduced in the present century is no innovation; it is a recurrence of an old system, but whereas now the payment is made by the State since the duties of a member are regarded as service to the State, in Tudor and earlier times burgesses attending parliament were paid by the city or town which they represented. This was due to the fact that although the burgesses were present to agree to the voting of money, their native city did not regard this by any means as their sole duty. In the fourteenth and fifteenth centuries Winchester members, in common with those from most other cities, were paid as a rule two shillings a day for their attendance, but they received further and comparatively large amounts for 'divers businesses done in the said parliament'.[1] Moreover, the City did not hesitate to refer to these payments as 'wages'. The Winchester burgesses in parliament were expected to bring forward appeals for the defence of municipal and even individual rights where there was danger of encroachment, for they were living in an age when land titles were constantly in dispute and civic liberties depended on special concessions and local custom.

During the reign of Philip and Mary, the City seems to have adopted a rather niggardly attitude towards its members of parliament, for in 1555 when William Lawrens and Robert Hodson were chosen they agreed to take eighteen pence a day only.[2] Two years later there was evidently some hard bargaining when Gyles White and William Lawrens were

[1] Furley, *City Government*, p. 111.   [2] 1st Bk. Ord., f. 108.

elected, for they promised to accept two shillings and eight-pence a day for both of them, that is, sixteen pence for each of them, so long as they were required to stay at Westminster.[1] The bargaining element entered into negotiations again in 1571 when Thomas Michelborne, one of the members, was granted a lease of ground in Buck Street on condition that he served during the whole of the next parliament and took only sixteen pence a day whilst he was there.[2] But with the election of Thomas Fleming, the Recorder, in 1586, the remuneration became two shillings per day, and it remained at that figure for the rest of Elizabeth's reign. It is known that the City paid Thomas Michelborne, but whether the three outsiders, John Caplin, John Woolley and Sir Edward Stafford, paid their own expenses it is difficult to say; it is most likely that they did so, for there is no record to show that they received any financial recompense from the City.

[1] Idem, f. 114.   [2] Idem, f. 163.

CHAPTER VI

The Executive

It has already been observed, in a previous chapter, that towards the end of Elizabeth's reign the executive power and the day to day government of the City had passed into the hands of the Mayor and a small group of former mayors known as the Mayor's brethren. On the Wednesday of each week, or oftener if occasion required, the Mayor was joined by a number of his brethren and the Recorder to deal with various matters. It was only when very important business was under discussion that members of the Twenty-four, other than former mayors, were called into consultation. As a rule, there were about half a dozen persons present at these meetings at the Guildhall, and it was the practice to record in writing the details of their deliberations and decisions together with other matters which had been brought to their notice. Fortunately, two of these early minute books have survived, though when they were re-bound at the beginning of the present century they were incorrectly entitled 'Proceedings of the Corporation'. From them can be ascertained the numerous and widely ranging affairs which occupied the attention of the City Fathers, and in this chapter an attempt will be made to summarize the business transacted by this executive body during the year 1598–99, when Edward Cole was Mayor for the second time.

In 1598 there occurred the Ulster rebellion of the Earl of Tyrone which moved Queen Elizabeth to dispatch against him the largest English force that ever went overseas in her reign. The citizens of Winchester became aware of this when the Mayor and his brethren, attended by the City officers, with all pomp and ceremony, marched to the market place and there read Her Majesty's proclamation 'declaring her princely resolution in sending over of her army into the Realm of Ireland'. It was not long before the first body of soldiers, 200 strong, under Captain Charles Wilmott, arrived in the City where they were billeted for the time being, and later provided, by order of the Queen's Council, with five carts to carry their equipment to the port of embarkation, Southampton. At the same time, in order to help in maintaining communications between London and Southampton, William Oram, a local dealer, was paid four pounds by the City to provide four post-horses for a period of ten weeks. One also reads that one of Wilmott's men, a 'pressed' soldier, immediately deserted and that 'hue and cry' was directed to Overton, Baughurst, Andover and Whitchurch for his apprehension. A week later the Mayor of Southampton wrote to the Town Clerk of Winchester informing him that one Thomas Hall, a soldier, had escaped and was making for widow Colson's house at Bub's Cross in the Soke (on St. Giles' Hill). The Town Clerk, realizing that the Soke came under the jurisdiction of the Bishop, sent the letter to the Bishop's officers so that search could be made. A watch was set in the City and a 'privy search' was made at night for Hall and other such persons, without much success. Next morning the Clerk heard that such a person as Hall had passed through Winchester the previous day and taken the road to Whitchurch, and thereupon he sent hue and cry after him from tything to tything to Whitchurch and thence towards Oxfordshire.

This procedure of hue and cry was being prosecuted with more vigour than previously towards the end of the sixteenth century. Prior to 1585 the inhabitants of the hundred or district within which a felony had been committed were held responsible for the depredations of the malefactors. It was found that although such inhabitants might do their utmost to apprehend offenders and bring them to justice, they were often baffled in their purpose by lack of co-operation on the part of adjoining hundreds and counties in following up the hue and cry which had been raised. In order to remedy this defect and to discourage offenders, who were only too ready to take advantage of the situation, the Act of 1585 stipulated that any hundred which showed negligence after hue and cry had been raised should be jointly responsible for any damages arising from such a felony, even though the offence had been committed elsewhere. It was also enacted that after this date no hue and cry or pursuit be lawful unless it were made by horsemen and footmen, and that the notice should be given 'with as much convenient speed as may be' to all neighbouring towns, villages and hamlets through which a fugitive might pass.

While the Mayor and his brethren were paying heed to military affairs, and incidentally augmenting the City armour by the purchase of ten new pikes from London, they were also giving effect to other royal proclamations and letters from the Queen's Council. Grants under the royal seal had been made to individuals permitting them to be the sole vendors or manufacturers of certain articles of trade. One of these was starch, and this particular monopoly had been granted to Sir John Parkington, but Winchester traders had conveniently ignored the Queen's proclamation announcing the grant, until letters from the Queen's Council drew the Mayor's attention to infringements within the City. Consequently eight prominent citizens were called before the Mayor and his brethren and given 'warning and admonishment for making, buying and otherwise dealing in starch'. A few days later, six more freemen, including a magistrate, were similarly dealt with. A further proclamation from the Queen forbidding the eating, killing and dressing of meat during Lent moved the Mayor and his brethren to appoint six freemen to make a diligent search every fortnight throughout the City for breaches of this latest regulation and to report the result of their activities to the Mayor.

At other times there were communications from higher authority concerning matters ecclesiastical which required immediate attention. Thus one reads of a warrant directed to the Mayor and Justices from Her Majesty's High Commissioners which caused the Mayor and one of his brethren, one of the Chamberlains, the two Constables and several others to proceed by night and, by virtue of the warrant, enter the County gaol, which was within the City, and carry out a thorough search both there and in other places specified in the warrant. The object of the search does not seem at all clear, and the only tangible result was the seizure of a man named Warnford who confessed that he was a recusant. He was passed on to the Commissioners, but as the record says 'what is done is not known to the Mayor and Justices'. Prior to this there had been a similar alarm when the Dean of Winchester and his fellow-commissioners were informed that there was at that time a seminary priest or Jesuit harboured within the City, who on the previous day had most boldly attempted to convert the Vicar of Hursley whilst the latter was lying ill in Winchester. The Mayor and his brethren were advised of this and on their orders the Constables made a very secret and diligent search throughout the City in all suspected places, but their efforts were of no avail and no such person was found.

This search may have been the aftermath of an incident which had occurred three days previously when the Bishop of Winchester and other Commissioners issued a warrant following the receipt of information that, in a certain house, several recusants, considered dangerous to the State, were secretly hidden. After consultation with his brethren, the Mayor called together the Constables and Sergeants-at-mace and entered the specified house. There were found old Mistress Goldsmith, a widow, together with her friend, also a widow, and a maid-servant named Churcher from Michelmersh. During the search the servant suddenly exclaimed that she had lost her purse containing four shillings; but the searchers supposed that she had done this perversely and falsely in order to slander them. Nevertheless a diligent search was made in the house in case the servant had lost it there through negligence. 'Afterwards for that still she persevered in her constant affirmacion that she had lost her purse the Maior, in regard of his particular creditt and the estate of the City, serched every of the persons aforesaid and not finding it in that serch went with his company to sermons', that is, to Sunday matins at the Cathedral. 'After sermon ended the Maior againe assembled all the serchers and apointed the Constables to serch one other parte which was not serched, viz. whether any of them had putt the purse within his codpisse or hose. Soe soone as the serche was entered into Richard Alderly, one of the Seriants, finding himself like to be discovered and his conscience touched, disclosed that he had taken up the purse and throwen it aside, and thereupon praying favor upon his knees was sent with an officer and brought it. Whereupon presently the Maior and aforesaid Constables and serchers went to the house and before old Mistress Goldsmith delivered the said mayde her sayde purse which she opened and told therein iiiis. iiiid. and a key which she acknowledged to be withowt diminucion even as she lost it.

'At one of the clocke in the afternoone the Maior repayred to the councell howse and cawsed the towne bell to be towled three several tymes to be advised by his company what was mete to be done concerning the impudent and slandrous accion of the said Richard Alderly. After three tymes towling the bell the Maior was assisted by Mr. Lane, Mr. White, Mr. Payce, Mr. Badger and Mr. Cooke, and upon examinacion of Alderly and consideracion of the case commanded his gowne and mace to be left in the councell howse and committed him to the Westgate unto Mr. Payce, bayliff, and not to be enlarged untill he putt in suertye to answere to the fact at the next sessions.' But as to the dangerous recusants for whom the search was made in the first place, not a word is recorded.

When the Mayor and his party had temporarily abandoned

the search in order to attend the Cathedral service, the two Constables decided to follow up another matter. They had heard that a citizen named Reding was suspected of taking advantage of the absence from home during 'sermon time' of a freeman named Sturt, and of living incontinently with his wife. The Constables inquired at Sturt's house, but his wife denied that Reding was there. However, when they entered they found him in her chamber hiding behind the bed. He was brought before the Mayor and his brethren and soon found himself in the Westgate and, like Alderly, awaiting the next sessions. Living cheek by jowl in small huddled houses within the narrow streets of Winchester, it was impossible to hide much of one's private affairs, and cases of immorality, in either its narrower or wider sense, quickly became known and were dealt with promptly and severely. For example, it was brought to the notice of the Mayor and his brethren that a certain Thomas Bryan, a carpenter, had kept company for several nights with Ellen Godden, a widow, in her chamber in the 'sisterne howse' or Sisters' Hospital. He was a stranger and wanderer who had come to the City without testimonial, and confessed that he had spent several nights in the chamber, and pretended that his purpose was to marry the widow. He was committed to prison, but on the following day he was further examined by the Mayor and one or two of his brethren, and as he promised to bring a certificate of his wife's death within ten days, he was set at liberty, provided that in the meantime he did not frequent the company of the said Ellen Godden.

The preservation of public order and the keeping of the peace were considered of primary importance. Although there is no evidence to show that Winchester citizens were unduly riotous or quarrelsome yet, as in all communities, there were occasions when hasty tempers led to misconduct which brought the offender before the Mayor and his colleagues for examination. William Brexstone, a freeman, was an unruly subject who on several previous occasions had disturbed the peace. He had failed to find sureties for his good conduct after former sundry misdemeanours, and was consequently committed to the Westgate in the safe custody of the Bailiffs. His brother, Cuthbert, had also been committed to the same place, but had escaped after assaulting the Sergeant-at-mace, and now the Constables and Sergeants were ordered to apprehend him 'wherever he may be met withal'. There is no record of his recapture, but his brother, William, after being held in custody for nine days was brought to the Guildhall before the Mayor and his brethren. 'He showed grete tokens of his sorowfulnes for his generall misbehaviors in the city, and thereupon after exhortacion to the performance of his duty, the company were satisfied to take bayle of him to kepe her Maiesties pece against all her her Maiesties subiects in generall and especiall to Mr. Richard Adderly, Constable, Mr. Richard Paice, high bayly, and Lancelot Thorpe, and to appere at the next sessions of boroughmoote.' But eight months later he was again in trouble, for it was reported that he and William Jennings between ten and eleven at night went down the High Street and met the brothers Wyatt and disorder and bloodshed ensued. Bloodshed had also been committed between John Beconshaw and Robert Jackson, a parson, at the Swan Inn outside Northgate, on the occasion of the felonious riding away of Beconshaw's gelding by a certain Captain Westmill, against whom hue and cry had consequently been raised. Apparently Jackson had been privy to the theft so the Mayor and his brethren sent him to the next sessions.

There were many occasions, however, when the minds of the Mayor and his peers were engaged on matters more pleasant than assault and battery, especially towards the end of the reign when it was customary to present sugar loaves to the Bishop of Winchester and to the City Recorder as New Year's gifts. In 1598 it was agreed that the former should receive a sugar loaf weighing eighteen pounds, while the latter had to be content with one of twelve pounds. Presents were also given to the Justices of Assize when they visited the City; thus it was decided, in the spring of 1598, that instead of sugar loaves or a gallon of sack or claret there should be given to the Justices a present of fish consisting of two couples of Iceland ling, two couples of Haberdon (salt or dried cod), and so many Holland ling as the accustomed sum of money would buy. The goodwill of the Mayor and his brethren was also shown when the newly appointed Bishop, Dr. Bilson, came into residence at Wolvesey, for which occasion it was agreed that their wives should call on Mrs. Bilson and present her, at the City's expense, with a sugar loaf weighing eleven pounds.

Such traditional customs, constantly recurring through the years, did not blind the eyes of the senior citizens to the needs of those who were less wealthy. In common with the rest of the country towards the end of the sixteenth century Winchester had an ever increasing amount of poverty, and rarely did a day pass without some measure being taken to give relief to the poor either by monetary contribution or by finding work for them. There was Dorothy Baker, 'an impotent creature living in the parish of St. Maurice', who lay bedridden at the house of her sister, Agnes Pratts, and received twopence only from the overseers of the parish. She was given an extra twelve pence from the City. Jane Waters was given a 'turn' and cards for the working of wool, and her allowance increased by twopence a day, on condition that neither she nor her children indulged in begging. Dionese Burton complained of lack of work; therefore she was given one or two pounds of tow to keep her occupied. Four shillings out of the alms of the Dean and Chapter was given to Joan Moore on condition that neither she nor her children became a charge on the City, and at the same time Gyles Tarrant was given twenty shillings for the bringing up of a young orphan girl.

Also there is a record concerning Harmon Moulton who declared before the Mayor and his brethren that seven years previously he received a child, bastard born, reported to be the child of George Leach begotten upon Agnes Orchard, which had been left with his wife during his absence. The said Agnes had given his wife to keep the child ten shillings in money, two potingers, two candlesticks, a baste pot, an old gown, one old bed and one old coverlet. He now sought help and advice.

As a remedy for unemployment, wool was bought in bulk and stored in the Council Chamber and afterwards given out in small quantities to those who were prepared to do the spinning. Such persons were paid for their labour and in certain cases 'turns' and cards were supplied to them. In the case of Thomas Fuller it was agreed that a currier's knife together with other equipment necessary for his trade should be given to him, and again there was a proviso that he should refrain from begging. In this instance the money to buy the tools was taken from that subscribed by the parishioners of St. Lawrence for the relief of the poor. Nor did the prisoners in the Westgate escape attention, for there is a note to the effect that they should be granted two shillings for their relief until the next gaol delivery. It is also evident that the generosity of the Mayor and his brethren extended beyond the city boundaries, for when the town of Tiverton suffered severely from fire in 1598 it was decided that a collection should be made 'from the better inhabitants' of Winchester to relieve the distress at Tiverton. This raised twenty-six shillings and eightpence to which was added thirteen shillings and fourpence from the city coffers, to make up the round sum of two pounds.

Special care and provision was constantly being made for orphans and the children of the poor by way of apprenticeship. One finds frequent references in the minutes to such matters. John Jevons was given leave to take Stephen Brexstone, son of the late Richard Brexstone, as an apprentice and was to receive three pounds six shillings and eightpence for so doing. Widow Hilson was lent twenty shillings towards placing her son with Thomas Tucker as apprentice, and was asked to repay that sum at the rate of five shillings quarterly. It was also agreed that twenty shillings should be paid to Harry Abbot on account of his taking Anthony Warde as an apprentice, and the same amount was granted Richard Humber for taking Stephen Brothers.

Besides the relief of the poor there were other matters of a financial nature which caused frequent meetings of the Mayor and his brethren. A bequest of one hundred and thirty-three pounds six shillings and eightpence made to the City by Richard Venables, a London merchant tailor, came up for consideration. It was decided that it should be divided into four equal sums of thirty-three pounds six shillings and eightpence which should be lent, free of interest, to citizens 'of fair name and fame', for fixed periods, provided security could be found. Needless to say, there was no lack of applicants for such loans from the trading community. Then there was the collection of the poor rate to be attended to, but before this could be done there was the usual assessment of the amount which the citizens, each according to his means, should be called upon to pay. The Mayor handed this duty over to one of the Justices, John White, who sent the final list to the overseers of each parish, and followed this up very shortly afterwards with warrants authorizing the overseers to distrain, in accordance with the statute, on such persons as delayed or refused to pay the amounts assessed.

There is one entry in the minute books, the last one recorded during the mayoralty of Edward Cole, which not only deals with finance but also shows the wide powers possessed by the Mayor and his brethren in determining the conduct of business in the Town Court. The entry runs as follows: 'To the intent that Mr. Mayor and Mr. Recorder of the Cytie may be induced more often to frequent the Courtes of the Cytie for the more spedyer proceedings to be had and good advice there to be given in iudiciall causes Yt ys agreed by the Maior and the more parte of his brethren that over and besides the fees now yelded there shalbe payed upon every judgment to be hereafter geven where the debt or damages shall amounte to the some of six poundes thirtene shillings and fourpence or above, the some of iiiid. upon every pounde to be divided as foloweth, viz. two partes thereof to the

Recorder, one fourth parte thereof to the Mayor, and the fourth parte to the Bayliffs of the Cytie.'

The above extracts from the minute books previously mentioned show that the matters which exercised the attention of the Mayor and his brethren varied a great deal in importance, ranging from merely trivial and parochial affairs to events of a weighty and national character. The former were generally decided and settled according to the terms of the City ordinances and local custom, while the latter called for action and judgment by the Mayor and his colleagues, acting as Justices of the Peace, in accordance with an Act of Parliament or Royal Proclamation. It will have been noted that cases dealing with the relief of the poor and the setting of poor people to work are constantly recurring. An explanation of these involves consideration of the social conditions prevailing at the time, and is therefore included in subsequent chapters on taxation, finance and health. Similarly, the interesting and possibly amusing entries referring to the search for recusants will be dealt with later when religion is considered, and those recording military affairs and operations will be recalled in the chapter on defence.

CHAPTER VII

City Finance

The ready acceptance of banking facilities as part of modern life tends to obscure the difficulties which, in earlier times, beset both individuals and corporations in their efforts to keep their assets, in the shape of money or securities or goods, in safe custody. Each corporation had to act as its own banker and the City of Winchester, according to the coffer accounts, kept all its money, securities and movable property of value, in a coffer placed within a settle in the Guildhall. It is recorded that in 1589 'the counsell howse of the Citie was founde broken open and the settle with twoo locks (within which settle was a coffer with fower locks fastened with a cheyne, the keyes whereof did remayne in the custodie of the cofferers accordinge to the auncient use of the citie) was also forciblie broken uppe and the saide coffer, the cheyne beinge broken, was carried awaie'.[1] At the time the coffer contained three seals, including the common seal of the City, about eighty pounds in coin and plate valued at sixteen pounds. In addition there were many bonds and securities for debts and loans, together with the account books. An inquiry was held, and by the scrutiny of certain books and documents and by the statements of persons to whom sums of money from the coffer had been lent, an estimate of the total loss was made.

In 1582 the City had entered into an agreement with the Lord Bishop of Winchester and the Dean and Chapter of the

[1] Coffer Accounts, 1589–1627, MS. City Archives.

Cathedral to accept one hundred pounds, of which Bishop Horne, who had died in 1580, had contributed forty pounds, and his successor, Bishop Watson, sixty pounds.[1] This money, known as the Bishops' Stock, was to be used by the Mayor, Bailiffs and Commonalty to help needy citizens by way of loans, apparently free of interest. The inquiry revealed that forty pounds of this stock, the repayment of a loan previously made to Jerome Adams, had disappeared from the coffer. Another stock called the Wiven Pine, the origin of which is unknown, was also held by the City, but its total value is not recorded. It came to light, however, that the same Jerome Adams had borrowed twenty pounds from this source and Michael Crosse had received ten pounds. For both sums Charles Newbolt, a former mayor, had stood surety but his bond had also been stolen. He now repaid twenty pounds and gave his bill for the remaining ten pounds. Two other sums of ten pounds each, which had been lent from Wiven Pine stock to two citizens and later repaid into the coffer, were also stolen. Robert Clifton's Stock was also mentioned at the inquiry, and it is noted that two more townsmen had each borrowed ten pounds of this stock but their 'obligations' were in the hands of the Town Clerk and not in the coffer, so that no loss had been sustained.

A citizen named John Holmede who had borrowed five pounds from the city funds had been summoned for not repaying this sum within the specified time, but unfortunately the Bailiffs had allowed him to escape from custody. Consequently the debt rested upon the Bailiffs, who had paid one pound immediately with permission to refund the remaining four pounds at the rate of five shillings per quarter. Thirty-five shillings of this had been repaid into the coffer and this was among the missing money. From the aforementioned Bishops' Stock Thomas Collie had borrowed fourteen pounds and his 'obligation' was now missing from the coffer. He had borrowed a further twelve pounds from the same source and for this he had given as a pledge several

[1] 1st Bk. Ord., f. 224.

pieces of plate which were now stolen. In addition there was now missing a bond for seven pounds previously borrowed. There was therefore a total sum of thirty-three pounds in the hands of Thomas Collie, and as he showed no signs of repaying it the Town Clerk was instructed to take legal action for its recovery. At the inquiry there also emerged the fact that the City had spent thirteen pounds on linen cloth for the purpose of giving work to poor people, and had then sold the cloth to Christian Smithe for ten pounds, the balance of three pounds being met from City funds. And again, it was found that a further sum of thirteen pounds, this time from the Bishops' Stock, had been lent to James Crooke without bill or obligation to enable him to buy wool for the setting of poor people to work.

The latter part of the inquiry was concerned solely with the disappearance of sureties, chiefly in the shape of bonds given for the repayment of money borrowed. An examination showed that these covered a sum amounting to about one hundred and sixty pounds and also included three silver spoons pawned ten years previously. In some cases it was possible to produce written evidence of the loan, but in others the record states that payment had been made 'as it is well remembered'. The object of the loan is rarely given, though one reads that Christopher Heycroft, a carpenter, was lent twenty shillings in consideration of his taking William Agullie to be his apprentice for nine years, at the end of which time or at the boy's death the sum was to be repaid; also, sixteen pounds was lent to Humfrey Norton in his lifetime towards the building of the City's house whereof he had a lease.

It is noticeable that at the time of the inquiry the repayment of many of the loans was long overdue, sometimes by as much as fourteen years. In one case, Thomas Whale had borrowed twenty-five shillings in 1575 to be repaid at the rate of five shillings quarterly, yet after making the first repayment in the same year the remainder was still unpaid in 1589. William Bethell, a former mayor, borrowed ten pounds in 1579 to be repaid the same year, and forty pounds in 1580 to be repaid in 1583, but six years later at the time of the burglary at the Guildhall neither sum had been repaid. In a few cases arrangements were made for repayment by quarterly or annual instalments, but in others legal claims were to be made in court against the borrower or, where he had died, against his executors.

There is no record of the recovery of the money, plate, or sureties which were stolen, nor of the apprehension of the thieves, beyond a marginal note in the coffer account to the effect that two obligations for ten and five pounds respectively in the name of John Stoner had been found, and an entry in the minute book of the Mayor and his brethren ordering that a reward of five shillings should be paid to a servant who had found the broken coffer and a few of the missing documents. It was decided that these together with other bonds in the possession of the Town Clerk should be placed in a box known as Mr. Mayor's box, and that Edward Cole, then Mayor, should have the custody of the thirty pounds already paid in by various borrowers and any other sums which might be repaid until such time as a more convenient and suitable place could be provided for the safe keeping of the City's assets.

It is apparent that according to modern standards there was considerable slackness in the handling of the City's finances. A comparatively large amount of money was available for disbursement as loans, and although a citizen was required to provide some security in return for financial assistance the recovery of the loan was rarely pursued by the responsible officers with promptitude. In the city archives there is an old paper manuscript showing the coffer accounts for the years 1589 to 1627. The first few pages of this book have supplied the material for the preceding account of the breaking open of the coffer in the old Guildhall in 1589. The remainder of the book is divided into two parts, the entries in the first part giving details of sums paid into the coffer from the year 1590 while simultaneous entries in the second half of the book show disbursements. It is a curious fact, however, that in 1598 this procedure was suddenly reversed, and from that date the first half of the book is devoted to sums paid out and the latter half to receipts.

There is plenty of evidence to show that these accounts are by no means complete and that many sums received or owing are not entered. According to the First Book of Ordinances, the Chamberlains of the City were required to render an account of their annual receipts for house and ground rents by Lady Day, but in the period 1590 to 1603 there are only six entries in the coffer account concerning such receipts. There were other important items which appeared very rarely, or not at all, on the credit side. The annual sum of forty pounds derived from the ulnage or duty levied on cloth at the time of sale in the County of South-ampton is mentioned once only, and one looks in vain for the sums paid by new entrants to the Merchant Gild and for the fines inflicted on those who refused to become members. Neither is there any mention of the sums paid by citizens to avoid holding such offices as that of bailiff. On the other hand there are many omissions with regard to sums expended. Only once is there any mention of the payment of members of parliament and the annual fee of ten marks paid to the High Steward has one solitary reference. There was frequent expenditure incurred in purchasing building materials and for labour in the reparation of City property, yet on only two occasions was money taken from the coffer to meet these charges. But the Chamberlains' accounts reveal that all these and many other monetary transactions actually took place; therefore, their omission from the coffer accounts can probably be explained by the assumption that many incidental expenses were paid directly by the Chamberlains, on the order of the Mayor, from the money received from various sources, such as rents. It seems that these officers kept just sufficient in hand to meet current expenses and paid any large surplus into the coffer. This would account for the occasional receipt into the coffer of sums amounting at times to thirty or forty pounds and also for the omission in the coffer account of smaller receipts and items of expenditure. In other words the coffer seems to have been used by the Chamberlains as a kind of safe deposit in order to avoid keeping large sums of money in their own hands, and as a reserve on which they could draw when called upon to meet any heavy expenditure.

The items recorded in the old coffer account during the last ten years of Elizabeth's reign are of great interest, for they cover many aspects of municipal activity and furnish details not only of the various sources of City revenue but also of the manner in which the financial resources were employed. One cannot but wonder, however, how the authorities with such a haphazard system of book-keeping ever knew at any given time what balance they had in hand. An examination of the total entries for this particular period of ten years shows that while three hundred and eighty pounds were paid into the coffer, approximately four hundred and fifty were taken out. But since there is a note to the effect that two bonds, in the name of John White who was Town Clerk for many years, for the total sum of seventy-eight pounds were lying in the coffer, it would seem that the City was, in fact, living from hand to mouth and managing to survive financially by a narrow margin.

Under these circumstances, all went well until some unexpected and extraordinary expenditure had to be met, as for example when a royal visit to the City was imminent, or when the City became engaged in a costly law suit. Concerning the visits of Queen Elizabeth to Winchester there is very little information in the municipal records. The coffer accounts give some details of such a visit in 1591, but as the accounts for previous years are missing, one has to search further afield for information regarding the other occasions when Winchester entertained Her Majesty. According to Nichols's *Progresses*, and Chambers's *Elizabethan Stage*, there was, in August 1560, a royal progress through Surrey and Hampshire when the Queen visited at least a dozen places including Winchester, where she stayed from the 16th to the

23rd of that month. Unfortunately the details of the visit and of the manner in which she was entertained are lacking. In 1574 the Queen made a journey through the west of England and after staying at Bristol, Bath and Salisbury, she arrived in Winchester on the 10th of September and stayed here three days. On this occasion the scholars of Winchester College welcomed Her Majesty with loyal verses in Latin and Greek, a copy of which still exists in the Bodleian Library.[1] There is an account of a visit in 1586 when the Queen left Bishop's Waltham on September 1st of that year and came on to Winchester to stay for five days, before going on to Tisted Manor, the home of Sir Richard Norton.[2] It is stated that this visit to Winchester cost the College £20 which was given to the Lord Treasurer for his favours and help in furthering College business, and another £5 given to his attendants and to Sir Francis Walsingham. It has also been claimed that the granting of the charter of 1587 to the City was the fulfilment of a promise made by the Queen during this visit. But as neither of the two authorities, Nichols and Chambers, make any reference to the Queen's journeying to Hampshire in 1586, there must be some doubt as to its occurrence.

Later, in 1591, the Queen made a progress through Surrey, Sussex and Hampshire during which she stayed with the Bishop of Winchester at Bishop's Waltham on September 8th and 9th.[3] She was at Farleigh Wallop on the 12th and in the meantime she had visited Warnford, Tichborne, Winchester, Abbotstone (near Alresford), and Wield, so that her stay in the City must have been short, in fact, she may have merely passed through it, staying just long enough to receive a welcome from the Mayor and citizens. It has been suggested that the Queen avoided the City on this occasion, the evidence supporting this view being a letter written by John Harmar, Headmaster of the College, in 1596, stating that when the Queen was last in Hampshire 'she had the scholars before her'

[1] Bodl. Rawl. MSS., Poet, p. 187.   [2] Cal. Cecil, MSS., iii, 178.
[3] E. K. Chambers, *Elizabethan Stage*, iv, 106.

at Abbotstone, where she was staying.[1] But the City coffer accounts tell a different story. On August 30th, 1591, the Mayor and his brethren agreed that £12 6s. 8d. should be taken out of the coffer to pay for a cup of silver and gilt to be presented to Her Majesty. Six days later there is another item in the accounts to the effect that £10 should also be taken from the coffer to be presented in the cup for Her Majesty, and two days after that a further £10 was taken out to make up the whole sum of £20 to be presented in the cup. There was further expenditure; ten shillings was given to Nicholas Marks for his journey to London to buy the gilt cup, and the various members of the Queen's household had to be 'rewarded'. Her trumpeters received twenty shillings and her marshal ten shillings, while the clerk of the market was given twenty shillings and the trumpeter who accompanied him ten. Five shillings was the reward of the purveyor and master of the buttery. It would seem that the City's water supply had suddenly become inadequate, for at the same time Francis Porke was paid eleven shillings 'in consideration wherof he hath undertaken to amende the common pumpe of the Citie and make the same welle in all pointes for presente use within fower daise next ensuinge'. Finally, to support the claim regarding this visit, there is an entry in the churchwardens' accounts of St. John's Church which reads 'iiis. for Drink, ringing for the Queen'.

But the greatest drain on the City's resources was caused by litigation. There are many instances of comparatively small sums being paid out to the Mayor and other prominent citizens to defray their expenses in travelling to London on legal business throughout the whole of the reign, but during the last twenty years of the sixteenth century quite considerable amounts were disbursed to meet lawyers' fees and other legal charges connected with suits to which the City was a party. The most important of these was the dispute concerning the will of Peter Symonds, details of which will be dealt with later, and two others relating to the setting up of markets

[1] Cal. Cecil MSS., vi, 237.

at Alresford and Bishop's Waltham respectively. In March 1592, the Mayor and seven of his brethren agreed that John White and Edward Cole, two former mayors, should be 'elected and entreated to travaile to London during this present parliamente aboute the affaires and busines of the Citie, viz. concerninge the landes geven by Mr. Peter Simondes, deceased, towardes the relief of the poore inhabitants of the Citie, and also concerninge the markets erected at Alresford and Waltham to the grete preiudice of the Citie, and that they travaile at the charges of the Citie and retaine counsaile and use advise in the premisses, and also that the some of tenne pounds shall be delivered to them owte of the coffer for which they shall accompte at their returne'.

Two and a half years later, in November 1594, it was agreed 'that there shalbe a quo warranto or anie other sute or meanes used at the charge of the Cytie for the deponyinge or avoydinge of Waltham market', and at the same time it was decided 'that suche prosequutinge shalbe of the cause towchinge the effectinge of Peter Symonds will for the erection of a hospitall by the same will devised as shalbe from tyme to tyme devised by Mr. Recorder and such other councell as shalbe retayned on the behalf of the Cytie and that Mr. Edward Cole ys appointed to sollocite the same this term and to lay out such charges as shalbe necessary thought meete'. There is a further record in October 1596 that 'A writt of Quo Warranto shalbe procured in this next Michaelmas terme at the charges of the Citie against the inhabitants of Bisshops Waltham concerninge their unlawfull usinge and keepinge of a common market within the towne of Waltham to the annusance of this Citie and of the inhabitants within the same'.

Nothing further is recorded in relation to the market at Alresford, but in December 1602, more than ten years after John White and Edward Cole had made their first journey to London on this matter, eighteen pounds were taken out of the coffer to be used in the City's case against Waltham market which was to be tried at Basingstoke, and three months later a further three pounds from the coffer were sent up to London in connection with the same case. This was obviously a costly and protracted business, the outcome of which unfortunately is not known. But it was by no means as costly as the law suit concerning Peter Symonds's will, for time after time between 1594 and 1600 various sums amounting in all to over two hundred pounds were required to meet the expenses incurred in these particular proceedings.

Peter Symonds was a native of Winchester who became a wealthy London mercer. He died in 1586 and by his will, a lengthy affair covering no less than seven large parchments, he made bequests to numerous individuals, corporations and charitable societies, including his brothers, John and William, both freemen of the City of Winchester, and to the City itself. He left his manor of Ingleby, in the parish of Shadwell in Essex, and his lands called Trinity Marsh in West Ham, with the profits and rents therefrom, after the death of his wife, to Mr. Bilson, Warden of Winchester College, his brother William, who at the time of Peter's death was Mayor of the City, and to four others and their heirs as feoffees in trust on condition that they should obtain a licence from the Queen for a hospital to be erected in Winchester to be called Christ's Hospital. In addition there was an annual rent of fifteen pounds for twenty-one years from lands held by Philip Beansted of Chidden, Hambledon, in Hampshire, to be devoted to the same purpose.

The date of the death of Peter Symonds's wife, upon which the appointed trustees were to take possession of the property, is not certain, but it was most probably shortly before March, 1592, since that was the date already mentioned when the City first sent representatives to London to deal with the legacy. The law suit which followed in 1594 was due to the fact that a certain Richard Symonds, who is not mentioned in the will and whose exact relationship to Peter Symonds has not been established, had in November of that year, contrary to the terms of the will, sold Ingleby and Trinity Marsh to Richard Higgins and Thomas Coke. The former of these two men shortly afterwards sold his share to Thomas Myll, who later re-sold it to the same Thomas Coke who held the other moiety. This person thereupon, by a deed in Chancery, entailed the whole property for the use of himself, his brother and their heirs. Therefore, in the following January, it was decided by the Mayor of Winchester and his brethren 'that a bill shall be exhibited in the Chancerie at the charge of the Citie concerninge the lands latelie given by Mr. Peter Simonds, and Mr. Seriant fflemynge' (the late Recorder of Winchester), 'Mr. Atturnie generall and Mr. Phillipps shalbe retained of the Cities counsell in this behalf and that the same cause shalbe from tyme to tyme prosequuted at the charge of the Citie and that uppon the recoverie of the saide lands the same charge so disbursed shalbe levied and paied in againe owte of the revenewes of the same lands and that such monie as shalbe necessarie be taken owte of the coffer from tyme to tyme as occasion shall require'. During the next four years sums varying from two to twenty pounds were taken out of the coffer and given to Anthony Dawley, Town Clerk, or to Edward Cole to pay counsel acting on the City's behalf. There is no doubt that great difficulty was experienced in raising the money necessary to prosecute the case in the Court of Chancery, and in March, 1599, it was found expedient to borrow two hundred and eighty pounds (probably well over twelve thousand pounds in modern currency) for a period of six months to meet further expenditure. For the repayment of this sum together with interest at the rate of ten per cent per annum Richard Cooke and Edward Cole stood bound for one hundred and five pounds, Charles Newbolt and William Beacham for the same amount, and Richard Ashton and George Pemerton for eighty-four pounds each.

The case went on for over five years and was finally settled in the Michaelmas term of 1600, when the recognisance in Chancery acknowledged by Thomas Coke to Richard Symonds was by order of the Lord Keeper cancelled and discharged, while Richard Symonds was committed to the Fleet prison and the property legally conveyed to Dr. Bilson, who in 1597 had become Bishop of Winchester, and the other trustees. It is recorded that on December 29th, 1600, the title deeds and other papers connected with the suit were placed in the coffer by Anthony Dawley, Town Clerk. It was not until 1605, however, that royal permission was obtained to proceed with the erection of the hospital in accordance with the terms of Peter Symonds's will.[1]

Chamberlain's Accounts

The financial year began on the Feast of St. Michael the Archangel (Michaelmas Day) and when the ensuing twelve months were ended the Chamberlains were required to present their account roll before the following Lady Day. Of the forty-five rolls which would cover the reign of Elizabeth, twenty-five are at present in the hands of the Corporation, and from these it is learnt that the Chamberlains collected money from many sources for they were, in effect, the city treasurers. With this money they met the various demands made upon them, and when they found that they could not meet any particular expenditure from cash in hand they appealed for a loan from the City coffer, for which they had to provide some form of security. In the course of a year a comparatively large amount of money passed through their hands, and more than one holder of this office found himself in financial straits at the end of his term and unable to hand over the balance due to the coffer. In such cases the Chamberlain was required to find sureties and was usually allowed to repay the debt by quarterly instalments; should he die before the whole sum had been repaid, his heirs or executors were called upon to discharge the debt.

A compotus or account roll consists of pieces of parchment, about eleven inches wide, stitched together to reach a length of twelve feet or more when unrolled. The writing usually covers both sides and the numerous items are arranged under various headings. For example, the Chamberlains' roll for the

[1] Proceedings of Corporation, B, MS., f. 54–56, City Archives.

year 1588–89, when translated from the abbreviated Latin in which it is written, can be summarized as follows:

	£	s.	d.
Arrears	8	18	10
Receipts in cash	48	4	4
Rents of assise, or fixed rents	7	16	3
Leases of old lands and tenements ..	59	12	8
Leases of lands and tenements formerly monastic property	26	17	10
Total ..	151	9	11
Public expenses	29	18	6
Fees and stipends	38	8	2
Rents paid	45	9	1
Stores bought and repairs to property ..	9	5	11
Total ..	123	1	8
Amount of surplus	28	8	3
Payments requiring auditors' approval ..	9	2	2
Amount to be placed in the coffer ..	19	6	1

This particular roll states that it was presented by the two Chamberlains, William Lane and Thomas Thorpe, and was approved by Charles Newbolt who was Mayor from September, 1588, until September of the following year, and by his successor, John Paice, who was Mayor on Lady Day when the roll was finally passed by the eight auditors, four appointed by the Twenty-four and four by the Commons. A complete translation of the roll would produce much repetition of items of no great interest or value, but some comment upon the main headings together with a selection of the more important details will show the chief sources of the City's income and the manner in which it was spent.

The arrears (arreragia) are taken from the account roll of

the preceding year. The cash receipts, which amount to nearly one-third of the total sum received, as can be seen in the above summary, came from many contributors. Thus there is included the sum of £40 paid by the collector of the ulnage or duty on woollen cloth for the county of Southampton, the total fees paid by entrants to the Merchant Gild at the rate of 3s. 4d. for each of the first six years, the fee of 1s. 6d. for the use of the City's crockery at dinners and other functions, rents of land and tenements belonging to Winchester Castle the custody of which had been granted to the City by the Queen in 1558, money from the sale of timber and other materials out of the City's stores and fees received for the sealing of pieces of finished broadcloth.

The rents of assise or fixed rents were divided into two categories. Firstly, there were those arising from land and property both in and outside the City which had been acquired by purchase or which had been erected by the City and, secondly, those accruing from lands and houses and other buildings which formerly belonged to monasteries and other religious houses (ad monasteria et alia loca religiosa). Such were the lands of St. Mary's Abbey, east of Colebrook Street, and of the College of St. Mary Kalender, on the north side of the High Street between Parchment and Shulworth (Upper Brook) Streets. The former holdings of St. Mary's Abbey numbered thirteen and included the large house of Richard Warneford, gentleman, in Wongar (Middle Brook) Street which paid 5s. a year, a house whose rent was 4s. opposite the George Inn which was occupied by Sir Thomas Sands, and a small corner cottage called Coppidhal near St. Giles' Hill within the Soke (prope montem sancti egidii infra sokam), which was let for 1s. per annum. The Kalender lands at this time seem to have been occupied by the Dean and Chapter, but they yielded nothing to the City because the Cathedral body claimed that the statute which brought about the dissolution of this college made no provision for such a payment.

It was the numerous leases of property which provided the

largest amount of money on the credit side, and on the roll they are set down in groups according to the parish or street in which the property was situated. Again there is a distinction, as in the case of the rents of assise, between old City property which yielded a total of £59 and the former monastic lands, granted to the City by Philip and Mary in 1554, which brought in about £26 per annum. Most of the streets of the City are mentioned, and it is interesting to note that the parishes named are the old, small parishes dating back in most cases to Norman times. Though some of their churches had long since disappeared or fallen into decay, and though some of the parishes were by this time united with others, the old names are still used in the account roll. One finds the parishes of Ode, at the corner of High Street and Wongar (Middle Brook) Street, St. Rowald in Shulworth (Upper Brook) Street, St. George in St. George's Street, and St. Pancras at the north end of Wongar Street, the sites of whose parish churches are described in the roll as vacant plots of land or as being occupied by tenements and gardens. Outside each of the four main gates of the City there were holdings granted on lease by the City. The pasture of the ditches outside Westgate and Northgate were leased to William Lane for £1 a year, and he also leased what was left of the former chapel outside Westgate for a further 3s. 4d. The herber (Orams Arbour), a large expanse of land outside the same gate, contained crofts and pastures and yielded the large amount of 59s. 8d. The most expensive lease was that of the George Inn at the corner of High Street and Jewry Street—as important then as in later days—which was £4, while the narrow lane which then led from Jewry Street to Staple Garden brought in a mere 4d. The 'newe house' near the common pump, not far from the City Cross, produced £2; two little shops near the cathedral graveyard yielded 2s. and 8d. respectively. In the parish of St. Mary Kalender there was the Pentice which consisted of a number of large houses leased by several of the more prosperous citizens at £1 per year. Further afield in the village of Twyford the City leased two fulling mills and a tenement to the heirs of Thomas Michelborne for £16, and for the fishbed in the river outside Durngate the sum of 1s. a year was received. The 'new lands' for which the City now granted leases, generally for forty years, included those formerly occupied by St. Mary's Abbey in Colebrook Street together with its burial ground (known as St. Mary's litten), and many other properties scattered throughout the City and the Soke which the Abbey once possessed. The College of St. Mary Kalender, Southwick Priory and Wherwell Nunnery also at one time owned tenements and gardens in the City and these, since their dissolution, are all found mentioned in the Chamberlains' rolls. The roll for the year 1588–89 mentions 175 separate properties which yielded rent to the City, and of these 115 are houses or cottages. In the account roll for the year 1446 the number of such houses is given as 40. It can thus be seen how the amount of property in the hands of the City had increased in the past 140 years, though it is evident that the bulk of it had been acquired during the past 50 years since the dissolution of the monasteries.

A close examination of the amounts paid as yearly rent shows that in Elizabethan times the rents of houses and of land were very low. Of the 115 tenements and cottages, 83 paid 10s. or less per annum. The remaining 32 included the mills at Twyford, the manor of Otterbourne, the George and King's Head inns, together with 13 houses which paid from 13s. to 16s. and 15 which paid from 20s. to 25s. All these are generally referred to in the rolls as large houses. Of the 83 houses which paid smaller rents, there are 30 yielding between 7s. and 10s., and 40 yielding from 4s. to 6s. 8d., a year. The latter are usually given in the rolls as cottages, while those habitations paying less, about 10 in number which pay 1s., 2s. or 3s. a year, are called small houses. It has been calculated that in those days a working man might not be paying more than 3 to 5 per cent of his wages in house rent; the occupant of a modern council house might well envy him.

In addition to the tenements belonging to the City, there

are 60 properties consisting of a large number of gardens and a few void plots of ground. Many of the houses and cottages had gardens attached to them, but there were many gardens in the City which were quite separate and which had previously been the sites of cottages and other buildings. For example, the parish of St. Thomas has by 1588 become somewhat depopulated, for there is an unusually large number of gardens in that locality, and incidentally their rents are comparatively high. The rent of a garden depended no doubt on its size and possibly on its position, and it is found to range from 8*d.* to 2*s.* 6*d.* per annum, with the majority paying either 1*s.* or 2*s.* Where the rent is much higher, it is usually indicated in the roll that the plot comprises two or three gardens or that it includes a stable. Also included in these lands are the sheep coops near the cathedral graveyard but standing in the market square which are leased at 5*s.*, and the Town pond in Danemark Mead, outside the City walls, leased at 6*s.* 8*d.* together with two smaller ponds near to it for which 1*s.* 6*d.* is paid. In order to reach these ponds the lessee had a special gateway made through the City wall for which he paid the lowest amount recorded in the roll, namely 1*d.* a year.

After recording £151 9*s.* 11*d.* as the sum total of all moneys received, the account roll reveals the manner in which this sum was spent. Under the heading of 'public expenditure', there are no less than 72 items many of which are both interesting and quaint. 45*s.* is spent on a sugar loaf weighing 27 lbs. at 20*d.* per lb. to be given to the Marquis of Winchester as a New Year's gift. Lord de la Warr also receives a sugar loaf but only half the size of the former and costing 20*s.* 8*d.* For baking half a fallow-deer, given to the Lord Marquis on the second of January, and for the wine consumed on that occasion, 3*s.* is paid. A week later the same nobleman is presented with a bottle of sack and a gallon of claret which together cost 8*s.* When soldiers break the lock on the Northgate the cost of replacement is 8*d.* The Justices of Assize are entertained by the City and the Chamberlains are ordered by the Mayor to pay out 11*s*. for a fresh salmon and 8*s*. for a fat sheep. Again by order of the Mayor, 20*s*. is given to the Royal Players when they appear before the citizens in March of that year. 'The grubbinge, sawinge and slittinge of the walnut tree and makinge and fillinge the sawpitt and amendinge the hedge' (which the scribe does not attempt to put into Latin), calls for an expenditure of 7*s*. In the Guildhall a quire of paper, fourpennyworth to be exact, is used. A shilling is given to Sergeant John Chapington for playing the fife, and 13*s*. 4*d*. to Thomas Bostock, a lawyer, for carrying out some legal business for the City. Fourteen yards of broadcloth at 7*s*. a yard for the liveries of the sergeant-at-mace and the beadle cost £4 18*s*. 0*d*. The repairs to the archery butts at Kingsgate and on the Castle Green require 7*s*. 8*d*., and the cleansing of the public washing-place and the latrines calls for an outlay of 6*s*. The musters, which are held periodically, are at the City's expense and the payments include 21*s*. 6*d*. for the dinner attended by the Mayor and various officers, 3*s*. for the drum and fife players, 15*s*. for armour, 8*s*. for 3 quarts of sack and 6 quarts of claret, 6*s*. for 6 lbs. of gunpowder and 9*d*. for 3 lbs. of matches. The beadle receives 4*s*. 4*d*. for clearing the weeds from the City walls, and a further 3*s*. 4*d*. for riding to Southampton with 'a strange lady' (*domina estranea*). One of the most noticeable features is the large amount of money spent on refreshment, and the final item in this section of the account roll records the sum of 6*s*. 2*d*. paid out for wine called 'Ipocrise' and cakes given to the Lord Marquis of Winchester by order of the Mayor.

The fees and stipends which show very little variation from year to year are paid out in 1588–89 as shown on page 131.

The next heading on the roll, namely, rents paid, is rather misleading. Although it includes the small sums of 5*d*. paid to the Bishop of Winchester for the rent of a cottage outside Westgate and 2*s*. 6*d*. for the rent of two houses in the parish of St. Pancras, the chief items are £4 to the Bailiffs of the City for quit rents, £10 for the Twyford mills which the City re-lets for £16, and £30 due to the Queen for the ulnage of

	£	s.	d.
To Sir Francis Walsingham, High Steward	6	13	4
To the Chamberlains	3	3	4
To the Town Clerk for his fee	1	0	0
To Charles Newbolt, late Mayor, second payment	10	0	0
To John Payce, present Mayor, first payment	10	0	0
To the Town Clerk for paper and parchment	1	0	0
To Thomas Fleming, Recorder	4	0	0
To James Ruddesbie, the tiler		10	0
To the Cofferers		1	6
To Owen Hammon, the City Armourer ..	2	0	0
Total ..	38	8	2

cloth within the county of Southampton. The sum total under this heading is £45 9s. 1d.

The roll then proceeds to give details of the amounts spent on repairs to property and on stores. Just over £3 is spent on stores which consist chiefly of timber in the shape of planks for building, and bricks and tiles. Repairs to City property cost £6, which seems remarkably low when one considers the large number of tenements and cottages which the City owned. But from the individual leases it is discovered that most of the City's houses were leased with a proviso that the lessee was responsible for repairs. Therefore, the expenses in the account roll under this heading are mainly concerned with such places as the Guildhall, the washing-place, the latrines, the City Cross and the Market House. For example, the pin-fold which was situated in what is now known as the Broad-way requires a new lock and key costing 8d., the weeding of the groundsel in the same pinfold costs 4d., the bricklayer and his mate receive 3s. for two days' work at the Castle, and the mason and his mate get 9s. 6d. for 6 days' work on the walls outside Eastgate.

Finally, the roll shows the total expenditure (summa

omnium allocacionum) as £123 1s. 8d. (Cxxiii^li. xx^d.), and the surplus of receipts over expenditure as £28 8s. 3d. Then there are enumerated several items of expenditure concerning which the Chamberlains are apparently in some doubt and which have been deferred pending the auditors' approval. These amount to £9 2s. 2d. There is therefore owing to the City coffer upon this account (et sic debet clave super hunc compotum) the sum of £19 6s. 1d., which is rather more than the average credit balance of £15 per annum for Elizabeth's reign.

CHAPTER VIII

Taxation

From the City records it is clear that in Elizabethan times there was both direct and indirect taxation and that each of these was levied not only by the central government but also by the local municipal authority, so that in all there were four kinds of taxation which a citizen of Winchester might be called upon to pay. Local indirect taxation, which has nowadays entirely disappeared, was paid on goods and merchandise entering the City and was collected at the gates or in the market and streets as a sales due. In the latter case it often took the form of rent for the setting up or occupying of stalls in the market or in the streets in front of shops. For example, for the occupying of the sheep coops alongside the cathedral graveyard the charge was one penny for every ten sheep per day. As a rule, however, the freemen of the City, as members of the Merchant Gild, were free from toll at the gates or paid it at a reduced rate, and it was the 'foreign' trader or stranger who paid most of these dues. Arrangements had been made with certain other towns for reciprocity of treatment, and in such cases the merchants of those towns enjoyed the same privileges as the local freemen when they came to Winchester. It is no surprise, therefore, to find that the total amount of money from import or market dues in the course of a year was comparatively small. These dues had originally been collected by the King's officers, but the City had long ago acquired the right to collect them and pay over to the Exchequer a fixed sum annually along with other royal dues. Thus, although they can be regarded as local taxation, they were in fact a form of national indirect taxation.

Strictly speaking, national indirect taxation took the form of customs dues, which were no new thing in Elizabeth's reign for they had been levied since the time of Edward I, and 'ancient customs' are recognized in Magna Carta. The proceeds from duties on exported and imported merchandise had been granted for life to each succeeding monarch since Edward IV, and by the middle of the sixteenth century they were regarded by Parliament as 'an ancient revenue annexed and united to the Crown'. In 1585 these duties were farmed at £24,000 a year, but this was considerably below their value as can be seen from the fact that in 1625 they had increased to £160,000. The main duties were three shillings a tun on wine, one shilling in the pound on other goods and merchandise, and an extra shilling in the pound on tin. The duty on wool and hides in the case of a native merchant was £1 13s. 4d. per sack, but in the case of a foreign merchant it was double this amount. This indirect taxation by way of custom duties did not prove at all burdensome to the average citizen even though it was increased from time to time by certain additional duties, known as impositions, which were levied upon various articles imported into the country.

The government could claim, partly by custom and partly by statute, that it was empowered to regulate trade, and so it is found that as a means of repression it levied impositions, and that at the same time in order to encourage trade in certain directions it granted monopolies. These trade monopolies and additional duties were regarded as a commercial necessity and no voice was raised against them for some time, but eventually it was realized that they had become an important source of profit to the Crown and were therefore a convenient means of evading parliamentary control. This gave rise to a bill, which was debated in the parliament of 1601, proposing the abolition of monopolies. It was disclosed that monopolies, which in former days had been granted to corporations to assist them in developing trade, as in the case of the Levant Company, had of late been granted under the royal seal to individuals permitting them to be the sole vendors or manufacturers of certain articles of trade, many of which were household necessities. This list included currants, iron, powder, playing cards, vinegar, sea cole, starch, steel, brushes, salt, saltpetre, lead, oil, and many others. Many abuses had crept in, and it was quoted in the House of Commons that as a result of the granting of a patent for salt in this country, that commodity was now sold at fourteen shillings a bushel whereas the former price was sixteen pence a bushel. Fear was expressed that bread would soon be added to the list. There can be no wonder, therefore, that this parliament, in which Thomas Fleming, late Recorder of Winchester, was Solicitor-General, expressed itself very strongly on this matter although the bill was prejudicial to the Queen's prerogative. But the Queen, with her usual adroitness, informed the House that she was as much opposed to the abuses as the members were, and would see that their grievances were redressed. This was a popular decision, for there was no doubt that the monopolies had become a source of irritation and complaint in all parts of the country. It has already been noted in a previous chapter how, in 1598, a number of Winchester traders had attempted to evade the monopoly on starch and had consequently been severely admonished by the Mayor and his brethren.

Direct taxation, when compared with indirect taxation, for both national and local purposes was a heavier burden on the citizen. National direct taxation was fixed by parliament at irregular intervals and took the form of Fifteenths, Tenths and Subsidies. From the time of Edward III it had been the practice to levy taxes amounting to a fifteenth and a tenth, or two or more fifteenths and tenths, on movable goods and chattels, the smaller fraction being levied on the counties and the larger on the towns. The assessment made in 1334 became more or less fixed, and the Fifteenth and the Tenth were to all intents and purposes a tax upon holders of lands and tenements of a definite value. After a time it was obvious that owing to changed circumstances this tax was unfair to certain districts and towns which had decayed, and on the whole was not touching all the resources of the country. Therefore a supplementary tax called a Subsidy was introduced. This tax in Henry VIII's reign became a direct tax of four shillings in the pound on the yearly value of land and two shillings and eightpence in the pound on personal property.[1] It will be seen that the rate on land is two-tenths and that on personalty two-fifteenths in the pound. In Elizabeth's reign the usual practice, though it varied occasionally, was to make each subsidy equivalent to two-fifteenths and tenths. Such a grant was made in 1559. There were therefore in this reign two somewhat similar national taxes, namely, fifteenths and tenths, and subsidies, which were combined in the parliamentary votes of almost every session. The fifteenths and tenths were assessed in Winchester, in whose records this tax is generally referred to as the 'Fifteenth', by five or six prominent citizens, usually former mayors, and the collection was undertaken by two citizens appointed by the two members of parliament for the City. This latter practice was probably a relic of the time when members who voted a tax were responsible for collecting it themselves. Thus, in April 1597, the Winchester burgesses in parliament, Mr. John Moore and Mr. William Badger, elected Richard Ashton and Thomas Salter, two freemen, as collectors of the tax for the City.

In Winchester the Fifteenth, like other claims made by the Crown, was not a varying sum but was compounded for at a fixed rate, and from the middle of the fourteenth century the amount had remained at £51 10s. 0d. Whenever a new demand was made the assessors' task was to revise the old list, striking out the names of those who had died or left the City and adding the names of newcomers, and then by spreading the burden as fairly as possible make an assessment of all those liable for taxation which would yield the total amount which the City had to pay.

[1] G. W. Prothero, *Statues and Constitutional Documents, 1558-1625,* p. lxxxi.

Taxation

Only a few of the taxation rolls relating to the Elizabethan period have survived. In those for the years 1581, 1585, 1589 and 1592 respectively, the names of the taxpayers and the amounts paid by each one of them are arranged according to the six aldermanries into which the City was divided. It seems best therefore to consider these four rolls collectively and compare their chief features. The rolls for 1581 and 1585 are for the first fifteenth, that for 1589 for the second fifteenth, while the 1592 roll gives details of the collection of both first and second fifteenths, that is for two fifteenths, and therefore the total amount of tax collected is approximately twice that recorded in the previous rolls, where one finds particulars of either the first or second instalment only. The information contained in these four rolls may be summarized as follows:

Table showing the number of taxpayers

Aldermanry			1581	1585	1589	1592
High Street	...	...	189	195	173	178
Jewry Street	...	...	40	34	40	24
Gold (Southgate) Street	...		38	34	33	37
Tanner Street	...	...	53	48	56	42
Colbroke Street	...	...	68	52	54	46
Northgate Street (Hyde)	...		27	32	28	23
Totals	...		415	395	384	350

Table showing amount of tax collected

Aldermanry	1581			1585			1589			1592		
	£	s.	d.	£	s.	d.	£	s.	d.	£	s.	d.
High Street	13	11	0	17	16	0	15	17	2	32	3	10
Jewry Street	1	16	6	1	17	8	2	12	2	2	2	4
Gold Street	1	18	2	2	13	8	2	19	0	6	4	8
Tanner Street	1	16	8	1	11	8	3	3	6	3	6	4
Colbroke Street	3	0	0	2	11	0	2	13	2	6	16	8
Northgate Street	1	7	10	1	1	10	1	1	0	1	16	8
Totals	23	10	2	27	11	10	28	6	0	52	10	6

An examination of these tables reveals several interesting and significant facts. The first table shows that the number of persons taxed was gradually decreasing over a period of eleven years just after the middle of Elizabeth's reign, whilst over the same period the amount of tax raised was increasing, so that whereas 415 persons paid £23 in 1581, there were 350, or 65 less, paying more than £26 at one instalment in 1592. Thus the average payment had risen from 1s. 1½d. to 1s. 6d. per person in eleven years. It can also be seen that the bulk of the population and the wealth of the City were centred in the vicinity of the High Street, where the average payment was 1s. 5d. in 1581 and 1s. 10d. in 1592, while in the remainder of the City which housed the poorer section of the community the average payment was rarely above 1s. 0d. The roll for 1581 shows that of the 27 taxpayers in Northgate Street aldermanry there were 18 who paid 4d. only. It is also noticeable from these tables that the number of taxpayers living in the aldermanry of the High Street nearly equalled the total number living in all the other five aldermanries, and that this aldermanry always provided well over half the total amount of tax raised.

The rolls for these four distinct years show that about one-seventh of the taxpayers were women, either widows or single women servants, and that just under one-quarter were classified as servants, both male and female, who paid 4d. only. When these figures are taken into consideration it becomes apparent that when the number of servants is deducted from the total number of taxpayers there were approximately 300 householders paying the tax. This means that since there were 650 householders in the City at this time, as disclosed in the first chapter of this book, there were about 350 of these, or more than half, who were not called upon to meet this obligation. These were undoubtedly the occupiers of cottages and smaller tenements whose goods and chattels were of so little value that they could not justly or reasonably be assessed for taxation. From all this it follows that there must have been a large amount of poverty in the City, a situation previously mentioned in dealing with the executive powers of the Mayor and his brethren, and one which will receive further attention towards the end of the present chapter.

At the other end of the scale one finds that in 1581 the highest amount of tax was paid by William Symonds, a wealthy cloth merchant and three times Mayor, who lived at the west end of the Pentice in the High Street, and was taxed at 12*s*. Sir Walter Sands, Captain of the City militia, paid 10*s*., Thomas Michelborne, a lawyer and member of parliament for the City, 8*s*., and six former mayors, four of whom were lawyers, were required to pay 6*s*., each. The remainder, except servants, were assessed at smaller sums ranging from 1*s*. to 5*s*. By 1585 William Symonds was paying 14*s*., and increases of 3*s*. or 4*s*. were paid by more than a dozen prominent citizens, chiefly former mayors and magistrates. Many freemen were now taxed at 5*s*., whereas they previously paid 2*s*. 6*d*. or 3*s*. 4*d*. The Mayor, Richard Birde, was raised from 6*s*. to 8*s*., but the Town Clerk, John Potinger, remained assessed at 3*s*. 4*d*. Mistress Joan Bethell, widow of a former mayor and natural mother of Peter Symonds the founder of Christ's Hospital in Winchester, paid 6*s*. 8*d*., while Lady Mary West, a prominent Roman Catholic and recusant, paid 5*s*. Similarly in 1589 and 1592 it is noticed that certain citizens were called upon for increased amounts in order that the total sum raised by taxation should not fall in proportion to the decreasing number of taxpayers.

The whole machinery of collection of Subsidies, as distinct from Fifteenths and Tenths, is described in detail in the Act passed in 1559, soon after Elizabeth came to the throne.[1] The Chancellor, Treasurer and other great officers of state appointed commissioners for the larger districts and boroughs, who in turn appointed collectors under them for the purpose of assessing and levying the tax. The collectors were to be persons having lands in their own right of the yearly value of £10 or in goods worth 200 marks at the least. The persons taxed were all those worth £5, which in 1587 was reduced to £3, whether it was in coin, plate, stock of merchandise, corn,

[1] Idem, p. 27–36.

household stuff or movable goods, or having lands, rents, fees, etc., to the yearly value of £1. Aliens were included and assessed at a double rate.

Only one Subsidy roll has survived in Winchester, namely that for 1588. This roll is prefaced by an indenture made between Thomas Cooper, Bishop of Winchester, Edward Cole, Mayor, and five other wealthy citizens, who were the commissioners appointed for the taxing, assessing and levying of the subsidy, on the one part, and Robert Colson and William Paige, inhabitants of the City, who had been deputed by the commissioners to act as petty collectors, on the other part. The sum to be collected is given as £25 3s. 0d., and this is the second instalment of the Subsidy granted by Parliament the previous year. The commissioners had obviously been responsible for the actual assessment, while the task of the petty collectors was to gather in the tax and pay it over to Richard Emerie, the high collector, who was a haberdasher and apparently a person with the requisite financial backing. The petty collectors were each allowed to retain 2d. in the £1 as a reward for their labours and a further 2d. in the £1 was to be given to the commissioners and their clerks to cover their expenses.

The indenture is followed in the roll by the 'extract', which is arranged according to seven ecclesiastical parishes and contains the names and amounts paid by 94 persons. The following table is a summary of this roll:

Parish	No. of taxpayers	Amount of tax		
St. Clement	8	£1	8	8
St. Thomas	22	5	4	0
St. Maurice	16	5	2	8
St. Peter in Colbroke	6	1	7	8
St. Bartholomew	6	3	2	4
St. Lawrence	22	5	17	4
St. Mary Kalender	14	3	0	4
Totals	94	£25	3	0

In this second payment of the Subsidy the rate is 1s. in the £1 on goods and chattels and 1s. 4d. on land. In the first payment, previously made, the rate was 1s. 8d. in the £1 on goods and 2s. 8d. on land, thus making a total payment for the whole Subsidy of 2s. 8d. in the £1 on goods and 4s. on land. It is noticed that no one is taxed on both goods and lands in this Subsidy roll since such a procedure would be contrary to the terms of the Act, which states that anyone taxed on his goods, chattels and movables at any taxation shall not be taxed for his lands or other real possessions and profits at the same taxation.

A study of this roll shows that the number of names appearing on it is less than a quarter of the number to be seen on the rolls for the Fifteenth and Tenth, and that only one in seven of all the householders in the City was called upon to pay this tax. The two small parishes of St. Lawrence and St. Mary Kalender, both adjoining the central part of the High Street, provided one-third of the taxpayers and had the same proportion of the tax collected, for it was here, as was shown in the tables dealing with the Fifteenth and Tenth, that many of the wealthier citizens lived. Of the 94 people named in the roll, 80 are taxed on their goods, 12 on lands; John White, the Town Clerk, on his fees, and one widow on her annuities. No servants are taxed though there are included the names of two aliens, Adam Vanderplant and Levyn Burte, each of whom is required to pay 4d. Seven women are included in the list; Mowlde Agulley, a widow, has land valued at £1, Christian Powlet is taxed on annuities worth £8, and five other widows possess goods which the commissioners assess at amounts varying from £3 to £10. The wealthiest man is still William Symonds who now pays 27s. on goods valued at £27, and following him comes Edward Cole, Mayor, who has to pay 13s. on goods worth £13. The valuation of the goods of others on the roll ranges from £3 to £10, and those whose possessions are of less value than the former figure are untaxed. Of the landowners Sir Walter Sands and Thomas Fleming, the City Recorder, are the most important, each having holdings worth £20, while the City itself, through its Chamberlains, has to pay tax on lands in the parish of St. Bartholomew which are estimated to be worth £10.

Those inhabitants who were called upon to pay this particular tax are often referred to in the City records as 'subsidy men', a term which may be regarded as synonymous with the phrase 'men of substance'. They were the more important citizens and no one of less standing, for example, was allowed to stand as surety for a person who had been arrested for committing a serious offence. There are also records of occasions when the total sum for which the City was liable could not be raised by taxation, as in 1591 when there was much sickness and a trade depression in Winchester. In that year forty shillings had to be taken from the Chamberlains' accounts to meet a deficiency, and again in 1600 the total collected fell short of the required amount by twenty-seven shillings.

In Tudor times it was customary for the sovereign, in order to meet temporary shortages, to borrow on a large scale from his or her subjects. Elizabeth took loans on at least six occasions, chiefly towards the end of her reign. Letters were written by the Privy Council to the Lords Lieutenant ordering them to prepare a list of the wealthier persons in their shires, showing the amount which in their opinions such persons might reasonably be asked to contribute. After revision by the Council, letters called Privy Seals were sent to the individuals in question calling upon them to pay over to the collector the sum at which they had been assessed. The loans were usually repaid, and though there was from time to time some discontent owing to the pressure brought to bear on unwilling lenders, the practice seems to have been generally accepted during Elizabeth's reign.

In December, 1588, after the defeat of the Spanish Armada, the Queen's Council decided to take defensive measures in order to repel any further attack by the enemy, and to help meet the cost of these preparations a further loan was necessary. In that month a circular letter was sent from the Council to the Lords Lieutenant of the counties saying that 'we require the names of all such as are known to be of sufficient livelihood and wealth within the shire, of whom you shall think Her Majesty may readily have by way of loan only for the space of one whole year, such particular sums of hundreds of pounds or of half-hundreds of pounds or at least not under the sum of £25, according as the abilities of the people shall seem meet to yield'. The Lords Lieutenant acted so promptly that by the end of the following month of January a further letter was sent from the Court at Richmond, signed by the Archbishop of Canterbury, Lord Burghley, Sir Francis Walsingham and six other Privy Councillors, addressed to 'divers persons whom we have cawst uppon in question and informacion geven to us to thinke to be of abilitie to lend such sumes of money as are particularly specified'.

In the copy of this letter preserved at Winchester, Sir William Kingsmill is named as 'a person both for his countenaunce and abilitie and also for his forwarde disposition to the furtheraunce of the service mete to be collector in that countie of Southampton'.[1] The privy seals which were enclosed were to be dispatched at once to the deputy Lieutenants, who were to send for those Justices who were considered well disposed towards this business. The latter were charged to deliver the privy seals to those persons in their respective districts to whom they were addressed and 'by way of friendly admonition and good persuation encourage them to yelde both willinglye and spedely to the sumes conteyned in the said privie seales by way of loane'. The reasons for the loan were to be carefully explained and a request was to be made for payment to the collector within a month. Where a person refused to pay he was called before the Lord Lieutenant, and if he could not then be persuaded to pay he was to be given to understand that an inquiry by a commission and a jury would be made of the true value of his lands and goods and a return made to the Privy Council and the Exchequer to be a permanent record, so that in time to come Her Majesty might

[1] MS., City Archives.

use it in determining that person's contribution for Subsidies, charges for musters and levies for men for service, and this would not be so favourable as the present low rate of assessment. Moreover, the names of such persons were to be certified to the Privy Council that 'such order maie be taken with them for their willfulness in suche tymes of peril as these are'.

Direct local taxation, as distinct from direct national taxation, consisted mainly of taxes levied from time to time for the repair of the highways and of bridges, and of more regular rates for the relief of the poor. The method to be adopted for the repairing of highways was laid down in an Act of Parliament passed in 1563. According to the terms of this act, the inhabitants of every parish in the City were 'bound' for the carrying out of the necessary road repairs within their parishes. In Winchester at that time many of the streets and lanes had become choked with weeds, rubble and dirt cast out from the brooks, gardens and saffron grounds, so that in winter time people could not conveniently pass through them; also, since every poor inhabitant was as far chargeable towards the amending of these highways within their parishes as the most substantial citizens, the poor people were not able to sustain the charges. Special arrangements had therefore to be made and it was decided by the Burgh-mote that four honest persons should be chosen to be supervisors and orderers for the work to be undertaken during the following twelve months, and that every year upon the Tuesday or Wednesday of Easter week a similar appointment was to be made, otherwise the Mayor was to have £2 deducted from his annual fee.[1] In addition the Mayor had to appoint six days in the year during which the work had to be done, and cause warning thereof to be given in every parish church yearly before Hock Monday (the second Monday after Easter Day) on pain of having a further £1 deducted from his fee.

The four supervisors had power to direct all repair work at their discretion and in default were fined £1 in excess of the penalty laid down in the statute. There were also appointed

[1] 1st Bk. Ord., f. 144.

six honest and substantial persons who upon the oath of their franchise were required to tax and assess impartially every inhabitant of the City, each one of whom had to contribute either in money or labour or both to the amending of the highways. The money was to be collected by the supervisors who had power to distrain for non-payment of the tax and to sell the distress within six days. Any person who refused to work when ordered to do so was to be imprisoned at the discretion of the Mayor.

In the first year when this ordinance came into force, it was decided that Shulworth (Upper Brook) Street should be repaired, and Harry Gest, James Waterson, Thomas Hodson and Steven Browne, all freemen, were elected supervisors. The six assessors were all former mayors and magistrates, and the days fixed for the work to be done were Monday, Tuesday and Wednesday in Rogation Week and the same three days of the week before Midsummer Day. Thus on six days of each year, in some part of the City, there must have been scenes of great activity when the accumulated filth of many years was removed and the underlying roadway put in good order. At the rate of one street a year, however, it must have taken nearly twenty years to repair the whole of the highways of the City.

Although there is this evidence of regular annual provision being made for the repairing of the highways, there does not seem to have been any system or foresight in providing for extraordinary or future expenditure and equalizing it over successive years. Therefore when unexpected or long-delayed reparations had to be carried out the only course was to levy a tax for such special purpose. A case of this kind occurred in 1599 when the north side of Eastgate Bridge (which crossed the River Itchen and is now known as St. Swithun's Bridge) collapsed, and work had to be put in hand immediately. The more prominent citizens were as usual assessed and taxed, and from the account rendered by William Symonds and Richard Cooke, the collectors of the tax, it appears that from 'the taxation of the inhabitants and the voluntary contributions of divers friends of the City' they hoped to collect nearly £22. No less than 50 inhabitants, however, refused to pay the amounts at which they had been assessed, and a full list of these appears in the collectors' accounts together with the sums which each one should pay. At the head of the list there is the name of Sir Walter Sands, one of the Twenty-four, who is liable for £1, and the amounts decrease until one finds the last twenty-one defaulters assessed at 1s. each. The total sum which they owed was over £11, or more than half the estimated income from this special levy. But the work was completed, and with the help of over £3 from the Dean and Chapter, £4 from the City coffer, £1 from the Chamberlains as part of the rent of the Castle Green, and other small sums, the collectors were able to meet their obligations.

In a former chapter dealing with the executive power of the Mayor and his brethren, examples were given of the matters which called for constant attention, and of these it was found that the most important and the most frequently recurring were the setting of poor people to work and the relief of poverty. The need for action in these particular matters, both on a national and on a local basis, became very pressing during Elizabeth's reign, and the consequent demand for money to alleviate the situation constituted the greatest item in direct local taxation. Although laws had been passed in the reigns of Henry VIII and Edward VI to deal with 'idle and loitering persons and valiant beggars', the nuisance caused by these persons had not abated, and Elizabeth's government found it necessary to pass a further Act in 1563. By this, on the Sunday after Midsummer Day, the Mayor was required to register the names of all impotent, aged and needy persons who were not able to live by themselves nor by their own labour, and after divine service in every parish church the householders and inhabitants of each parish had to appoint two able persons to collect the charitable alms of the parishioners. The following Sunday these collectors were to approach all and sundry and ask them what weekly contribution they were prepared to make towards the poor and to enter the same in the register. The collectors afterwards distributed the alms among the poor 'without fraud, covin, favour or affection', seeing that the more deserving got the greater amount, that those who were able to work were put to labour, and that none went and sat openly begging.

Those who refused to contribute were brought to the notice of the Bishop, and if they then obstinately refused to show charity they were to appear before the Justices who had power to assess and tax them for a weekly contribution. Failure to pay in this case resulted in imprisonment. In Winchester there were two collectors for each of the parishes of St. Clement, St. Thomas, St. Peter in macellis, St. Lawrence, St. Mary Kalender, St. Maurice and St. Peter in Colbroke Street. The Mayor acted as treasurer for the poor and the distribution was overseen by one of the Bailiffs and a member of the commonalty.

It was found, in spite of this Act of 1563, that the country still continued to be 'exceedingly pestered with rogues, vagabonds and sturdy beggars', and in 1572 all previous Acts were repealed in favour of a new one. In future all persons over fourteen years of age found begging or wandering were to be apprehended and tried at the next sessions. If found guilty of vagrancy, they were to be whipped and burnt through the gristle of the right ear with a hot iron unless some person of substance was willing to take them into service for a whole year. If a person who had been burnt in this way, being eighteen years old or more, offended again after sixty days from the date of his being marked, he was to be treated as a felon. This Act, attempting a definition of the term 'rogues, vagabonds and sturdy beggars', indicates the various types of person who made up the hordes which wandered through the country, and which, in Hampshire, were to be found on the thoroughfares leading northwards from Southampton and Portsmouth and in the forests and woodlands further north and west. The following are included: 'all persons that be or utter themselves to be proctors or procurators without sufficient authority, and all other idle persons using subtle, crafty and unlawful games or plays, and some of them feigning themselves to have knowledge in physiognomy, palmistry or other abused sciences, and all persons being whole and mighty in body and able to labour, having not land or master nor using any lawful merchandise, craft or mystery; and all fencers, bearwards, common players in interludes and minstrels, not belonging to any baron of this realm or towards any other honourable personage of greater degree; all jugglers, pedlars, tinkers and petty chapmen; which said fencers, etc., shall wander abroad and have not licence of two justices of the peace; and all common labourers being persons able in body using loitering and refusing to work for such reasonable wages as is taxed and commonly given; and all counterfeiters of licences and passports, and all users of the same knowing the same to be counterfeit; and all scholars of the universities of Oxford and Cambridge that go about begging, not being authorized under the seal of the said universities; and all shipmen pretending losses by sea; and all persons delivered out of gaols that beg for their fees not having licence from two justices of the peace.'

It was necessary not only to repress the above-mentioned idlers and beggars, but also to provide for the deserving poor, aged and impotent. For this purpose, it was enacted that 'habitations and abiding places' should be established for them. The Mayor was required, as in the previous Act, to have a register compiled showing the names of all deserving poor persons and also to compute the total cost of their support. Instead of an appeal being made to charity, all inhabitants were assessed at weekly rates which were so fixed that in the aggregate they met the total cost of poor relief. In addition, the Mayor had to arrange for all aged and disabled persons to be inspected once a month, and those who were not natives or who had resided for less than three years in the City were removed to their place of birth or to their last permanent place of abode. In Winchester this inspection was undertaken by the Mayor and his brethren every fourth Thursday. The penalty for refusing to pay the weekly rate for the relief of the poor was imprisonment, and if any of the poor who were able to work refused to do so they were whipped and placed in the stocks. Four years later an Act was passed for the setting of the poor to work. In every city and town a store or stock of wool, hemp, flax, iron and other stuff was to be provided and handed over to needy persons to be wrought into yarn or other matter, and payment was to be made for the labour involved. This practice continued throughout Elizabeth's reign and there are constant references to it in the Winchester records. The raw materials were stored in the Guildhall from which place they were distributed to the various applicants, and sums varying from ten to twenty pounds were spent from the City coffer on several occasions to replenish the stock and to purchase equipment for teaching children and poor adults the various processes, especially those connected with the woollen industry.

The Act of 1576 had called for the establishment of institutions to house the poor and the Hampshire justices, more enterprising than those of many counties, set up in Winchester a House of Correction, the articles for the use and management of which have fortunately survived. The governor of the house undertook to keep eighty men and women at work, giving them as much for their labour as they would obtain elsewhere and reserving the sum of one penny per head weekly for their lodging and washing. Many skilled occupations were to be provided; for the men, spooling and quilling of yarn, weaving of kerseys and serges, wool combing, cloth dyeing, the making of hats, gloves, wool-cards and nails, with grinding of wheat and malt, frilling of cloths, and other less skilled occupations as occasions arose; for the women, spinning, carding, sorting of wool, carding of hatters' spools, knitting of hose and dressing of flax. All unskilled workers committed to the house were to be set to learn one of the above crafts under competent instructors, and were to be detained for at least five years, devoting three years to learning the trade and two to working at it in order to repay the institution for their board, lodging and tuition. The house was to be self-supporting, each inmate working for his own maintenance, and though the governor was willing, if the supply of vagrants in Hampshire should fail, to take in at the appointment of the justices as many poor men as would make up the total number, these were not to be impotent, diseased or unable to work, but must be in a fit state to earn their keep. The discipline of the house partook also of the nature of a punishment, for persons could be sent there by the justices for pilfering, disorderly conduct, or any offence which did not rank as a felony. Strangely enough, also, parents or masters might send their unruly children or lazy servants there for correction, by means of a justice's warrant, paying for their lodging and making whatever allowance they pleased for food for the delinquents. Persons who escaped from the house before the end of their term were on recapture to be committed to gaol and branded as rogues, after which they were to return to the house of correction, there to remain until by permission of the governor they might sue the justices for release.

But in spite of all the provisions which were made, poverty still persisted and beggars were to be found loitering in the towns and cities or roaming the countryside. Further vigorous action was therefore taken in 1598 when two more Acts were passed. The first of these repeated many of the provisions of the former acts concerning setting poor people to work, apprenticing young people and by means of local taxation buying further supplies of raw materials. Where a parish was not able to raise enough money for this purpose, other parishes were to be called upon to help, and where inhabitants were slack in paying their poor relief tax the overseers were to obtain a warrant from the local justices and distrain upon their goods. There had evidently been considerable laxity in this matter of executing the warrants held by overseers. In March, 1598, three overseers in Winchester admitted that though they had warrants to distrain on those within their parishes who refused to pay to the poor, they had not distrained. They were immediately commanded by the Mayor and his brethren to perform their duty and put the warrants into effect. Besides refusal to pay, there was undoubtedly some slackness in collecting the tax, for one reads of a former mayor and magistrate, Charles Newbolt, who owed 17s. 10d. for the relief of the poor over a period of time. But this was rectified when the Mayor deducted this amount from a bill for 32s. 10d. which Newbolt had submitted for his labour in clearing out the brooks.

The second Act of 1598 dealt with the punishment of rogues, vagabonds and sturdy beggars. Despite all the former measures taken for its repression begging still continued, and following this second enactment it is recorded that the Mayor, deploring this practice of begging, especially in the Cathedral Close, issued a stern warning that offenders would be publicly whipped at the post. This was in accordance with the statute which laid it down that anyone taken begging was to be stripped naked from the middle upwards and openly whipped until his or her body was bloody, and forthwith sent from parish to parish to his or her last permanent place of abode. Dangerous rogues were to be banished out of the kingdom or sent to the galleys.

From the foregoing pages it can be seen that in Elizabeth's reign the various attempts to deal with pauperism by means of the voluntary payments of the inhabitants failed, so that finally it was decided to make the maintenance of the aged and the invalid poor a statutory charge on the parishes. The able bodied were called upon to work or undergo imprisonment, but the impotent and the deserving poor were fed and housed by the parish overseers while the children were apprenticed to a trade. To meet the cost of these measures a weekly rate was levied on all inhabitants according to their means, and although there were attempts at evasion the system seems to have worked satisfactorily for a considerable time afterwards. At Winchester the weekly levy for the relief of the poor formed the major portion of the direct local taxation which the citizens had to bear. This was in some degree due to the fact that the burden of local taxation in the City had been reduced, except in the case of poor relief, by the large income derived from the rents of the City's properties. In former times the cost of repairing the walls and gates and the expense of sending two burgesses to parliament had necessitated a separate tax on the townsfolk, but by Elizabeth's time such items of expenditure were charged to the Chamberlains' accounts where the income from rents, and particularly from the former monastic lands granted to the City by Philip and Mary in 1554, was sufficient to relieve the inhabitants from a considerable amount of local taxation.

CHAPTER IX

Justice

The charter granted by Elizabeth to the City in 1587 gives details of a court which was to be held in Winchester 'for the preserving of the peace and to hear and determine within the city aforesaid all manner of murders, felonies, misprisions, riots, routs, oppressions, extortions, forestalling, regrating, trespass, etc.', at which the Mayor, Recorder and Aldermen are empowered to act as Justices of the Peace and representatives of the Crown. Immediately following the paragraph in the charter which gives this information, there is a clause stating that 'the Justices of the Peace for the county of Southampton shall not hereafter in any wise intermeddle with the said city or the liberties thereof, nor shall have or exercise any jurisdiction or authority concerning any causes, matters or things whatsoever arising or appertaining to the said city'.

A Court of Sessions for the county of Southampton had been held at Winchester since 1344 when Edward III, by statute, established such courts in the various counties of England to hear and determine felonies and trespasses done against the peace. It has been thought that the word 'hereafter' in the clause quoted above implied a new departure, and that the City was henceforth to be independent of the Court of Sessions for the county and have its own Court of Sessions.[1] But such assumption is erroneous, for there is ample evidence that Winchester had its Court of Sessions,

[1] J. S. Furley, *City Government*, p. 136.

quite independent of the county, long before 1587, and it becomes clear, therefore, that Elizabeth's charter did not establish such a court but merely confirmed the right of the City to hold it. In 1551 it was enacted by the Burgh-mote that two sessions of the four Quarter Sessions were in future to be held at the same time as the two Burgh-motes, that is, one between Michaelmas and Christmas Day, and the other between Easter and Whitsuntide.[1] There is also in existence a mutilated record of a Quarter Sessions Court for the City dated 1527, and much earlier still the Chamberlains' roll for 1467 shows the receipt of money from fines inflicted by the Mayor and Justices at the Sessions Court.

But such evidence of the existence of the City Court of Sessions in pre-Elizabethan days is not really necessary, for the answer to the query concerning the establishment of this court is to be found in letters patent of Henry VI, dated June 7th, 1442, wherein is contained the following: 'We have granted to the said Mayor, citizens and their successors for all time to come that they may elect from themselves four aldermen, as often as there may be need, and the Mayor and three or two of the same . . . may have for all time to come full power for examining, hearing and determining there, as well in the presence as in the absence of ourselves and our heirs, all and several matters, complaints, defaults, causes and articles . . . which pertain to the officers of the justice of peace of the labourers, servants and artificers and are wont and able in every way to be examined and heard and determined before Justices of the peace . . . together with the punishment and correction thereof as fully and entirely as Justices of the peace have had and exercised in the county of Southampton and elsewhere, and that Justices of the peace in the said county or other Justices of the peace do not hereafter interfere in any quarrels, causes, articles or matters whatsoever, that in any way regard or pertain to justices of peace, that arise in the said city and liberty in such manner that the said Mayor, aldermen and upright men or their successors may proceed to

[1] 1st Bk. Ord., f. 9.

the determination of any felony without special licence or order of ourselves or our heirs in any way whatever.'

Unfortunately most of the files of the City Quarter Sessions held in the latter half of the sixteenth century have disappeared; only a few remain and these are in such a fragmentary condition that they are of little value. But to compensate in some measure for this loss, there have survived many manuscripts dealing with the proceedings of the City Court of Record. This was the ancient and already existing City Court of the Mayor and Bailiffs which Elizabeth's charter further sanctioned as 'a Court of Record in the Guildhall every Wednesday and Friday in every week, held by the Mayor and Commonalty', dealing with 'all manner of pleas, plaints, and actions, covenants, contracts, etc.' arising within the City. Although the court is called in the charter, the Court of the Mayor and Commonalty, thereby suggesting that it may have had its origin in the Burgh-mote, there is no record of the members of that assembly having any judicial powers, and as far as the court rolls show the only service rendered by the citizens was that of serving on the jury. Strictly speaking, this court was the Queen's Court with the Mayor and Bailiffs acting as representatives of the Crown, as is shown on the first parchment of the roll for the year 1580-81, as follows:

'Curia domine Regine tenta in Civitate Wintoniae ultimo de Septembris Anno Regni Domine nunc Elizabethe Dei gratia Anglie ffrancie et Hibernie Regine ffidei Defensor etc., Vicesimo secundo in Guihalda civitatis predictae coram Edwardo White maiore civitatis predictae Jacobo Vibert et Johanne Twyne ballivis eiusdem civitatis secundum consuetudine civitatis illius a tempore quo non extat memoria in eadem civitate hactenus usitata et approbata etc.'

(The court of our Lady Sovereign held in the city of Winchester on the last day of September in the twenty-second year of the reign of our present Lady Elizabeth, Queen, by the grace of God, of England, France and Ireland, Defender of the Faith, etc., in the Guildhall of the aforesaid city before Edward White, Mayor, of the aforesaid city, James Vibert and John Twyne, Bailiffs of the same city, according to the custom of that city which from time immemorial in that city up till now has been usual and established, etc.)

This City Court of Record is mentioned as early as the reign of Henry III, whose charter dated 1227 confirms to the City 'the use of its own court, and with certain exceptions exempts citizens from the necessity of pleading elsewhere; accepts the custom of the City as defence in pleas of the Crown; it allows all questions affecting land tenure within the City to be decided according to the custom of the City, and continues to the City its own customary procedure.[1] The local customary law of a town was not identical with that of other towns, and though the tendency from the twelfth century onwards was to subordinate local law to the common law of England, many points still survived in which local law retained its individuality'. A document of about the year 1278, *The Ancient Usages of the City of Winchester*, supplies an explanation of the procedure of the Court of Record during the thirteenth and fourteenth centuries, but in the sixteenth century local custom and usage had developed into such a complicated mass of unwritten law that the Burgh-mote in 1580 attempted to clarify the situation.[2] In that year it was ordained that 'whereas the auncient usages and customs of this Citie are now partlie growne out of memorie by reason whereof some doughtes are likelie to arise about the same what have been holden for usages and what have not to the greate preiudice and daunger of the citizens of this Citie beinge bounde by their othes to performe the same whereof for the most parte theie are ignorant To avoyde which inconvenience and to thende that the saide usages reduced into

[1] Furley, *City Government*, p. 120.

[2] *The Ancient Usages of Winchester*, transcribed and translated from the Anglo-French version preserved in Winchester College, Clarendon Press, 1927. There are two versions in English (XVth Century) in the City Archives.

certeyntie may bee better knowne and dewlie observed to the common benefite and weale publique of this Citie It is now agreed that it shalbe lawfull for Mr. Mayor of this Citie and the more parte of his brethrene uppon conference with thauncient men of this Citie of most knowledge and experience in that behalf and uppon the vewe of the olde rolls to set downe in writinge under their hands such customes and usages of this Citie as they shall finde lawfull and meet to be observed And the same so by them set downe in writinge and none other shalbe from thence forth dewlie observed and kepte for usages within this Citie'.[1]

What was set down in writing as a result of the above ordinance has been lost, so that the only reliable source of information regarding the court proceedings is the rolls and the documents connected with them which have survived. The court rolls remaining from the Elizabethan period constitute a broken series covering less than half the forty-five years of that reign. Each roll, coinciding with the annual period of the Mayor's term of office, consists of a dozen or more parchment skins varying in length from twelve to twenty-four inches, written on both sides in the careful and characteristic handwriting of those times. The language is Latin, but for the most part abbreviations and symbols are used instead of complete words and these occasionally present some difficulty to the translator though their exact meaning was no doubt quite clear to the scribe who used them. At times the roll gives an English equivalent in order to make the meaning more explicit, particularly when mentioning goods and articles of trade; for instance, 'tres mappas vocatas three diaper napkins', 'unum modium pomorum vocatum a bushell of frute' and 'iiii dolea vini vocata iiii hoggeshedds of gascoyne wyne'.

The roll for the year 1580–81 commences on September 30th, as shown above, shortly after the election of Edward White as Mayor. It shows that during the next twelve months the Town Court sat on forty-seven occasions, each one being

[1] 1st Bk. Ord., f. 216.

on Friday, with breaks of two weeks at Christmas and Easter respectively and one week at Whitsuntide. The number of cases dealt with at any one sitting of the Court is never more than ten nor less than four, and no single case is ever concluded at one hearing. The record of the first court in this particular roll is shown as follows:

veredictum.	Edwardus Noble queritur versus Jacobum Clement. Jurati videlicet Thomas Colley et socii sui electi triati et iurati super sacrum suum quod defendens est cul-
respectatur Iudicium usque proximam curiam.	pabilis de dictione et pronunciacione predicta verborum anglicorum in narracione predicta recitata modo et forma prout predictus querens versus eum narravit et assidant damna ipsius querenti occasione dictionis et pronunciacionis verborum illorum ultra misas et custagia sua in hac parte ad xx^s et pro misis et custagiis illis ad x tunc respectatur inde Iudicium hic usque proximam curiam.
continetur ex assensu partium statu quo nunc usque proximam curiam. pro licentia concordandi iii$^{d.}$	Petrus Bedham queritur versus Thomam Bedham. Petrus Bedham queritur versus Stephanum Browne.
continetur ex assensu partium statu quo nunc usque proximam curiam.	Edmundus Bedham junior et Margaria uxor eius queruntur versus Edwardum Gardener et Katherinam uxorem eius.

In the first of these cases Edward Noble is pleading against (queritur versus) James Clement, and it is gathered from the previous roll that it is a case of slander which has occupied the attention of the Mayor and Bailiffs for several weeks. It has now reached the stage when, according to the marginal note, a verdict is given, and the footnote goes on to say that a jury, consisting of Thomas Colley and his associates, declares the defendant guilty of uttering the words quoted by the plaintiff, and that they assess the damages at twenty shillings and the costs and expenses at ten shillings. Judgment is deferred, says the marginal note, until the next court. It is found from the roll that at each of the three succeeding courts judgment was still deferred and then at the fourth court, one month after the jury's verdict, leave was granted to settle the matter out of court (licentia concordandi), for which the usual fee of threepence was paid. But there is no record to show upon what terms settlement was reached.

In the second case Peter Bedham pleads against Thomas Bedham and the previous roll shows that this is a case of debt. The marginal note states that it is held over with the assent of both parties, in the state in which it now stands, until the next court. When this case is followed up through the succeeding weeks it is found that it was adjourned at each of the next two courts, after which leave to negotiate (licentia interloquendi) was granted at the two following courts, and when attempts to assemble a jury at three more courts had failed, the case was adjourned until June 9th. On that date there was still no jury available. The case was again called on the 16th, and 23rd, of June, and on the latter date a writ of habeas corpus was issued, but as this did not produce a jury on June 30th, an order was given to distrain on the goods of the men summoned for jury service. This was repeated a week later and at last, on July 14th, a jury was sworn, and it then declared that Thomas Bedham owed Peter Bedham £14 8s. 0d., and not £23 7s. 2d., as the latter had claimed. The judgment of the court was deferred for a week, and then for another week until July 28th, more than ten months after the case first came to court, when the jury's verdict was accepted, and Peter Bedham was allowed his £14 8s. 0d., but fined for making false clamour (pro falso clamore), that is, for making a claim for more than his due.

In the third case, the same Peter Bedham pleads against Stephen Browne. The marginal note states that leave to settle the case out of court is granted on payment of threepence (pro licentia concordandi, iii^d).

In the fourth and last case, Edmund Bedham, junior, and his wife, Marjory, plead against Edward Gardener and his wife, Katherine. Reference to the previous roll shows that the plaintiffs complain of slander. The marginal note states that both parties have agreed to an adjournment until the next court, the case remaining in statu quo. At the next court the defendants were unable to deny the charge, so a writ of inquiry was issued to ascertain the amount of the damages. After the case had again been called at the three following courts, it was adjourned until March 3rd. On that date the jury, after inquiry, assessed damages at two shillings and the costs and expenses at three shillings and fourpence. Judgment was deferred for one week, and then for another week after which, for some unknown reason, the case is never mentioned again.

When a case first appeared before the court there were entered on the roll the names of the two parties engaged in the suit and the nature of the plaint, whether debt or trespass. There were also entered the names of the attorneys, when such persons were employed, and the name of the person who acted as surety for the defendant. For instance:

ponit loco suo Jo: Stoner
Ricardus Birde queritur versus

ponit loco suo An: Alderley Johannem Pratte de placito transgressionis super casum. Per plegium Christoferi Genens.

ponit loco suo Jo: ffoster
Johannes Brooker queritur versus

in propria persona sua Zacharram Chadde de placito debiti.

In the first example, Richard Birde, through his attorney, John Stoner, makes plaint against John Pratte, who is represented by Anthony Alderley, in a plea of trespass on the case, which was a plea whereby a party sued for damages for a wrong such as negligence or breach of contract not under seal. Christopher Genens acts as surety for the defendant.

In the second example, John Brooker, through his attorney, John Foster, makes plaint against Zachary Chadde, who appears in person to defend himself in a plea of debt.

The parties to a suit more often than not made use of attorneys. It was recognized that plaintiff and defendant might make attorney in any kind of plea if the opposing party were present. This acted as a safeguard should either party repudiate the action of his attorney if he lost his case. Attorneys were not necessarily persons with legal knowledge; they were merely persons empowered to act on behalf of the people who employed them. The names of the three attorneys mentioned above constantly recur in the court rolls of this period, with the phrase 'ponit loco suo', showing that the party is acting through him. The attorney's fee and other charges sustained in bringing a suit to the City Court of Record were approved by the Mayor and Bailiffs as shown by the following statement:

'Costs and charges sustayned by William Mondaye, playntiff, againste Barthomewe Lardener in placito debito (plea of debt),

In primis thentringe and servinge	iiii^d·
Item counsels ffee	iii^s. iiii^d·
Item the Attorneis ffee	viii^d·
Item the Warrante of attorneie	ii^d·
Item the fylinge the declaration	iiii^d·
Item for Judgment	iiii^d·
Item for execution and servinge	viii^d·
Sum awarded by the Court	v^s. x^d·

During this period of its history the Court of Record dealt mainly with cases of debt and trespass. This is in accordance with the terms of Elizabeth's charter which limited its jurisdiction to pleas, plaints, covenants, contracts, etc. In much earlier times the City Court had dealt with murder, felony, misprision, etc., but these offences had passed to the County Court of Sessions in 1344, and at a later date to the City Court of Sessions. When the rolls of the City Court of Record are closely examined it is found that cases of debt form the greater part of its business. When the verdict in these cases went against the defendant, an order was made for the sum in question to be repaid immediately to the plaintiff, who was also awarded damages for wrongful detention though these rarely came to more than a few pence whatever the amount of the debt, together with the costs and expenses of the suit which usually totalled a sum of five or six shillings. When the debtor could not repay, his goods were distrained and if the sum realized from their sale failed to reach the amount due, he was sent to prison until he or his friends had satisfied the claim. If the court found that the plaintiff had claimed more than his just due, he might make partial recovery of his debt but he was fined for making a false claim. Trespass covered assault, slander, breach of covenant and any action by which the rights and interests of another person were invaded. In successful cases of trespass the damages awarded to the plaintiff varied considerably from a few pence to twenty shillings or more, and the costs awarded by the court similarly varied from three to ten shillings. These details were usually written in a very abbreviated form on the court rolls, but the depositions of the parties were not included. Whereas the rolls always consisted of parchment, the depositions were recorded on separate sheets of paper many of which have, fortunately, been preserved, and from them the three typical examples given below have been chosen.

ASSAULT

'Thomas Burton attachiatus est ad respondendum Ricardo Roberts de placito transgressionis et unde idem Ricardus per Johannem Mathewe attornatum suum queritur quod predictus Thomas Burton sexto die Maii Anno Regni Domine Regine nunc octavo hic apud civitatem Wintoniae infra etc., vi et armis viz. etc., in Johannem Hobbes servientem predicti Ricardi Roberts insultum et affraram fecit et eundem Johannem Hobbes adtunc et ibidem verberavit et maltractavit Ita quod de vita sua desperabatur per quod predictus Ricardus Roberts servicium predicti Johannis Hobbes per duas septimanas amisit ad grave dampnum ipsius Ricardi ac contra pacem dictae domine Regine unde dicit quod deterioratus est et unde producit sectam suam.'

(Thomas Burton was attached to answer Richard Roberts on a plea of trespass, whereby the same Richard, through John Mathew, his attorney, pleads that the aforesaid Thomas Burton on the sixth day of May in the eighth year of the reign of our present Lady Sovereign, here in the city of Winchester, did with force and arms commit assault and violence upon John Hobbes, servant of the said Richard Roberts, and then and there beat and maltreated the same John Hobbes so that his life was despaired of and the said Richard Roberts lost his services for two weeks, to the great damage of the same Richard and against the peace of the said Lady Sovereign, whereby he says he is injured; whereon he brings his suit.)

Debt

'Johannes Bedham summonitus est ad respondendum Nicholao Andrewes de placito quod reddat ei xl^s quos ei debet et iniuste detinet Et unde idem Nicholaus per Antonium Alderley attornatum suum dicit quod cum predictus Johannes Bedham quinto die marcii mutuatus fuisset de eodem Nicholao predicto xl^s solvendos eidem Nicholao cum inde requisitus fuisset tamen Johannes Bedham licet sepius requisitus predictos xl^s eidem Nicholao nondum reddidet sed illos omnini huiusque reddere contradixit et adhuc contradicit unde dicit quod deterioratus est et dampnum habet ad valenciam vi^s viii^d Et inde producit sectam suam.'

(John Bedham is summoned to answer Nicholas Andrewes on a plea that he should repay forty shillings which he owes him and wrongfully withholds; and hereon the same Nicholas through Anthony Alderley, his attorney, says that although on the fifth of March the aforesaid John Bedham borrowed from the same Nicholas the said forty shillings to be repaid to the same Nicholas when thereafter he should demand it, nevertheless John Bedham although frequently asked had not yet repaid the said forty shillings to the same Nicholas, but until now had constantly refused to repay it and still refuses to do so, whereon he says he is injured and has damage to the amount of six shillings and eightpence, and thereon makes his suit.)

'Et predictus Johannes Bedham per Johannem Mathewe attornatum suum venit et non potest dedicere quin ipse debeat prefato querenti xviiiˢ iiiiᵈ parcellum predictorum xlˢ quos semper paratus fuit solvere prefato querenti et adhuc est denarios illos profert hic in curiam paratus ad solvendum Et quoad residuum viz. xxiˢ viiiᵈ dicit quod ipse non debet prefato querenti modo et forma prout predictus querens versus eum narravit Et ad legem suam inde faciendum petit admitti et admittitur unde lex se quarta manu.'

(And the aforesaid John Bedham through John Mathewe, his attorney, comes and is not able to deny that he owes the said plaintiff eighteen shillings and fourpence, parcel of the said forty shillings, which he was always prepared to pay to the said plaintiff and still is, and brings that amount of money into court ready to pay it, and as for the remainder, namely, twenty-one shillings and eightpence, he says that he does not owe the money to the plaintiff in the manner and form which the said plaintiff has stated against him; and he seeks to be allowed to make his law thereon, which he is permitted to do with the fourth hand.)

TRESPASS

'Johannes Crowche attachiatus est ad respondendum Waltero Michell de placito transgressionis. Et unde idem querens per Johannem Mathewe attornatum suum queritur quod predictus Johannes Crowche xv⁰ die Decembris vi et armis etc., domum predicti Walteri Michell fregit et intravit et tres mappas vocatas three diaper napkins valoris viˢ viiiᵈ, unam mappam vocatam one holand napkin valoris viᵈ, unam mappam vocatam lokara napkin valoris iiiiᵈ et unum modium pomorum vocatum a bushell of frute valoris iiiˢ iiiiᵈ de bonis et catallis predicti Walteri Michell ad tunc et ibidem iniuste cepit et asportavit et alia enormia ei intulit et dampnum ipsius Walteri Michell et contra pacem dictae domine Regine unde dicit quod deterioratus est et dampnum habet ad valenciam xxviˢ viiiᵈ. Et inde producit sectam suam.'

(John Crowche is attached to answer Walter Michell on a plea of trespass, whereby the same plaintiff through his attorney, John Mathewe, pleads that the aforesaid John Crowche on the fifteenth day of December did, with force and arms, break and enter the house of the said Walter Michell and then and there from the goods and chattels of the said Walter Michell seized and carried away three diaper napkins worth six shillings and eightpence, a holland napkin worth sixpence, a Lokara napkin worth fourpence, and a bushel of fruit worth three shillings and fourpence, and inflicted on him other illegalities to the great damage of the same Walter Michell, and against the peace of the said Lady Sovereign, whereby he says that he is injured and has damage to the amount of twenty-six shillings and eightpence, and thereon he brings his suit.)

'Et predictus Johannes Crowche per Johannem Stoner attornatum suum venit et defendit vim et iniuriam et dicit quod ipse in nullo culpabilis de transgressione predicta modo et forma prout predictus Walterus Michell versus eum narravit Et de hoc ponit se super patriam etc.'

(And the aforesaid John Crowche through John Stoner, his attorney, appears and denies force and wrong, and says that he is in no way guilty of the said trespass in the manner and form which the said Walter Michell has stated against him; and hereon he puts himself on his country.)

It will have been noticed that in the above case of debt the defendant was summoned to appear in court, while in the cases of trespass and assault (the latter also counting as trespass) the defendants were attached. In all cases of trespass, attachment was the general rule, but in cases of debt a freeman of the City was summoned to appear at the court, and moreover, by the ancient custom of the City, he was entitled to three summonses before he need put in an appearance by himself or by attorney. Where the defendant was not a freeman, he was attached whatever the charge against him. Thus, Thomas Burton, although a freeman, was attached in the above case of assault, while John Bedham, also a freeman, in the case of debt was summoned to appear. John Crowche was not a freeman and was attached for trespass, but whatever the charge he would still have been treated in this way. A person who was attached was either arrested (per corpus) or some of his goods were seized to ensure his obedience to the order of the court. But arrest or forfeiture could be avoided if security for the defendant's appearance could be found. This procedure was governed by a long-standing ordinance to the effect that 'the suertie of every foren person' (that is, a stranger) 'which shalbe arrested or attached upon any accion shalbe amerced at every courte in which the defendant shall not make an appearance in manner and forme followinge that ys to saye At the first courte v^d, at the seconde v^d, at the thirde courte vi^d, at the fowerth courte viii^d, at the fyveth courte x^d, at the sixt courte xii^d, and at the seventh courte xiiii^d, which amounteth to v^s, and then at the seventh courte a Capias' (writ of arrest) 'shalbe awarded against the suertie of the defendant to answere in the stede and place of the defendant.'[1, 2]

If a defendant pleaded guilty and wished the case to be dealt with summarily, he sought judgment (petiit iudicium) or, as it was sometimes expressed, put himself on the grace of the court (posuit se in gracia curiae). But when he contested the case, there were two alternatives open to him; he could either make or wager his law, or he could place himself on

[1] Idem, f. 107.   [2] Amerced = fined.

his country. In the case of debt already quoted, John Bedham, the defendant, was permitted to make his law upon the fourth hand (lex se quarta manu). This procedure, sometimes known as 'wagering his law', called for the production by the defendant of a number of persons, in this case four including himself, who would swear to his innocence. Such persons, called compurgators, varied in number but they were rarely less than two or more than nine. When John Crowche was charged with trespass he denied the offence and placed himself on his country, that is to say, he asked for a jury of twelve men. It would be the Sergeant's duty to find the required number of honest and loyal men for the next court. This would be no light task for him as the number of men liable to serve in this capacity was limited to the sixty or seventy freemen. Jury service had become a heavy and tiresome burden, so much so that in 1573 it was decided by the Burghmote that in cases of debt, 'for avoydinge of muche trouble growen to the citizens of this Cytie by reason of their apparance in juries upon light and smale causes', the defendant should not be allowed trial by jury unless the debt was for an amount exceeding twenty shillings.[1]

An ordinance enacted four years earlier in 1569 shows that difficulty was experienced in bringing debtors to court, and also that there was a suspicion that the Sergeants of the City were in some measure responsible for this state of affairs. It runs thus: "fforasmoche as dyvers evill disposed persons myndinge to lyve upon other mens travayle have gotten into their handes by the way of buyinge and contracting other mens goodes and not payinge redy money for the same, after which tyme entendinge to defraude their sayed creditors have kept their houses and other secret places so that the seriantes of this Cytie cannot serve process duelie against them And also yt ys thought that some of the sergeants beinge corrupted by such debtors have not done their diligence in servinge of process against such as aforesayed by reason wher of many simple and well meaninge people have byn

[1] 1st Bk. Ord., f. 171.

greatlie delayed in recovering of their debtes against such persons so kepinge their houses to their greate hurte and damage and delaye of justice and to the greate ignomie and slaunder of the Cytie and discredit of other good cytizens myndinge trulie to pay their debts, ffor remedy wher of yt ys agreed by the mayor and thole comminaltie of the sayed Cytie that yt shalbe lawfull from henceforth for the mayor for the tyme beinge and the most parte of his brethrne from tyme to tyme to authorize any person of this Cytie to arrest any person so that he so authorized have a precept under the seale of thoffice of the maioraltie and that the same arrest shall stande and be in as good force and effect as though the Sergeant had done yt and that the like ffees be payed to the bayliffes as have been accustomed when the Sergeantes have done the like.'[1]

When a plaintiff successfully sued for debt and the debtor was unable to meet his obligation, the decision of the court was enforced by taking distress. This meant that certain of the defendant's goods and chattels were seized, nominally by the Bailiffs but in practice by the Sergeants, and sold within fourteen days.[2] With the money thus realized the Bailiffs satisfied the claimant and handed over the surplus, if any, to the defendant. A person who had been distrained could, however, recover the whole of his goods at the end of a year and a day, if he could satisfy the claim that had been made upon him. If the debtor had no goods and chattels upon which distress could be levied, he was imprisoned until such time as he and his friends could raise enough money to fulfil the obligation. Distress took many forms. In a case, quoted below, in the Pie Powder Court, it consisted of 54 lbs. of yarn. Occasionally it took the form of livestock or tools and trading appliances. But mostly it was taken in household articles and furniture as shown in the following case:

'An inventory of goods and cattalls of John Browne

[1] Idem, f. 157.
[2] Idem, f. 255 (formerly the period was forty days).

dystrayned at the sutte of Wylliam Caplyn and praysed by Jamis Waterson and Wylliam Mosse as foloyth the iiii^th day of August in the yere of our lord 1559.

Item a chafer of brasse, v brasyn potts, ii
    kyttylls, ii skylletts weyying C and vi^li at
    iiii^d the pownd   xxix^s. iiii^d.
Item ii rakes of iron weyying liiii at ii^d   ix^s.
Item ii fether beds and a tabull in the hawle   xxxvi^s. viii^d.
Item a cobberd and old bolsters   xv^s.
Item a grett chest   xii^s.
Item ii joinyd formes   v^s.

                    The hole score is v^li xvii^s.'

The outstanding feature of the proceedings of the City Court of Record as revealed by the court rolls is the number of times the court was adjourned for one reason or another, and the delay which consequently ensued. The defendants generally showed, as was quite natural, a reluctance to come to court. Unless they had been arrested by the Bailiffs in default of finding security they rarely appeared at the first summons, and freemen, when charged with debt, took full advantage of their privilege of not appearing until three summonses had been issued. Freemen could also ask for a 'day of town' (dies ville) which gave them a delay of another week, and any person, citizen or stranger, plaintiff or defendant, at any court could put in an 'essoin', which was an excuse for non-attendance through sickness, absence from the City or engagement in the Queen's service. As already shown, absence by a defendant at seven successive courts resulted in the person who had acted as his surety being fined five shillings and brought to court to answer the original charge made against the defendant. But most frequently the defen- dant or his attorney asked for leave to negotiate (licentia interloquendi), which with the plaintiff's assent was invari- ably granted for at least one week and often for two or three. There were cases where such leave was granted until a definite date several months ahead. When a defendant in a case of debt admitted his guilt, the court proceeded to deliver judgment either at the same sitting or within the next two or three weeks, but in cases of trespass it was customary to issue a writ of inquiry which necessitated the assembly of a jury to assess the damages sustained by the plaintiff, and this usually took several weeks.

The cases which were most quickly terminated were those in which the parties asked leave to settle the case out of court (licentia concordandi), for which a fee of threepence was charged, and a considerable number were settled in this way. Where a defendant refuted the charge against him it was not unusual for the plaintiff to ask for a day of replication, which would give him a week's respite in order to prepare his reply. Thus the weekly sittings went on (unless, of course, the plaintiff withdrew his charge, in which case he had to pay a fine), until the defendant elected either to wager his law or put himself on his country. In the former case he brought his compurgators with him to the same sitting and judgment was given, but in the second case it was necessary for the Mayor and Bailiffs to issue a 'venire facias', a writ empowering the Sergeant to summon twelve men to serve on the jury. When the Sergeant had reported at several consecutive weekly courts, as he invariably did, that he could not form a jury, a writ of habeas corpus was issued. Armed with this the Sergeant renewed his efforts and if, after a fortnight, the jury-men failed to appear the officers were ordered to distrain on their goods. This never failed at the end of a week or possibly a fortnight to bring the jurymen to court where they gave their verdict on the case. But judgment was always deferred, generally for a week but occasionally for several weeks. Then came the final delay, namely, deferment after judgment had been given and pending execution, but this was rarely for more than a week. It is not surprising, therefore, that many cases dragged on for more than twelve months, particularly when it is remembered that in addition to the above causes for delay it was permissible for a suit, with the assent of both parties, to remain in statu quo for an indefinite period.

In addition to the suits recorded in the rolls there was other business which came before the City Court of Record, namely, breaches of the Assize of Bread and irregularities presented by the Aldermen of the street-wards. At a special court held each autumn the Mayor, Bailiffs and a jury of twelve citizens fixed the weight of the penny loaf for the next twelve months, adjusting it to the current price of wheat and other grains. Thus the price never altered, though the weight varied according to the harvest. To guard against the breach of this assize and to protect the householder, an officer was appointed by the Mayor, who himself was Clerk of the Market, to weigh once a month the loaves of bread offered for sale by the bakers of the City. When bread was found lacking in weight or badly baked, the baker was brought to court and fined, and it is evident from the records of such cases that punishment was meted out on the principle that the greater the deficiency in weight the larger the fine inflicted. These proceedings were recorded on small pieces of paper and not on the court rolls, partly in English and generally in very untidy handwriting. Many have been found amongst the manuscripts connected with the court, and the following is an example showing, in the case of each offender, the amount of the fine and the deficiency in weight of the loaf.

'Assisa panis capta coram Willelmo Goodwin maiore civitatis Wintoniae ac clerico mercati per cartam etc., xviii° die Marcii anno regni Elizabethe dei gratia etc., primo.'

(The Assize of Bread taken before William Goodwin, Mayor of the City of Winchester and Clerk of the Market, according to the charter etc., on the eighteenth of March in the first year of the reign of Elizabeth, by the grace of God, etc.)

The obolus (halfpenny) whyt loff

vii[d.]	Johannes Deninge	caret (lacks)	vii ozs. viii dwts.
vi[d.]	Georgius Spenser	caret	vi ozs.
vii[d.]	Ricardus Burton	caret	vi ozs. viii dwts.
vii[d.]	Thomas Whelar	caret	vii ozs. vi dwts.

The obolus (halfpenny) wheten loffe.

iii^d.	Ricardus Burton	caret	vi ozs. viii dwts.
vi^d.	Georgius Spenser	caret	x ozs.

The 1^d. wheaten loffe
Omnia bene (all is well)

The 1^d. bred of all graynes

xii^d.	Thomas Whelar	caret	xxxiii ozs. iii dwts.
xii^d.	Georgius Spenser	caret	xxvi ozs. viii dwts.
xvi^d.	Ricardus Burton	caret	xxx ozs. and cowrse stuff

For several centuries the City had been divided, for purposes of better government, into six aldermanries or streetwards. In charge of each one of these was an alderman who, amongst his other duties, was responsible for the preservation of law and order and for the cleansing of the streets. Later, the Aldermen became Justices of the Peace and it was found necessary for them to hand over what in modern times would be termed police duties to their appointed deputies. Whereas in earlier times it was the Alderman himself who, with his fellows or associates (socii), made inquiry into nuisances and breaches of the many ordinances, in Elizabeth's reign it was the deputy who carried out these duties and afterwards made out the presentment or report of irregularities and brought the offenders to court. The presentments, very few of which have survived from this particular period, are on sheets of paper and, in contrast to the court rolls, badly written in English. Abbreviated transcriptions of four of these, each for a different aldermanry, are given below with marginal notes showing how each offender was treated. It will be admitted, without doubt, that they give an interesting glimpse of social conditions in Winchester at that time.

The presentmente of Nycolas Barsdall and his felows the xiii day of January 1575.

xii^d.   In primis we present Steven Knight for making a dounghill at his garden hedge by Sir Henry Seymours house.

xx^d.

Item we present John Whit and Frauncis Wodshaw that theyr servauntes do lay theyr fylthy pottes in the way by Saint Peters churche.

iii^s. iiii^d.

Item we present John Write for brewing and typling the same in his howse and baking.

No action taken.

Item we present Robert Agullye for streking of Gyles Blonden his maid the xxi day of December at vii of the clocke in the night and now she is in fere of him to go abrode, also we present the said Robert for that he mett Joan Makes the xi day of January last past at vii of the clocke in the night and did request her company but she wold not grant him his request, then he did axe of her wherfor he shoulde not have to do with her as well as Nicolas Rokesbury did, Also Thomas Parkers maid have made complaint to us for the lyke matter.

xii^d., except Lane.

Item we present Mr. William Lane, Christopher Jenens, Bartylmew Lardner and Andrew Haselbye for letting theyr dogges go abrod without moselles contrary to the ordinances of the City.

vi^d.

Item we present Andrew Haselbee and Wylliam pavier for keping hoggstyes over the water the wiche is a great anoyance to the quenes lyege people.

A byll of presentmente made by Mr. Johnson and hys company the 12 day of January in the year of ouer lord god 1576.

xvi^d.

Item we present John Adderley for layeing of wedes and robbell out of hys orcherd in to the heywey in southgeat stret whych makyth the heyway very faultey.

vi^d.

Item we present Jeames Veybart for straw that is throuen out of hys barn a in to the heyway at fawkners corner whych maketh the heyway verey yell.

173

Item we present Alles Strong that lyeth in the postern house for kepyng of yllwell and lyvyng unqueatly wythe all the dewellers ther about.

No action.

Item we present Robert Agolley for hyrkenyng under onyest mens windos and mysseusyng of mayed servantes as they goeth in their masters beyseynes in the nyet sesun.

xii^d.

Item we present franceyes Wodshoues servant and John Sadlers servant for throwyng out of fylthey pyspouttes in to the stret out of all good order.

xii^d.

On the eighteenth day of June in the twenty-seventh year of the reign of Queen Elizabeth, John Paice and his fellows, sworn for the said Lady Sovereign, present as follows, etc., Anno Domini 1585.

In primis we present John Winter, Margery Woodward, the Lady Mary West, Mary Tavernar, and Alice Croke her servants, Arthur Rudsbey, Mistress Mary Warneford, Richard Hamden, and also Mistress Brabon, for that they and everey of them have not resorted to their parysh church by the space of one moneth last past.

Item we present William Brexstoen, William Cheapman, Edmund Bedham, junior, Richard Kent, John Typper, John Abbot and Richard Harvey for that they and every of them have unlawfully betweene January and Maye last killed six calves a peice contrary to the statute in that case made and provided.

Each one xl^s.

Item we present Nicholas Marcks, Robert Vincent, John Pett and Robert Agulley for that they and every of them do sell ale and bear without licence contrary to ordinance and statute.

xx^s.

Item we present Christopher Smyth, Justinian Cheapman (and thirteen others) for that they

Each one vi^{s.} viii^{d.}	and every of them have not frequented archerye nor used to shoot in longe bowes by the space of one moneth contrary to the statute.

Each one
vi^{s.} viii^{d.} and every of them have not frequented archerye nor used to shoot in longe bowes by the space of one moneth contrary to the statute.

Each one
xii^{d.} Item we present Mr. Penigere, Mr. Whithed, Mr. Sands, esquire (and ten others), for that they nor any of have not caryed awaye the soyle and filth that was latlye ridd out of the brookes.

The presentment of Richard Adderlie and his fellowes made the xi daie of June 1589.

Each one
ii^{s.} In primis we presente Thomas Greene, William White, and Edward Eridge for that they and everie of them doo washe theire sheepe skins in the ryver at the wasshinge place to the grete annusance of the Quenes liege people.

Let speech
be had
with the
Chamber-
lains. Item we presente John Potingere and Harrie Grewe, Chamberlains of the Citie, for that they have not sufficientlie repaired the wasshinge place but doo suffer the same to growe ruinous and in decaie in default of plankes and bordes under foote.

No action. Item we presente Alice Collins, Christian Trusle, for that they and everye of them is a comon skold and disturbitors of ther neybours.

THE COURT OF PIE POWDER

The Mayor and Bailiffs, as already shown, were called upon to administer justice in the many cases which were brought before them every Friday in the City Court of Record. But there was another court where their services were required, namely, the Court of Pie Powder (Curia pedis pulverizati), or in Anglo-French pie poudré, meaning 'dusty foot', the nickname of the travelling merchant for whose convenience such courts had originally been established by the Statute of Acton Burnell, in 1283, and the Statutes of Merchants in 1286 and 1288. In the first place, these courts were connected with fairs and markets at which the owners' stewards were the judges with power to administer justice for all commercial plaints and injuries in those fairs or markets. Thus in medieval times the famous fair on St. Giles' Hill, Winchester, had its Court of Pie Powder, for the period of the fair only, under the jurisdiction of the Bishop's officer. This court, however, had no connection with a similar one held in the City with the Mayor and Bailiffs as its chief officers. The City Court of Pie Powder was one set up, as in other cities and towns, under the original statute, to facilitate the recovery of debts locally and to save the suitors the expense of going to the central courts.

The sittings of the City Court of Pie Powder were not confined to times of fairs or market days, but were held throughout the year on any day of the week, including Sunday, as occasion arose. Moreover, it was not an uncommon occurrence for this court to hold several sittings at hourly intervals during one day, sometimes starting at eight in the morning and ending at six in the evening with a break of two hours at midday. These frequent sittings and the avoidance of lengthy adjournments, which were all too common in the City Court of Record, caused the Winchester Pie Powder Court to be used increasingly not only by citizens but also by non-burgesses from places as far away as London and Exeter.

Thus in many of the cases both plaintiff and defendant were strangers to the City. In 1579 Robert Williamson, yeoman, of Bishop's Waltham, sued Hugo Okeshott, yeoman, of Newton Valence, for debt, and John de Howe, glassmaker, of Buckholt in the County of Southampton, made a similar plaint against Thomas Jones, glass carrier, of Taunton in the County of Somerset. In other cases in the same year the plaintiff was often a Winchester resident as, for example, when Thomas Michelborne, gentleman, of Winchester, sued Thomas Rowles of Titchfield for debt, and Simon Braxton, a butcher of Romsey, was summoned by Walter Sandys, esquire, of Winchester, on a similar charge. At other times both parties were inhabitants of the City and one reads,

amongst many other cases, of John Shafte, yeoman, of the
aldermanry of Hyde Street suing John Williams of Winchester for trespass. The court was thus used by all and sundry
irrespective of their place of habitation. Two husbandmen of
Botley, William Smith and Thomas Potter, brought their
dispute here for settlement, and so did two yeomen, Francis
Angles of Itchen Abbas and John Aylinge of New Alresford.
But it is noticed that although freemen of the City often
appeared in this court as plaintiffs, they never came as
defendants. They obviously took advantage of their ancient
right which allowed them to be prosecuted only in the City
Court of Record and not elsewhere. It is also clear that in
Elizabeth's time the use of the court was no longer confined
to merchants visiting Winchester, but it served a much
wider need and had, in fact, become a popular court where
there was as little delay as possible.

From the files of the Court of Pie Powder two cases of
debt have been selected and an account of each one is given
below:

On the 23rd day of December in the twenty-second year
of Elizabeth (1579) Edward Sone (of Winchester), through
his attorney, John Stoner, pleaded that Nicholas Neve (also
of Winchester) should repay him the £3 1s. 0d. which he
owed him and wrongfully withheld. For lack of security the
defendant was attached by the seizure of goods and chattels,
namely, fifty-four pounds yarn, which remained in the
custody of the Bailiffs, and the defendant was due to appear
in court for the first time at 8 a.m. on the same day. At which
hour, when the case was duly called, the plaintiff's attorney
was present but the defendant was absent.

(In the plea roll the above information appears thus:
'xxiii⁰ die decembris anno Elizabethe Regine xxii⁰ Edwardus
Sone—ponit loco suo Jo: Stoner—queritur versus Nicholaum
Neve de placito quod reddat ei iiiˡⁱ xiiᵈ quae ei debet et
iniuste detinet. Defendens attachiatus per bona et catalla sua
videlicet per liiiiˡⁱ fili lanei vocatas liiii poundes of yarne
remanentes in custodiam ballivorum pro defectu securitatis

et habet horam viii^a ante meridiem eiusdem diei ad quam quidem horam partes predictae exacte fuerunt et predictus querens per attornatum suum predictum comparuit et predictus defendens non comparuit.')

The case was called again at 4 p.m. on the same day with the same result. Owing to the Christmas recess, the case was adjourned until 8 a.m. on January 8th, but neither at that court nor at those at 10 a.m. and 4 p.m. on the same day and at 8 a.m. on the following day did the defendant appear. As he had the six courts allowed to him and had not appeared, an order for distress to be taken was issued and Thomas Colley and Anthony Warren were appointed to appraise the goods distrained by 4 p.m. on the same day (January 9th). The time allowed was insufficient, so the appraisers were given until 10 a.m. on January 13th, when they appeared again and said that they had not completed their task. But on January 16th at 2 p.m. they came to court and upon oath stated that they had valued the goods at £3 1s. 0d. Judgment was given that the plaintiff should receive that sum together with 2d. for detention of the amount owed and a further 9s. 3d. for costs and expenses of the suit, making a total of £3 10s. 5d., and that the yarn should be sold. Four days later the sergeant-at-mace reported that the sale had realized £3 16s. 6d. Whereupon £3 10s. 5d. was paid to the plaintiff's attorney and the remaining 6s. 1d. was given to the Bailiff, James Vibert, 'for the use of the defendant, Nicholas Neve'.

Walter Sandys, Esquire, of Winchester, through John Stoner, his attorney, pleaded that Henry Haywood, yeoman, of Ashley, for whom Anthony Adderley acted as attorney, owed him £40 and would not repay him. The defendant had been arrested but had found surety for his release in William Brexstone. The case was tried on May 20th, 1581, at 10 a.m., when the attorneys of both parties appeared and the defendant's attorney asked for the agreement and the endorsement upon it to be read openly in court. From this it appeared that Walter Sandys had let to the aforesaid Henry Haywood, for a period of ten years, a rabbit warren at Langley in Hampshire for the sum of £40, on condition that at the end of the ten years the lessee should leave on the warren 300 couples of breeding rabbits, both male and female, to be viewed by impartial persons elected by the lessor, Walter Sandys. After the reading of the agreement the defendant's attorney asked leave to negotiate until 2 p.m. the same day, when further leave was sought and this was repeated at later courts until the sixth occasion when the defendant's attorney admitted that his client had no defence. The court thereupon decided that Walter Sandys should receive his £40 together with 3*d.* for detention of the debt and 8*s.* 8*d.* for costs and expenses. A week later, the plaintiff's attorney asked for execution of the sentence and the defendant, who was present in court, was committed to prison in the Westgate of the City until such time as he could pay (as the plea roll says 'defendens presens in curiam committitur prisone domine Regine de le Westgate civitatis predicte ibidem moratur quousque etc'.).

An examination of the documents connected with the Courts of Record and Pie Powder gives the impression that the work undertaken there by the Mayor and his colleagues took up a considerable amount of time and was, in the main, rather tedious. There were always numerous cases to be tried in both courts, and though the Court of Record met only on the Friday of each week the Court of Pie Powder averaged about two sittings per week. Thus for three days of every week there was work in the courts for the Mayor and Bailiffs, and, after 1582, the Recorder. In the Court of Record these officers had to deal with many cases of a trivial nature arising from breaches of local ordinances and their work here somewhat resembled that of a modern police or petty sessional court, while in the Court of Pie Powder, where cases of debt followed each other with monotonous regularity, their task approached that of a modern County Court judge. Throughout the records there is evidence of the way in which the administration of justice in those days was greatly hindered by the cumbersome and wearisome procedure. But the attendance of the Mayor, Recorder and Bailiffs and other officers at these courts, burdensome though it may have been, was not the only duty required of them, for they were called upon from time to time to examine persons who had been apprehended on suspicion by the constables and their helpers. From the depositions of such persons, an example of which is given below, it was decided whether or not they should be brought to trial.

'23 ffebruary 1598.

Thexaminacion of Robert ffurnesse of Tichfild, teyler.

He also professeth to be a musician upon a harpe, and saith that on friday last he came to Bisshops Waltham and lodged at the house of Nicholas Dyer and accompanied Thomas Monday there who is skilful upon the base violl and William Noble of Portsmouth met they there who plaieth upon the violett. And there they continued from friday last untill Wenisday last and then came to the soke of Winchester and there lodged and had no other errand there but to use there minstrelsy and make merry and to gett somewhat if they could. But saith that they played not in Winchester with there instruments onely at there lodging the morning they tuned there instruments and soe they brought them up into the City intending to play amongst there friends but did not play as he saith for he saith he was apprehended before. This deponent hath byn acquainted with Thomas Monday these xx years past and with Noble he hath byn abowt one moneth past.

Thexaminacion of Thomas Monday of Bisshops Waltham, shomaker.

He saight he hath skill on a base vyall and came in company with Robert ffurnesse and William Noble to Winchester on Wednisday night last and lodged at William Warrens in the soke but saith they played not on there instruments either in the soke or in the towne. They came this tyme to see there friends and to gett somewhat if they could.

Thexaminacion of William Noble, saylor.

He also saith that he is a musician and came lately from sea and fell acquainted with Dionese Tucker of Stockbridge whom he intendeth to take to his wife and is purposed to goe to sea againe as sone as the Rose Lion can be made reddy. He came on Wednisday night last to Winchester in the company of ffurnesse and Monday who also are musicians and they brought there instruments with them intending to gett some mony here by there minstrelsy to help bere there charges. But this deponent saith that they did not use or exercise there instruments in this city or in any place because they were apprehended before by the officers. He pretendeth that he was at sea when the statute on this behalf was made and being now advertised thereof he promiseth that henceforth he will not offend against the same.'

Endorsement on the back of the above manuscript:

'Examination of Robert ffurnesse Thomas Monday William Noble minstrells taken in Winchester and committed to Westgate by Mr. John White one of the Justices of the City where they remayned 2 dayes and then discharged by the Maior and the said John White, 24 February, 1598.'

CHAPTER X

Trade

In a previous chapter dealing with the Burgh-mote, it was
stated that originally the Merchant Gild of the City was
composed of merchant craftsmen who, by virtue of the
successful completion of their apprenticeship and admission
to the Gild, had acquired the status of merchants. Although in
Elizabeth's time candidates for admission to the Gild were no
longer presented by the craft to which they belonged, and
even though the doors had been opened to citizens who had
not served an apprenticeship nor been engaged in trade or
commerce, yet membership of the Gild was the essential
condition of the independence of a craftsman.[1] No one who
was not a member of the Gild could keep a shop, buy or sell,
without paying a fee to the Bailiffs for the concession. This is
quite clearly shown by the ordinance of 1563 which declares
that artificers, other than freemen and those engaged in the
various branches of the cloth trade, could not set up 'their
occupations, mysteryes or crafts' within the City unless they
were prepared to pay 3s. 4d. per week to the Bailiffs.[2] Provision was made, however, that persons who brought foodstuffs into the City on certain appointed days should not be
required to pay. This imposition which must have proved a
very heavy burden to all artificers continued to be levied until
1573, when 'for dyvers good consideracions' it was declared
null and void, and instead it was decided that 'every mayor
for the tyme beinge with the more parte of his bretherne shall

[1] J. S. Furley, *City Government*, p. 74.   [2] 1st Bk. Ord., f. 136.

yerelie before the feast of the nativitie of Christ and so from henceforth as often as he and they shall thinke meete taxe or assesse what every occupier artificer or craftsman of the sayed Cytie beinge no freeman or clothier and such as belonge to cloth makinge and workinge upon that arte onlie shall paie for occupyinge his arte mysterye science or occupation within that yere'.[1] Two years later it was further decided that no one, except those already engaged in such trade, should be allowed to sell by retailing textile goods, such as linen, wool and silk cloths, velvets, mercery and haberdashery.[2]

From the wording of the oath taken by an entrant to the Merchant Gild, it would appear that a freeman's duty was to be loyal to the King and the City, to bear his full share of taxation and public office, to see that Winchester cases were tried in Winchester courts, to be obedient to the Mayor and Bailiffs, and not to use his franchise for the purpose of showing undue favour to any other person. All this implies that the object of the Merchant Gild was not to further sectional or self interest but, as a body which had in its hands the government of the City, to further its general prosperity. But there is no doubt that even as far back as 1158, when Henry II by charter granted freedom from tolls to members of the Merchant Gild at Winchester, there was another object, namely the protection of the gildsman from competition when engaged in business both inside and outside the City. This protection was strengthened from time to time by ordinances enacted by the Burgh-mote, and the process was continued in Elizabeth's reign when, no doubt, the freemen held the view that their own personal interests and those of the City were identical.

Only three lists of artificers, showing the amounts at which they were annually assessed, are now available; these are for the years 1594, 1597 and 1598.[3] For 1594 the list shows the names of 53 artificers assessed at a total sum of 85s. 7d., the highest individual assessment being 20s. and the lowest 1d., while seven are not required to pay anything at all. In only a

[1] Idem, f. 172.   [2] Idem, f. 182.   [3] Idem, f. 274, 288, 290.

few cases is a person's occupation given; thus one finds William Goodall, butcher, assessed at 1s. 4d., William Goodall, shoemaker, at nothing, John Taylor, another shoemaker, at 1s. 0d., and William Colson, apothecary, at 2s. 6d. By 1597 the number of artificers had fallen to 36, and by 1598 to 34, and the total amounts of the assessments are 36s. 8d. and 32s. 10d. respectively, showing a decrease in numbers and revenue which may have been due to a decline in trade following the serious outbreak of the plague in 1593.

In addition to the Merchant Gild, there were craft gilds which were of a later origin. In England they were well established by the fourteenth century, but as early as the twelfth century the term 'gild', applying to craft fraternities of weavers and fullers, is found in the Winchester records. The object of these gilds was the regulation of the particular trade or occupation so that the interests of the workers were safeguarded while at the same time honest work was secured. Later there is mention of other fraternities in Winchester, such as that of the tailors and hosiers, but the word most frequently used to denote an organized body or society of skilled or trained men engaged in a particular trade or occupation is 'mistery'. Although the craft gild was really industrial or commercial in scope, it often had some religious connection; for example, an ordinance of 1437, which was still in force in 1552 but was repealed in Elizabeth's reign, gives the order which was to be observed in the procession which took place on Corpus Christi Day in Winchester:

'It is accordid of a sartayne Processyon in the ffeast of Corpus Christi of diverse artyficers and crafts within the said Cytie beinge that is to saie that Carpenters and hellyers shall goo together fiyrst Smythes and Barbars second Cooks and Bochars thyrd Shomakers with two lyghts ffourthe Tanners and Tapeners ffyvethe Plummers and Sylke men sixt ffysshers and furryers seventhe Taverners eight Weyvers with two lightes nenigth ffullars with two lightes tenthe Dyars with two lights eleventhe Chaundlers and Brewers twelvth Mercers with two lights thyrtenthe the Wyves with one light and

John Blake with an other light ffourtenthe and all theis lights shalbe borne orderlie before the said prossession before the prists.'[1, 2, 3, 4]

By the charter granted by Elizabeth in 1587 the City received authority for the creation of corporations or companies of the various trades or occupations within the City and for the drawing up of regulations for such bodies. There is in the records, however, evidence that such companies, which were really the old craft gilds under another name, had existed for some three or four centuries previously in Winchester and that they were still flourishing in the fifteenth century. But there is no payment from them to the Chamberlains in the middle part of the sixteenth century, and in the reign of Mary, 1552–58, there are several references in the Chamberlains' rolls to the fact that the fraternity of the fullers and weavers, which had been one of the oldest and most important of the craft gilds, was no longer functioning. Between the years 1575 and 1580 there was renewed activity, and during this period the brewers, fullers and weavers, shoemakers and cobblers, and the tailors and hosiers were each incorporated into companies with new regulations. The appropriate clause in Elizabeth's charter of 1587 was quite possibly inserted in order to give royal sanction to these companies which had been so recently reconstituted.

THE INCORPORATION OF BREWERS

In 1575 the common brewers of the City complained that their business had suffered to such an extent that they were unable to provide liquor as in time past, and that this state of affairs was due to the fact that there were many petty brewers in the City who brewed and sold by retail when malt was cheap and in plentiful supply, but left the City when it was dear.[5] Therefore in times of plenty the common brewers, through competition and low prices, made very little profit,

[1] Idem, f. 5.   [2] Hellyers = tilers or slaters.   [3] Taperners = weavers.
[4] Plummers = dealers in plumes and feathers.   [5] 1st Bk. Ord., f. 189.

but when contrary conditions prevailed in times of dearth they still had to continue brewing, often at a loss, without providing a satisfactory service for the community. It was therefore decided by the Burgh-mote that Christofer Genens, George Moulton, beer brewers, and Richard Alison, William Budd, John Stoner and John Mathew, ale brewers, who were the common brewers at the time, should be incorporated into a Corporation or Company of Brewers, and should have the power to elect two of their company annually to be wardens.[1] If any one of the six proved obstinate and would not accept the provisions made by the Burgh-mote he was to be deposed and another freeman elected in his place, for it was made quite clear that only freemen could be of the company which was limited to six in number. Should there be any dispute between the wardens and the others concerning the matter of brewing, it was to be settled by the Mayor and his brethren, and if their decision was not accepted then the corporation or company was to be dissolved and their incorporation declared void.

No inn-keeper or retailer of beer or ale was to be allowed to brew for consumption within his premises upon pain of paying forty shillings, nor was any other person in the City, except members of the Company of Brewers, allowed to brew to sell upon pain of a similar penalty. The common brewers were allowed to sell beer or ale without being regarded as retailers, provided that they sold it within twenty-four hours of the tunning and in quantities of not less than one gallon per person. Only one brewer dwelling outside the City was allowed to brew and bring his beer into the City, and this was Thomas Pulley of the Soke, who was granted the privilege of being a common brewer because he had for many years served the City both in times of dearth and plenty of corn. Should the said Thomas Pulley break any of the regulations as a brewer, another was to be appointed in his place on payment of a fee of four pounds.

No inn-keeper or retailer of beer or ale was allowed to take,

[1] Idem, f. 189.

except by way of a gift and even then without fraud or favour, more than one gallon of beer or ale into his premises for the purpose of selling it unless it came from one of the Company of Brewers. For a breach of this and all other regulations within the articles of incorporation the fine to be levied on innkeepers and retailers was forty shillings. Neither was an inn-keeper or retailer allowed to bring into his premises any beer or ale which had been brewed with the inn-keeper's own malt, wood or hops, or which had been brewed fraudulently by others for him. The strength and price of beer and ale which they sold were not to exceed those set by the common brewer, and if any common brewer attempted to brew specially for any particular inn-keeper he was disenfranchised out of the Company and the inn-keeper was debarred from keeping an inn until he had paid the fine levied by the Mayor and his brethren. In all cases of non-payment of fines it was lawful for the wardens to distrain for the same and to sell the distress within fourteen days. Where a citizen did not submit quietly to such distress or started a suit or action in connection therewith, he was, if a freeman, disfranchised. If he was not a freeman the distress was to be taken by the Mayor's sergeant and sold by him within fourteen days after it had been appraised by two persons appointed by the Mayor in the City Court.

The wardens of the Company were empowered to search at all times and in all places, quietly and without disturbance, for any offence against the regulations and to call upon any Bailiff, Constable or Sergeant to assist them. Anyone disturbing them in their search was liable to a fine of twenty shillings, and if unable to pay then suffer imprisonment. No one could become a member of the Company of Brewers unless he had previously been an apprentice in the City or paid an entrance fee of twenty shillings, and in any case no one was admitted to the Company unless he was a freeman, that is, unless he had been admitted to the Merchant Gild. The wardens were elected before the September meeting of the Burgh-mote, at which meeting they took their oaths before the Mayor to carry out their duties faithfully. They paid twopence to the Town Clerk for entering their names and every new member of the Company paid him fourpence for the same service. It was left to the Mayor and the Twenty-four to determine any scruple or doubt arising from these regulations and to revoke or change them upon 'good and wise cause for the preservation of the common wealth of the Cytie'. Finally, it was ordered that if the Mayor should 'fortune to be remyse slacke or negligent and not put in execution all those thinges and every of them which are specified and conteyned in this ordinance', then forty shillings were to be deducted from his annual fee.

The Incorporation of Taylors and Hosiers

In 1566 the tailors and hosiers of the City complained that 'at diverse quicke tymes of worke and against highe feastes' outsiders came into the City and took houses for the purpose of plying their trade, and that others came in and worked secretly in inns and other places and then departed, much to the detriment of resident tailors and hosiers.[1] For the reformation of this abuse the Burgh-mote decided that these tradesmen should be allowed to elect two wardens to rule and correct all such things as appertained to their craft. No one was to be allowed to set up for himself as a tailor or hosier within the City unless he was a freeman or had been an apprentice to a freeman and, in the latter case, paid five shillings. Strangers coming to the City later and who had not been apprenticed in the City could set up provided that the wardens considered them 'expert and conninge' in the craft, and that they paid twenty shillings. All persons admitted to the craft had to be sworn before the Mayor that they would be obedient to the wardens.

Fines were inflicted upon all who failed to keep the various rules and regulations, and the money thereby collected was divided equally between the common box of the craft and the

[1] Idem, f. 143.

chamber of the City. Wardens who failed to deal with the grievances of their members were fined 3*s*. 4*d*. No journey-man was allowed to work more than fourteen days without paying 12*d*. Failure to comply with the lawful commands of the wardens resulted in a fine of 3*s*. 4*d*., and failure to carry out the rules ratified by the Mayor and his brethren was punished by a heavier fine of 6*s*. 8*d*. Twenty shillings was the penalty for enticing a servant or apprentice from his master, and for giving instruction in the craft to anyone who was not an apprentice the penalty was 26*s*. 8*d*. A member of the craft who worked or opened his shop windows on a Sunday was fined 3*s*. 4*d*., to which was added 12*d*. a day until the fine was paid, and no member was permitted to engage in any other craft while he was a tailor or hosier except that of selling woollen cloth.

These regulations could not have proved altogether effec-tual, for fourteen years later in 1580 one finds the tailors and hosiers making the same complaint as before concerning interlopers coming into the City.[1] The Burgh-mote there-upon revoked the old grant and agreed that fourteen citizens, all tailors or hosiers then trading in the City, should be incor-porated to form a Company of Tailors and Hosiers. The wardens were elected annually and they were to be presented and sworn before the Mayor 'well trewlie and indifferentlie to make serches of the offenders contrarie to this present ordinance and to present trewlie all offenders offences and defaultes which they shall fynde contrarie to any article herein conteyned and to doo their best endevour to levie and gather all fynes forfeytures penalties and paymentes in this ordinance limited by them to be levied'.

The wardens, with the consent of the Mayor, had the power to elect others to the Company, but they could not refuse to admit a person who had completed his apprentice-ship in the City provided he paid 3*s*. 4*d*. Those who had not been apprenticed had to pay the exorbitant fee of five pounds. New members had to be presented and registered at the Town

[1] Idem, f. 211.

Court of Record where they swore to observe and keep all the regulations of the Company and paid the Town Clerk two shillings for entering their names on the roll. Persons, not being members of the Company, who persisted in setting up as tailors and hosiers forfeited ten shillings for every week in which they pursued their craft. Journeymen employed by a member of the Company paid sixpence and were not allowed to leave one member to serve another without licence, while any member guilty of enticing a journeyman or apprentice was fined twenty shillings. The penalty of 26s. 8d. for teaching the craft to anyone but an apprentice, and that of 3s. 4d. for working or opening the shop windows on Sundays were still enforced. In order to ensure a high standard of workmanship, it was decreed that if any member destroyed or spoilt any garment or material entrusted to him he should adequately recompense the owner or be disenfranchised from the Company. Wardens who failed to take proceedings against such an offender were themselves liable to a fine of four pounds.

It was lawful for the wardens to call together the Company from time to time to transact necessary business and to search the houses and shops of members to ascertain whether the regulations were being strictly observed. Those found to be offending were fined 6s. 8d., and were not permitted to carry on their business until this fine had been paid on pain of paying another 12d. for every day they opened their shops. Should these fines be left unpaid the wardens of the craft or the Mayor's sergeant were entitled to enter the premises and distrain on the offender's possessions, and after these had been appraised in the Town Court to sell them, the Mayor's sergeant taking eightpence for his labours. In addition, the wardens were enabled by the articles of incorporation to devise further regulations for the Company, but these required ratification by the Mayor and his brethren in whom was vested the right of settling disputes and controversies arising from the interpretation of the regulations.

THE INCORPORATION OF SHOEMAKERS

'Earnest and pitifull complayntes' were made by the shoe-makers and cobblers of the City that their 'trades sciences and misteries' were being used by sundry and divers persons, who not having served any apprenticeship came to the City daily, with the result that such persons did 'either ignorantlie or for wicked lucre and gaynes sake utter and sell to the people bootes shooes sterkoppes and pantaples made of faultie deceatfull and evell tanned leather to the greate hurte and deceat of the people', and also that by their entering the City in this way the number of shoemakers and cobblers had increased to such an extent that the trade of the resident craftsmen was diminished, and they were now unable to meet the taxes and other charges for which they were liable.[1, 2] Consequently it was agreed by the Burgh-mote in 1580 that a Company of Shoemakers and Cobblers should be incorporated to consist of ten shoemakers and six cobblers.[3] The articles of incorporation were almost identical with those drawn up for the tailors and hosiers, except that a person who had not been apprenticed with one of the Company had to pay no less than six pounds thirteen shillings and fourpence and provide a dinner for all the members and their wives on being admitted to the craft, while a cobbler who had not been similarly apprenticed had to pay thirty shillings. The distinction between a shoemaker and a cobbler was strictly maintained, the former not being permitted to mend old boots and shoes except for his own family, nor the latter to make new boots and shoes.

THE INCORPORATION OF FULLERS AND WEAVERS

In 1577 the fullers and weavers of the City complained that certain persons, unmarried and under thirty years of age and not worth ten pounds of their own goods, had set up as

[1] Sterkoppes = short gaiters or buttoned buskins.
[2] Pantaples = pantofles, slippers.   [3] 1st Bk. Ord., f. 205.

masters in their trade and refused 'to serve in these occupations accordinge to the lawes of the realme', and also that many who had not been apprenticed to fullers and weavers had likewise set up in these trades.[1] As a result, they said, 'the nomber of them doo daielie so increase that such persons of these occupations as have heretofore kepte householde and borne the brunte of divers and sundry grete charges within the Cyty for wante of sufficiente worke are neither able to sett any jornyman on worke neither yet have worke sufficiente for themselves wherebie they might susteyne theire poore famelies and beare the saied charges to theire grete decaye and overthrowe yf remedie be not speedelie had therin'. It was thereupon decided that twenty fullers and seventeen weavers of the City should be incorporated as a Corporation or Company of Fullers and Weavers with two of each occupation elected annually as wardens. The articles of incorporation were substantially the same as those for the tailors and hosiers and for the shoemakers and cobblers, but in this case a person who had not been an apprentice could be admitted to membership on payment of forty shillings.

There was a long-standing ordinance of the City, quoted in the *Black Book* under the date 1412 and repeated in 1525, to the effect that no one except a freeman was to be allowed to have an apprentice, and at later times there are records of the drafting of further ordinances for enfranchising freemen's sons and their covenanted and indentured servants.[2] As has already been shown the master tradesmen of the City were members of the Merchant Gild and it was in their interest to see that any depletion in the ranks of that body was made good by the admission of suitable candidates. To accomplish this they favoured the sons and servants of freemen to the exclusion of others, and made sure that apprenticeship was legally recognized. In 1567 the method of enrolling the indentures for apprentices was set out and approved by the Burgh-mote.[3] In future every indenture had to be brought

[1] 2nd Ledger Book, f. 219.　　[2] 1st Bk. Ord., f. 135, 137.
[3] Idem, f. 153.

192

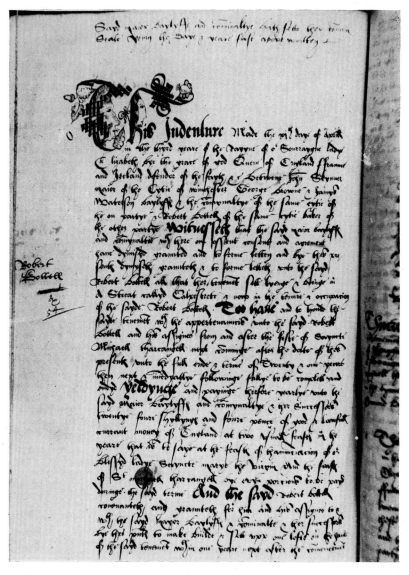

8. Lease of a tenement in Calpe (St. Thomas) Street to Robert
Bottell (Second Ledger Book, f. 48).

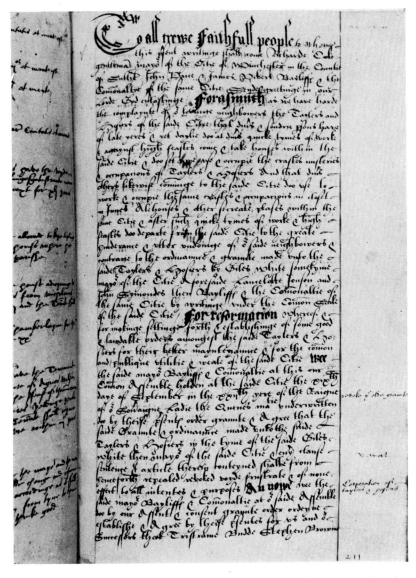

9. The Incorporation of Tailors and Hosiers (First Book of Ordinances, f. 143).

into the City Court of Record before the Mayor and at least one alderman within three months after the sealing and there acknowledged and enrolled in a book 'accordinge to the custome of the Cytie of London'. The master paid sixpence to the Mayor, and to the Town Clerk, for enrolling, twelve pence. Failure to comply with this ordinance rendered the indenture void and the master liable to a fine of 6*s*. 8*d*.

In the ordinance concerning the Corpus Christi procession, there are twenty separate trades and crafts mentioned and it may be assumed that these were the occupations which in the fifteenth century were recognized as 'misteries'. In the City records of Elizabethan times only four incorporations are mentioned and the details of these have been given above. There may have been others, but the fact that all trades and crafts in the City were not incorporated is clearly shown by an ordinance of 1595 agreeing that 'all the occupiers artificers trades misteries and sciences of the Cittie shalbe incorporated and divided into fellowships under the comon seale of the Cittie'.[1] There is plenty of evidence, however, that several trades and occupations, though not mentioned specifically as being incorporated, were of considerable consequence and played a necessary and important part in the life of the City. At a time when beer was one of the staple foods and not a luxury, inn-keepers and tiplers (as retailers of beer and ale were then called) tended to be a numerous body, and in the interests of a community in which brewing was a domestic industry their activities, like those of the common brewers, had to be regulated. Not only were their premises visited at least once a week by the Bailiffs and Constables, but from time to time their numbers were limited by ordinance. In 1540 it had been decided that there should not be more than twenty-four of them and that 'they be of good behavyer and honest conversation and that they have ther signes accordinglie'.[2] Later in 1567 it was agreed that none of the inn-keepers or tiplers 'shalbe dismyssed but as they shall die or departe out of the Cytie, or otherwise offende the lawes, so

---

[1] Idem, f. 283.   [2] *Black Book*, p. 167.

shall the number of them be diminished to the nomber of xviii', and that thirteen of these should supply the High Street, and of the remainder there should be two in the aldermanry of Colebrook Street, and one in each of the aldermanries of Tanner (Lower Brook) Street, Gold (Southgate) Street and Northgate (Hyde) Street.[1] But eight years later, because it was found to be unworkable, this ordinance was declared void, and thereafter at the discretion of the Mayor and his brethren inn-keepers and tiplers were appointed as required to meet the needs of the population.[2]

Throughout this period it is found that ordinances are constantly being enacted and later repealed to meet changing conditions, and it becomes increasingly clear that the City authorities kept a close watch on the activities of all who engaged in trade and commerce in Winchester, particularly those who dealt in foodstuffs, whether they resided in the City or outside. The general policy was, firstly, to prevent any one person from following more than one occupation so that the honest trader or craftsman, especially if he were a freeman or a resident, did not encounter unfair competition, and secondly, to protect the citizens against fraudulent dealing. As an example, the inn-keeper or tipler had to confine his activities to the sale of beer or ale, and he was not allowed to compete with the bakers by baking bread for sale. The supply of beer, bread and meat, the staple food of the people, was constantly under consideration, and the ordinances and amendments to them dealing with this matter are extremely numerous. Also the large number of cases arising from the infringement of these regulations which were brought into the City Court shows how difficult was the task of city government in this respect. As in the case of other trades, the number of bakers was limited by the Mayor and his brethren, and persons from outside the City, that is, 'foreign' or 'strange' bakers as they were called, were allowed to bring in their bread on market days only and sell it between six o'clock in the morning and two in the afternoon.[3] The con-

[1] 1st Bk. Ord., f. 151.   [2] Idem, f. 189.   [3] Idem, f. 112.

sumer was protected by the 'assize of bread' which has been described in the preceding chapter.

On market days when 'foreign' traders were admitted to the City much of the business was conducted in the market place on the north-west side of the cathedral. At other times the High Street was the trading centre, and it was there that the principal traders had their shops with stalls or 'bulks', upon which they laid their wares, protruding into the street. This was a practice which often brought them into conflict with their neighbours and which from time to time required official investigation and judgment by the Mayor. But a few occupations were confined to certain localities within the City. The curriers of leather and the dyers were obliged to stay in the region of the 'brooks', while the butchers and fishmongers each had their own shambles. Resident butchers carried on their trade in Fleshmonger (St. Peter's) Street near the church of St. Peter in macellis, that is, in the shambles, and an attempt by them in 1604 to open shops on the other side of the High Street, under the Pentice where there were several cloth merchants, was strongly and successfully resisted.[1] 'Foreign' butchers were admitted to the City on sufferance. For over a century they had been allowed to stand near the church of St. Maurice, on the south side of the High Street, on Saturdays only, and even then they had to finish trading by five o'clock between Easter and Michaelmas and by four o'clock from Michaelmas to Easter; after 1566 they had to close down an hour earlier than these specified times.[2]

In that year it was ordained that 'no bocher stranger comynge to the Citie doo bringe any veale to sell that shalbe blowen or otherwise unlawfullie stuffed'.[3] The slaughtering of cattle had to be regulated by all butchers so that meat should be sold during the whole of Saturday and on the Sunday following before eight in the morning, and it was also required that all foreign butchers should bring into the City the hide and tallow of all cattle which they had slaughtered

[1] Idem, f. 308.   [2] Idem, f. 139.   [3] Idem, f. 149.

outside the City. Later it was ordered that they should bring 5 lbs. of tallow with every quarter of beef and 1 lb. with every sheep, and that these should be sold at the same prices at which the City butchers were compelled to sell upon pain of forfeiture of their meat.[1] All tallow went to the common chandler of the City at a controlled price in order to ensure that there was a constant supply of candles, the price of which was fixed by the Burgh-mote at $2\frac{1}{2}d$. per pound. Any butcher who refused to carry out these regulations was driven from business by having his shop door and windows closed and not being allowed to follow this occupation in any shape or form. The trade of candle-making was protected by an ordinance which declared that 'no person other than the chaundler of the citie and John Jenens and such other as have bynne or hereafter shall be apprentice to the arte of a tallowe chandler within the same Citie shall use or exercise the arte neither shall sell or utter in grose or by retaile anie tallowe candelle openlie or privilie other than such candells onelie as they and everie of them shall have and buie of the tallowe chandler of the citie after the rate of thirteene for twelve'.[2]

The fish shambles were situated on the north side of the High Street below Staple Garden and it was there that the resident 'fishers' plied their trade. Though they had to be reminded occasionally that the casting into the street of trade refuse and fish water was an intolerable nuisance, they do not appear to have troubled the City officers unduly. The same cannot be said of 'strange fishers' who came to the City from outside and tried to sell their fish at all times and in all places. Ordinances forbade them to stand elsewhere than 'in the place to them limited' or to sell before six o'clock in the morning in summer or seven in winter.[3] Neither were they nor any one on their behalf to sell their fish secretly or in inns. At one time there was some disorder created by fishmongers selling in the vicinity of the City Cross, but the City officers arrived and compelled them to retire to a more suitable place.[4] There

[1] Idem, f. 247.   [2] Idem, f. 237.   [3] Idem, f. 1.   [4] Idem, f. 135.

are many references in the records to the Mayor and his brethren deciding on 'suitable places' where these particular tradesmen might stand and sell, but no definite place is mentioned until 1583, when it was agreed that the sale of saltfish other than in shops should take place 'beneathe the signe of the Bell', an inn standing on the west side of Wongar (Middle Brook) Street at its junction with the High Street.[1]

An ordinance of 1515 had declared it illegal to sell or buy with any weights or measures unless they bore the King's seal, and in 1531 it had been agreed 'that everie Maior shall delyver to the Maior next followinge the seale of the office of the mairaltie, with the seale of the Staple, the brasin busshel, the brasin galon, the brasin yarde and the seale of measures'.[2,3] From the time of Magna Carta there had been attempts by Act of Parliament and by Proclamation to regulate weights and measures but for many years there was much variation in local usage. Though the yard was stabilized at an early date, the bushel and the gallon do not seem to have been fixed until the reign of Henry VII, from which time the standards were to be of brass whereas they had formerly been of iron or at least sealed with an iron seal. The bushel, gallon and yard mentioned in the ordinance of 1531 as being in the Mayor's keeping are still preserved at Winchester and were the standards employed to secure honest trading during the reign of Elizabeth and for some years later. The bushel is of bronze and contains 2,124 cubic inches as against the Imperial bushel of today which contains $2,219\frac{3}{4}$ cubic inches. It bears a central band inscribed: Henricus Septimus Dei gratia Anglie et Francie: and this is interspersed with the badges of Henry VII, the greyhound in leash, Tudor roses and a portcullis. The gallon is of brass and contains $272\frac{1}{4}$ cubic inches as against $277\frac{1}{2}$ cubic inches of the present Imperial gallon. On the band there is a greyhound in leash, Henricus, the Tudor rose, Septimus, a portcullis, and on the handle a Welsh dragon. The yard dates from the time of Henry I; it is a bronze hexagonal rod, re-standardized at one end with a

[1] Idem, f. 231.   [2] Idem, f. 8.   [3] Idem, f. 12.

Roman E for Edward I, and at the other end with 'h' for Henry VII. It is four-hundredths short.

With these standard weights and measures at their disposal the City officers kept a constant watch for fraud and trickery, and brought offenders before the Mayor and his colleagues in the City Court of Record where the guilty, as shown by the court records, were severely punished. Two other practices which were regarded as fraudulent, namely, 'forestalling' and 'regrating', were also subject to heavy fines. Forestalling was the term applied to the buying, generally in small quantities, of goods before they were offered for sale in the market. The price paid was usually lower than the fixed market price and the payment of any market dues was avoided. Regrating was an attempt to buy up all available supplies of any one commodity by meeting 'foreign' traders outside the City walls in the hope of making a corner in the market and re-selling later at an enhanced price. Both were common offences, and the ordinances which forbade buying and selling before a certain hour or secretly in inns and other places were aimed at their prevention.

Sunday trading was regarded with great disfavour. All merchants and artificers dwelling in the City were required on every Sunday throughout the year to close their shops, cellars and warehouses, and shut all shop windows so that no wares or merchandise were on view. An exception was made in the case of butchers and 'all men and women bringinge geese ducks capons pultry wyldfowle piggs Wotmeale' (oatmeal) 'and any other kinde of victuall or wares to the Cytie'.[1] These persons were allowed to sell between six and eight o'clock on Sunday mornings, but not later on pain of forfeiture of their wares. This ordinance was made 'for that purpose that as well citizens as straungers maye the better serve and please god and intend there dyvine service the sabott day whiche is the Sondaye and renownce worldly occupations which tendythe to the detryment of there soules'.

Of the various trades and crafts which were carried on at

[1] Idem, f. 4.

this time in Winchester there can be little doubt that the woollen trade in all its branches, including carding, spinning, weaving, fulling and dyeing, gave employment to most people. In medieval times it was the premier industry in the City owing to the fact that Winchester was, for some years during the fourteenth century, one of the fourteen staple centres in this country for the collection and examination of wool before it went abroad and before it was delivered to the home manufacturer.[1] But although by Elizabethan times the woollen trade had declined in the City, it still turned out quantities of 'chaluns' or blankets, and a rough coarse cloth known as 'burel' cloth. The comparative importance of this local industry may be judged partly by the relatively large number of master weavers and fullers, twenty of the former and seventeen of the latter, who formed the Company of Weavers and Fullers at their incorporation in 1577.

This trade was localized in the north-east part of the City, in Tanner (Lower Brook) Street and Buck Street (Busket Lane), through which passed two branches of the River Itchen. The fullers took the cloth from the weavers and were responsible for all the finishing processes, except the dyeing, and these included the cleaning from grease by the use of fuller's earth, shearing, and the thickening of the cloth. It was these processes which required abundant water. Between Buck Street and Eastgate was the ground known as Coitbury, granted to the City by King John, where formerly stood two fulling mills, both of which had fallen into decay by the end of the fifteenth century. Adjoining this piece of ground were small meadows in which were the 'rack' or 'tenter' houses, the rack or tenter being the wooden frame to which the cloth was fixed by tenter hooks to be stretched and straightened before it was delivered to the dyers. Rack and tenter (tentorium) are frequently mentioned in the sixteenth-century leases of certain properties in this locality, and there is usually included in the lease a clause calling on the tenant to keep the rack in repair.

[1] Furley, *City Government*, p. 99.

No mention is made of fulling mills being in operation or even in existence within the City at this time. The only mill actually situated inside the walls was St. Mary's Abbey Mill in Colebrook Street, which had once been a corn mill and in Henry VIII's time was used as a grindstone factory. On the main branch of the river running through the Soke on the east side of the City there were Durngate and Segrim Well Mills, both of which were grist mills owned by the Bishop of Winchester. What is now known as the City Mill, outside Eastgate, was also at one time ecclesiastical property belonging to the Nunnery of Wherwell. The site was granted to the City by Queen Mary in 1554, and is described as a messuage or tenement which was once a mill. It was let at a rent of 6s. 8d. a year, the City reserving the right to rebuild the mill there. It never exercised this right, but in subsequent leases it inserted a covenant that the tenant should rebuild the mill. This covenant was disregarded and nothing was done until as late as 1743, when James Cooke, a tanner of the Soke, rented it and commenced building. Therefore, as far as can be ascertained, there were no fulling or power mills connected with the woollen industry in the City, but there were two fulling mills at Twyford, to the south of the City, for which the Chamberlains collected an annual rent of sixteen pounds. They were leased from time to time to prominent citizens and this points to the fact that they were connected with the fulling trade in the City, which along with the other branches of the woollen industry was undoubtedly a 'domestic' occupation carried on in the tenements of the workpeople and in the store-houses of the master craftsmen.

The comparative wealth and financial standing of individual merchants, freemen and prominent citizens is often disclosed by the amounts at which they were assessed for payment of taxes and other liabilities; also from their wills one can often gain some knowledge of the amount of their worldly possessions. But with regard to the poor inhabitants, particularly in the absence of testamentary evidence, the task is not so easy. It is obvious, as was shown in a previous chapter, that considerable numbers of the population were living from hand to mouth on the verge of poverty, and that a proportion of these were totally dependent on charity. Between the comparatively wealthy and the more numerous poor, however, there was a large class of working people engaged in various trades and occupations whose rates of remuneration can be seen in the certificate drawn up by the Mayor and Justices in 1563 for the regulating of the wages of 'artificers, labourers, servants of husbandry and apprentices'.[1] This certificate can be summarized as follows:

Women servants, 18 years of age and upwards.
    Best service, 20s. 0d. per annum, livery 8s. 0d.
    Common service, 16s. 0d. per annum, livery 8s. 0d.
Women servants under 18 years of age.
    Wages per annum—meat, drink and necessary apparel.

DAY WAGES FOR ARTIFICERS

A freemason, a master carpenter, a rough mason, a brick-layer, a plumber, a glazier, a carver, a joiner, a chief helier, being able to set forth by plot or to take charge of any work in their several sciences.

Easter to Michaelmas	*Michaelmas to Easter*
without food and drink 10d.	without food and drink 9d.
with food and drink 6d.	with food and drink 5d.

DAY WAGES OF COMMON WORKMEN OF ABOVE SCIENCES

Easter to Michaelmas	*Michaelmas to Easter*
without food and drink 8d.	without food and drink 7d.
with food and drink 4d.	with food and drink 3d.

[1] In accordance with the Statute, 5 Elizabeth, Cap. IV.

Chief sawyer
without food and drink 9d.   without food and drink 8d.
   with food and drink 5d.   with food and drink 4d.
Common sawyer
without food and drink 7d.   without food and drink 6d.
   with food and drink 3d.   with food and drink 2d.

    Easter to Michaelmas   *Michaelmas to Easter*

Apprentices
without food and drink 6d.   without food and drink 5d.
   with food and drink 3d.   with food and drink 2d.
Labourers
without food and drink 7d.   without food and drink 6d.
   with food and drink 3d.   with food and drink 2d.

ANNUAL WAGES FOR JOURNEYMEN AND SERVANTS OF THE CRAFTS

	best	common sort
Servants of clothiers.	66s. 8d.,	40s. 0d.
Woollen cloth weavers.	„ 43s. 4d., „	„ 33s. 4d.
Tucker, fuller, cloth-worker, shearman, linen weaver.	„ 50s. 0d., „	„ 40s. 0d.
Shoemaker, glover, cutler, smith, farrier, furrier, currier, capper, hatmaker, felt-maker, bowyer, fletcher, arrow-head maker, miller, tanner.	„ 53s. 4d., „	„ 33s. 4d.
Hosier, tailor, baker, spurryer, cook, cooper.	„ 40s. 0d., „	„ 26s. 8d.
Pewterer, butcher, rippier.	„ 60s. 0d., „	„ 40s. 0d.
Brewer, dyer.	„ 80s. 0d., „	„ 53s. 4d.
Sadler, chandler.	„ 50s. 0d., „	„ 33s. 4d.

Trade

There are several features of the above summary which seem to call for comment. In the first place, the remuneration of women employees appears rather small for even the best could not command a higher wage than twenty shillings per annum, though one must not lose sight of the fact that they were provided with food, clothing and accommodation free. At a time when there was increasing poverty in the City such emoluments would no doubt prove attractive, and with a decline in the various branches of the woollen trade and the consequent lack of work for women workers, the younger women under 18 years of age were likely to prefer security in the shape of meat, drink and livery, even without monetary reward for their work, to unemployment and poor living conditions in their own homes. Secondly, it was the workmen engaged in the building and allied trades who were paid daily wages, and these ranged during the summer months from 10*d.* for the foreman and highly skilled operative to 7*d.* for the labourer, with a deduction of 1*d.* during the winter. But when food and drink were provided by the employer, a further 4*d.* was deducted, an amount which was equivalent to half the average daily wage. Thirdly, journeymen and workers in other crafts who were hired, in accordance with the statute, for periods of not less than one year, were paid an annual wage, and it is to be noted that there were two rates of wages for each trade, one for the 'best' and one for the 'common sort', the rate for the latter being from 65% to 80% of the former. One cannot but wonder who decided whether a craftsman was of the best or of the common sort, and by what standards the rate for each individual craft was fixed. Why, for example, was a brewer or a dyer paid twice as much as a baker, or a cook, or a tailor? Possibly the law of supply and demand operated, and a superfluity of bakers and cooks kept their wages low while a scarcity of brewers and dyers had the very opposite effect.

CHAPTER XI

Health

Many ordinances enacted by the Burgh-mote during the fifteenth and sixteenth centuries were designed to prohibit practices which were inconsistent with the maintenance of a healthy city. Their frequency reveals the prevalence of unhealthy conditions, and an examination of their details helps one to realize the deplorably low standard of sanitation which then existed. The root of the matter lay in the practice of keeping large numbers of animals within the walled and confined city, and in the inadequate means at the citizens' disposal of getting rid of both domestic and trade refuse. From the earliest times the eastern and lowest part of Winchester had been intersected by open streams, all branches of the River Itchen which flowed from north to south immediately outside the eastern wall of the City. These streams, or 'brooks' as they are always called in the records, provided a ready supply of water for domestic purposes, but at the same time offered a very easy way of getting rid of refuse and of this the inhabitants had been only too ready to take advantage. From 1489 it had been the rule that if 'any man cast any donge, straw, dede hogge, dogge or catte or any other fylthe into the water wherby the water mought be stoppid', he should be fined twelve pence.[1]

The brooks ran through Shulworth (Upper Brook), Wongar (Middle Brook), Tanner (Lower Brook) Streets and also alongside Colebrook Street. Since 1543, in Henry VIII's

[1] 1st Bk. Ord., f. 9.

time, it had been the duty of every householder whose property adjoined any one of the brooks to cleanse and scour his portion of it within eight days of being ordered to do so by the alderman of the street-ward, under pain of paying the heavy penalty of ten shillings.[1] In 1554 it was ordained that the brooks should be stopped yearly on the second Monday after May Day and that they should be 'scallied scowred and lett go within ten dayes then next and immediatelie folowinge'.[2] If the householder failed to stop the brook he was fined 6s. 8d., while the penalty for failure to clean and scour it was imprisonment. Four years later, the date for cleansing was altered to the last Monday in August, and further provision was made that 'every man betweene Ascension Daye and Trinitie Sondaye shall drawe the wedes owte of the brokes before his grownde'.[3] In 1561 the ordinance was again altered and it was now agreed that 'the brokes shalbe scoured of such depithe and profundite as of ancient tyme hathe byn accustomed' and 'stopped yerely the wednisdaye in witsun weike'.[4] This procedure for keeping the brooks clear of rubbish was observed annually, except on one or two rare occasions. In 1558, the first year of Elizabeth's reign, the stopping of the brooks was dispensed with 'for the greate sycknes in the Citye', and again in 1564 'for diverse consideracions and specially for avoydinge the danger of the plague now remayninge, which god for his mercye ceasse', it was decided that no penalty should be levied for not obeying the ordinance.[5, 6]

The disposal of trade refuse was a constant problem and many efforts were made to overcome the nuisances created by various traders and to restrict to specified localities the activities of those occupations which by their nature were likely to be offensive. Curriers of leather were not allowed to work except in certain houses upon the brooks, and shoemakers were permitted to burn their shreds or parings of leather only between nine o'clock at night and four in the

[1] Idem, f. 14. [2] Idem, f. 105. [3] Idem, f. 117.
[4] Idem, f. 128. [5] Idem, f. 120. [6] Idem, f. 138.

morning.[1,2] Butchers were forbidden to throw 'intrayles or other vile things in the river of the Cytie or elsewhere within the saide Cytie to the noyance of their neighbours, but onlie in the place accustomed called abbies bridge and there nother but where the same intrailes and other vile things be cutt iiii inches longe at least'. Any dyer who poured into the river his 'wodegore', that is, the dirty, slimy waste matter deposited in the preparation of blue dyestuff or woad, 'after the sone risinge in the morninge and before sone sett', and did not wait until night time to get rid of the waste, was fined sixpence for each offence.[3] Similarly, glovers were not allowed to wash their skins at the public washing-place in Colebrook Street nor to hang the skins in the water between certain hours.[4] It was also forbidden to grind or to mill woad or to lay it out to dry within one hundred yards of the High Street, under the heavy penalty of twenty shillings.[5] If any fishmonger watered his saltfish and threw the water out of his door, he was compelled by ordinance to throw twice as much clean water after the fish water.[6]

The shopkeepers and traders were by no means the only persons whose activities came under the watchful eyes of the City officers, for it was found necessary to formulate many regulations dealing with sanitation which were directed at the ordinary householder. There was a long-standing ordinance which required every inhabitant within the City to make clean the street, and carry away the dust and soil, before his house every Saturday on pain of paying threepence to the Bailiffs in default, and an equally ancient ordinance ordering every tenant who was responsible for repairs to his house, or otherwise the owner, to pave in front of his dwelling. But these were not enough to prevent the accumulation of filth outside the houses. An ordinance of 1563 declared that 'no person shall laye anye ded dogge ratte or horse or anye other ded carreyne in anye strete or highwaye nether in anye other place excepte he burye the same sufficientlye' upon pain of a

---

[1] Idem, f. 7.   [2] Idem, f. 178.   [3] Idem, f. 1.
[4] Idem, f. 170.   [5] Idem, f. 131.   [6] Idem, f. 135.

fine of 6*s.* 8*d.*, half of which went to the person giving information.[1] Later in 1577 there were enacted three ordinances from the tenor of which it is gathered that a determined effort was to be made to put an end to various nuisances which were proving offensive not only to the Mayor and his brethren but also, one would imagine, to the more reputable citizens. These ordinances are quoted in full:

'Item wheras the lane leadinge throughe Staple garden into Bridnestreate by reason of much fylthe there cast ys very noifull to all such as passe that waye And also dyvers other streates and lanes of the saied Cytie aswell by castinge of donge dust and other fylthye things as also by doinge their other needes of easement which is to be done in pryvies or other meete places ys likewise very fylthye and noifull to all suche as shall passe by the same, ffor avoydinge wherof and the great infeccions and other inconveniences that may arise therebie yt ys first agreed that the sayed lane shalbe paled uppe with a dore locke and keye necessary for all suche as carry their dust and other ffilthie thinges into the common place of staple garden which keye shalbe alwayes remayninge at the house in the whiche Dorothe Mathew widow now dwelleth redy alwayes for any person that shall have occasion to occupie the same.'

'Item yt ys agreed that every person that shall laye any filthe duste or dounge in any streate or lane of the Cytie without their owne house or groundes or the groundes of any other person hired and meete for that purpose shall forfayte and lose for avery tyme vi^d. to the use of the taker of any person committinge such facte, And yf the offender presentlie upon the fact committed have not sufficient to pay or having sufficient shall refuse to paye the same then he or she so refusinge or not havinge to pay shall suffer suche correction for that faulte as by the discretion of the Mayor and the more parte of his bretherne shalbe thoughte meete And yf yt shall fall owt that the facte was committed by any mans sonne daughter or servante with thassent of the master or

[1] Idem, f. 136.

dame, father or mother, of such offender that then suche
father or mother, master or dame shall paye the sayed for-
fayture of vi^d., And yf they refuse to paye yt that the refuser
shalbe committed by the Mayor to warde there to remayne
untill he or she have payed the same Provided alwayes that
they that have stables maye cast out their dounge so yt be
carryed awaye within xxiiii houres after the castinge out
therof.'

'Item yt ys agreed that all persons of or above the age of
twelve years which shall doo his or her needes of easement
meete to be done in pryvies and other appointed places shall
doo yt in any streate or lane of the sayed Cytie beinge taken
with the facte or the facte may be proved by lawfull witnes
shall forfayte and lose for every tyme vi^{d.} to the use of the
taker of any suche offender which yf the offender shall refuse
to paye by himself or some frende presentlie he or she so
offendinge shall have such other punishment as shalbe
thought good from tyme to tyme by the Mayor or his
sufficient deputie.'[1]

For many years it had been unlawful to keep pigs or to
erect a pig-sty within the bounds of the High Street, but it
seems that the law was more honoured in the breach than in
the observance for the ordinance forbidding the practice was
on several occasions re-enacted. To put a stop to the wandering of pigs through the streets of the City it was ordained in
1573 that 'no person shall permyt any of his or her or their
hogges or weynlinge piggs to go or be within any place of the
Cytie out of their own groundes', the penalty being two
shillings for every pig over one year old and one shilling for
every pig under that age.[2] Half of the fine went to the beadle
or to any person who brought them to the town pound or
pinfold, which was probably sufficient incentive to urge any
impecunious individual to indulge in a pig hunt through the
by-ways of the City. At the same time it was agreed that no
person should 'kepe any hogstie or donge myxton' (dung
midden) 'to the common anoysance of the quenes liege

[1] Idem, f. 196.   [2] Idem, f. 172

people', upon pain of forfeiture of 3*s.* 4*d.* a month. It was the duty of the Bailiffs to see that these regulations were enforced, but there had obviously been some laxity on their part for in 1584 it was enacted that no hogsty should be kept within one hundred yards of the High Street, that the penalty for offenders should be increased to ten shillings, and that if the Bailiffs failed to levy this forfeiture then the Mayor should authorize his own Sergeant to levy by distress the same penalty upon the offender.[1] The Sergeant was to keep half of the fine and 'the bayliffes in respecte of theire negligence to have nothinge'.

The natural and abundant supply of clear water which Winchester possessed has already been mentioned in connection with the cleansing of the brooks. There are many references to these streams in the old records, particularly in the court rolls, from which it is evident that any interference with the water by way of diversion or defilement was severely punished. The streams supplied the householders with water for domestic purposes and in all probability for drinking also, though there was a common well and pump situated near the City Cross and there were other wells in private houses and grounds. The Aldermen of the street-wards presented in the City Court of Record the offenders who had, for example, washed dirty clothes in the brooks instead of at the common washing-place or thrown in rubbish instead of taking it to Abbey Bridge, which like the washing-place was in Colebrook Street at a point on the south side of the City where the streams left the City boundary.

Although there is ample evidence that the Burgh-mote made innumerable rules and regulations in order to improve the sanitary condition of the City, one cannot refrain from thinking that many nuisances were allowed to continue and were dealt with only when there was a public outcry. In 1554 Soranzo, the Venetian ambassador in London, wrote of the plague as follows: 'They have some little plague in England well nigh every year for which they are not accustomed to

[1] Idem, f. 230.

make sanitary provisions, as it does not make great progress; the cases for the most part occur amongst the lower classes, as if their dissolute mode of life impaired their constitutions.'[1] It is not surprising to learn that the plague was prevalent in Winchester on many occasions in Elizabeth's reign, as indeed it was in many other parts of the country. Mention has already been made of 'greate sycknes in the Citye' in 1558 and of the 'plague now remaynynge' in 1564, but there were at least three other occasions, namely in 1583, 1593 and 1603, when pestilence again visited the City.

During the sixteenth century a number of epidemical and contagious diseases grouped under the common name of the 'plague' brought death and misery to the towns of Britain. The records of many towns and villages testify to the number of outbreaks that occurred and show how some suffered much more than others.[2] Cambridge, during the first half of the century, was rarely free and on twelve occasions it was necessary to shorten the University terms. Possibly many of these outbreaks were due to fevers brought on by insanitary conditions and were not cases of plague. Oxford had six outbreaks throughout the century, while Chester had five. In the latter half of the century the plague apparently became more widespread; towns and villages were attacked more fiercely, some of them on more than one occasion. Leicester, Lincoln, Northampton, Norwich and Nottingham, all of them large towns, record outbreaks between 1550 and 1600. The provincial town which suffered most was Norwich where, during a period of twelve months in 1579 and 1580, 5,000 people out of a total population of 17,000 died.

Between the years 1500 and 1550 the most feared and the most fatal disease was the 'sweating sickness' or 'sweat', so named because the first sign of illness was that the victim began to sweat profusely.[3] It appeared for the first time in

---

[1] Cal. State Papers, Venetian, V, 541 (1554).
[2] J. H. Thomas, *Town Government in the XVIth century*, p. 135.
[3] Idem, pp. 137–8.

England in 1485, and it is considered that it was introduced by the hired soldiery brought by Henry VII from Normandy. Although it may have been no more than a kind of low fever in the region of its origin around Rouen, among a susceptible people in England it developed a very malignant nature. The disease attacked rich and poor, well nourished and ill-fed alike, and from its sudden and fatal nature it became known in some parts of this country as 'Stopgallant' and 'New Acquaintance'. After the first outbreak of the 'sweat' in 1485, nothing more was heard of it for twenty-three years. Then it reappeared in 1508, 1517, 1528, and for the last time in 1551. After that date nothing more was heard of it in England, at least not under that name.[1]

Records show that during the reigns of Edward VI and Mary (1547–58), there were in this country outbreaks of sweating sickness, pestilent fevers and influenzas, while in 1557 a severe influenza epidemic swept across Europe.[2] It seems probable that the 'greate sycknes' which, as already mentioned, afflicted Winchester in 1558 was an influenza which had so marked a symptom of sweating that it could be compared to the true 'sweat' of 1551. This view is supported by a statement made by Dr. John Jones in his 'Dyall of Agues', written about 1564.[3] He relates that when he was staying near Southampton in 1564 he became a victim of this particular sickness, which was so virulent that half the populations of Southampton, Portsmouth and the Isle of Wight were suffering from it, and goes on to describe the similarity of its symptoms with those of the 'sweat' of which he had seen so many cases in previous years.

Throughout the medieval period there are many references in various chronicles and in town records to outbreaks of plague and pestilence, but it would be unsafe to conclude that all these were outbreaks of the same kind of plague, namely bubonic, such as the Black Death of 1349, for pestilence, or 'pestis', was a generic name for all epidemic diseases

[1] C. Creighton, *History of Epidemics in Britain*, p. 263.
[2] Idem, p. 304.   [3] Idem, p. 403.

and included fevers, dysentery, agues and delirium, as well as boils and botches. Where the last two afflictions are mentioned in the records, it is indicative of the presence of bubonic plague, since 'botch'—referring to the inflamed swelling in the glandular parts of the human body—was the name given to this kind of plague down to the Elizabethan and Stuart periods.[1] It was the botch, which after a period of dormancy, again became active in 1563–64 in London, and there are references for the same years to outbreaks of plague at Canterbury, Derby, Lichfield and Winchester. In London the death-rate was high; in the last week of September, 1563, the number who died from plague was 1,128, and between June and December of that year there were 17,404 deaths.[2] The outbreak lingered on for two or three years and it was still prevalent in Winchester in June, 1564, when the Burgh-mote considered it unwise that year to cleanse the brooks.

It seems that the endemic incidence of the plague was tolerated up to a point, but whenever it showed signs of exceeding this limit strenuous efforts were made to keep it in check.[3] One may doubt whether the measures taken made any difference; the outbreaks came at intervals, reached their peak, subsided usually after some months, and left the town more or less free of plague until suitable conditions, due in some measure to carelessness regarding sanitation, brought about another noticeable epidemic. Although there were severe outbreaks in London and some provincial towns during the twenty years following the epidemic of 1563, there is no mention of plague in the Winchester records until 1583. In that year orders were agreed upon 'to avoyde the infection of plague and other diseases, in other places dispersed'. These orders have the appearance of what may be termed panic legislation and show clearly that past ordinances had not been carried out as well as they might have been. Rubble, filth and dust had to be cleared immediately from before front and back doors on pain of a fine of 6s. 8d., and if not removed within three days the fine was to be 20s. Every inhabitant

[1] Idem, pp. 207–8. [2] Idem, p. 305. [3] Idem, p. 312.

had to throw five buckets of water in the 'cannell' or gutter running down the middle of the street and rake from it and carry away all the filth between 6 a.m. and 8 p.m., upon pain of a fine of 3s. 4d., or distress of goods and chattels. The Aldermen had to inspect the streets every week to see that they were clean. Dogs and bitches were not to be allowed to go at large and if found abroad were to be killed. The paving before the doors of houses was to be repaired at once. Four women were appointed to examine houses and persons suspected of infection and were to be remunerated for their services. Lastly, 'the orders appoynted in the Citie of London and now imprinted' were to be observed in Winchester in such manner as was thought good by Mr. Mayor and the greater part of his brethren. Amongst these orders were those requiring that a cross of St. Anthony should be painted in blue on the door of each infected house, and that a white rod, two feet long, should be carried for forty days by those who came from plague-stricken houses.

Ten years later, in 1593, there was an outbreak which was far more serious and which called for more extensive preventive measures. No person of whatsoever degree in the City was allowed to receive into his house or custody anyone coming from an infected place, and if anyone was found in the City who had come from such a place he or she was to be expelled at once. This necessitated a thorough search for strangers who, although they might not have come from an infected area, were permitted to stay in Winchester for one night only. Care was taken at the gates where the usual night watch took charge from 9 p.m. to 5 a.m., while a special warder took over during the day-time to examine all suspected persons, especially footmen and those who carried packs of merchandise. In spite of these precautions, a certain Christian Wilson, wife of James Wilson of Kingston or Guildford, both infected places, came into the City with her two children to stay with her mother, widow Shapton. She was immediately expelled with a passport to return to her husband and with the City's charity of two shillings for their relief.

At the same time the Mayor and his brethren, fearing an outbreak of fire in the City, devised regulations for its prevention. These stipulated that the Chamberlains should provide at the City's expense ten leather buckets, that every Alderman should provide himself with two leather buckets and every one of the Twenty-four with one each. It was also hoped that similar buckets would be made available by every gentleman inhabiting the City 'according to their proportion'. The Chamberlains were required to have, in addition, 'two ladders and ropes for the hooks thereof to be in readiness'. Every householder was ordered to have standing at his door, both day and night during the summer time, a tub of water to be cast out in the morning and then refilled, on pain of imprisonment. It was also decreed 'for the swete preservation of the Citye all common nusances forthwith be viewed and the penalty of the ordinances executed upon the offender'.

During the three months following the outbreak of the plague in July, artificers and others engaged in trade were forbidden to receive any wares or merchandise brought by the carrier from London, and anyone transgressing this order was to have his shop windows immediately shut down and not allowed to reopen them for one whole month. The only person who is recorded as having disregarded this order was Anthony Bird, an alderman and magistrate. In September of the same year he was accused before the Mayor and his brethren of having gone to London and brought back certain goods. After the hearing he was given the alternative of being imprisoned in St. John's House for fourteen days or of having his shop windows shut down and barred from selling any wares for the space of one month.

It had been the practice since Norman times to ring the curfew in the City each night and each morning, and for this purpose the bell in the steeple of the church of St. Peter in macellis, in Fleshmonger (St. Peter's) Street, had been used. But it was now realized that owing to the steeple having shown signs of decay the ringing of the curfew had been temporarily suspended. It was therefore decided that 'St.

Peters steple be withall spede reedified at the charge of the Chamberlains of the Citye', an operation which eventually cost ten pounds, 'and that in the mean tyme St. Lawrence bell to be used and made knowen to be used for the towne bell upon all cawses of assemblye or daunger And therefore to be rung at 4 in the morning and 8 in the night'.

Extraordinary measures were taken to ensure that no infected person entered the City, and for this purpose special attention was given to the watch which was kept at the gates. This duty was placed in the hands of the Aldermen, two of whom were allotted to each of the gates, Westgate, Eastgate, Southgate and Kingsgate, and three to Northgate through which came the traffic from London, to 'viewe and surveie dailie the sufficiencie of the warders'. As the number of Aldermen, according to the terms of the charter of 1587, was six, it seems probable that their deputies were called upon to assist with this supervision of the gates. The watch was to be maintained day and night and the Constables had to deliver every Friday into the Mayor's hands the names of all the watchmen and porters assigned to the various gates. The duties of these men stationed at the gates were quite clearly laid down. 'All suspicious persons, rogues, idle persons, disorderers of caryinge of woodde and breakinge of hedges, and stealers of powltrie and piggs, late and nighte watchers unorderlie goinge owte and comynge in erlie and late both on foote and an horsebacke', and all persons coming from infected places, namely London, Farnham, Alton and other places, wishing to enter the City were to be brought at once by the warder to their inn where they were to be examined by the inn-keeper, and if they were not fit persons to be received they were to be dismissed from the City. Westgate and Eastgate only were to be used by horsemen; all other gates were to be shut and only the wicket gate at each one to be opened, and none to be allowed to pass through except those coming to the market with corn, wood or other provisions, and those who were well known to come from places not infected.

A further precaution was taken by having a proclamation read at the fair at Weyhill, near Andover, announcing that on the occasion of the fair to be held at Winchester on St. Edward's Day no one would be allowed to bring into the City any wares except horses and cattle, turner's ware, cooper's and joiner's ware, butter, cheese, corn and grain. Smiths, nailmen, butchers and fishermen would be permitted to enter provided that they did not come from an infected district. It had also been thought wise to restrain people from gathering together in crowds, and to this end an order had been given prohibiting bull-baiting which always attracted large numbers of people. But it was found that contrary to this express commandment and public notice a great concourse 'had nevertheless in open and manifest contempt assembled themselves in places adioyninge to the Citie and there haunted bulbaitinge and other such unlawfull exercises'. It was decided that the persons who had offended in this way should 'for their contempte to the danger of the inhabitants of the Citie and evill example of others' be committed to prison.

In spite of these precautions the plague was still present in the City in the December of 1593, in which month the Mayor and his brethren had to take action concerning an infected house occupied by Thomas Jonson, which was shut up with its occupants and no one allowed to enter. But a woman, known as Pierce the Bagman's wife, went there and took away some yarn 'to the danger of herself and of the inhabitants'. She was therefore committed to the Cage of the City, to remain there 'until furder order be taken' with the door of the Cage closed upon her, and a written notice fixed to the door 'expressinge her contempte, disobedience and danger'. In the same month it was decided to segregate all those suffering from the pestilence and to erect a house for this purpose at the City's expense near the Town Ponds, which were outside the City walls in Danemark or Hyde Mead. Although a special tax, payable weekly, had been levied on all the inhabitants to meet the cost of the precautionary measures which had been taken, it was now found that with this extra expense the contributions were insufficient to meet the whole charge. It was therefore agreed that a sum of five pounds should be taken from the rents derived from property owned by St. John's Hospital, which was in the hands of the City, and devoted to the relief of poor and infected persons.

A rather unusual situation arose concerning a house and shop owned by William Goodall. The shop had been declared an infected place and consequently closed, meanwhile Goodall and his family retired to the adjoining house and went into quarantine. After a while the Mayor and his brethren decided that the danger of further infection had passed, that the shop might be reopened and that Goodall might re-start his business. During the period of closure the City authorities had made a contribution towards the relief of the family, but now when the question of discontinuing the relief arose there was a difference of opinion in the council chamber. Five of the Mayor's colleagues thought that relief should cease immediately, while five others claimed that it should continue for some time longer. A definite decision was reached by the Mayor giving his casting vote in favour of the continuation, and it was finally decided that the relief should be paid for another fortnight. This is the only case noted in the whole of the records of the Mayor giving a casting vote or even of a majority vote being mentioned.

Elizabeth's reign ended as it began with the plague again occupying the attention of the Mayor and his brethren. In 1603 there was a repetition of the orders dealing with the appointment of warders to keep watch on the gates and on infected houses, and provision was made for messengers to attend to the needs of infected persons. Durngate, a postern gate at the north-east corner of the City, was closed and the keys deposited with the Mayor, and the Constables were warned once more to be diligent in keeping out of the City all wanderers and suspected persons. On this occasion the plight of the infected people was such that contributions towards their relief were invited from sources outside the

City. As a result, the Sheriff of the county of Southampton, Sir Benjamin Tichborne, gave forty shillings, Sir Walter Raleigh twenty shillings and Lady Russell nineteen, while the City Recorder, who was one of the members of parliament for Winchester, brought from London five pounds given by the Lord Chancellor and over three pounds contributed by certain judges.

The foregoing account of attempts which were made to produce a clean bill of health in Winchester nearly four hundred years ago leads one to believe that the necessary measures were taken more or less sporadically as occasion demanded, and that as far as the majority of the inhabitants were concerned there was a general air of complacency during the intervals between the various outbreaks of sickness.[1] It may appear surprising that with such insanitary conditions the City did not have epidemics far more frequently and of a more serious nature. But what is more surprising is to find John Trussell, attorney, historian and twice Mayor of the City, writing some thirty years after the death of Queen Elizabeth as follows: 'The scituation of this Cittie is placed in an ayre exceeding good, sweet, temperate and healthfull, of that clensing qualitie that fewe that come from other places to plant heer, no not one amongst forty, but att their first coming they are entertayned with a sharp but short fever, which so throughly clenseth them from all peccant humours, that after their full recoverye their health for the most parte uninterupted hathe no need to challendge any healpe from Aesculapius or his schollers. I affirme yt bowldly and trewly that experience hathe and dothe approve yt that the puritie of the ayre is sutch that neither physitian, apothecarye or surgeon did ever growe rytch by their practice in this place.'[2]

---

[1] The details concerning the outbreaks of plague in Winchester in 1593 and 1603 are to be found in two manuscripts erroneously entitled 'Proceedings of the Corporation, A and B', which record the meetings of the Mayor and his brethren between 1589 and 1605, as previously mentioned in Chapter VI.

[2] John Trussell, 'Origin of Cities', MS., f. 27.

CHAPTER XII

Defence

The ancient city of Winchester lay within the fortified walls though, as pointed out in an earlier chapter, the large suburb on the north-west side and the Soke on the south-east were considered as part of the City. Until recently it was thought that the former Roman town, whose ground level was from four to six feet below the present street level, was much smaller than that enclosed by the medieval walls, but more recent excavations have suggested that this was not so, and it is generally agreed that the Roman plan gave the main pattern to the later lay-out which comprised an area of 138 acres. This was in the shape of an irregular quadrilateral measuring 860 yards from the Eastgate to the Westgate with the High Street joining the two gates, and 780 yards from the Northgate to the Southgate which were joined by a street intersecting the High Street at right angles. At the south-west angle of the City stood the royal castle. Even before the Norman Conquest every freeman was under an obligation to help with the maintenance of fortifications and the repair of bridges and to serve in the fyrd or militia.[1] But afterwards, the citizens of Winchester were excused military service, though they had still to maintain their own walls and gates (except Southgate and Kingsgate, which were kept in good order by the Priory of St. Swithun), and this obligation was discharged by payment of murage. It is very probable that at one time the obligation had taken

[1] J. S. Furley, *City Government*, pp. 102–3.

the shape of personal service which at a later date had been compounded for in the form of a money rate.

In various rolls dating from the thirteenth century onwards there are references to the ruinous state of the walls and fortifications, and to the orders issued by the Mayor and Bailiffs for their upkeep and repair. There are also records of the inability of the citizens to raise sufficient money to meet the cost of the reparations, and of petitions to the King for financial assistance for this purpose. But in the sixteenth century less is heard about the walls although it was reported to the Burgh-mote in 1564 that the Marquis of Winchester had defrayed the cost of their repair, and following this it was ordained that 'to thentent the walles of the Cytie may be kepte and preservyd frome ivye springalles and weeds which hathe byn the chefist decaye of the same walles the Mayor shall yerely geve commandment to the chamberlaynes to cause the same ivye springalles and weedes to be ridd betweene the last daye of Maye and the fyrst daye of Julye'.[1,2] Throughout the reign of Elizabeth there appears in the Chamberlains' rolls an annual expenditure of 4s. 4d. (that is, one penny per week) for this purpose. At the same meeting of the Burgh-mote it was agreed that 'whereas William Lawrens hathe latelye purchased one medowe plot lienge nighe to the towne ponde and can not convenientlye come into the same medowe with cart and cariage it shalbe lawfull to the said William Lawrens his heyres and assignes to make a sufficient gate for a carte to passe throughe the towne waule where nowe he hathe a doere And that he shall have from hensforthe free ingresse egresse and regresse into and from the sayde grounde bye and throughe the same gate with carte and other cariage for ever. Provided that he shall shut the same gate att all tymes at the commandment of the Mayor for the salvacion of the Quenes Citye and yeldinge yerlie to the Cytie a pennie'.[3]

The above-mentioned William Lawrens was a lawyer who

[1] 1st Bk. Ord., f. 138.   [2] Springalles = saplings.
[3] 1st Bk. Ord., f. 139.

held the office of Mayor on four occasions during his life-time and sat as one of the burgesses for the City in all Queen Mary's parliaments. He was again elected as one of the bur-gesses to Queen Elizabeth's first parliament, and in this capacity he presented to Sir William Cecil, Secretary of State, the following petition: 'After our humble com-mendacion unto your Honourable Lordeshipe It may please the same to call to remembrance our former sute made unto your Lordship to be a meane for us to the Quenes Majestie for the obteyninge of the Constableshipe of the Castle of Winchester And for as miche as the Quenys Majestie of whome we had a graunte is departed this present liffe whose sowle Jesu pardon And therefor the graunte voide We humblye beseeche your good Lordeshipe to revive our sute again to the Quenis Majestie that nowe is and to be a mediator for us that we maye have leike graunte of her grace for the custodye of the said Castle.'[1]

In March, 1559, there came the reply, in Latin, of which the following is a translation: 'Know that by our special grace we give to the Mayor Bailiffs and Commonalty of our City of Winton the office of Constable of our Castle of Winton and the custody thereof besides all commodities rents profits emoluments to the said Castle pertaining And also all lands and pastures in the said castle called the Castle Green with the ditch both within and without the Castle called Castle Ditch And we ordain and constitute the said Mayor etc., Constable and Guardian of the said Castle To have and to hold enjoy and occupy the said office and the said lands and ditches to them and their successors etc.'[2] Immediately, the Mayor and his brethren, to show their gratitude to William Lawrens for the services which he had rendered, decided that for his life-time or as long as he lived in the City he should have the free use of the herbage of the ditch on the east side of the castle.[3] Eighteen years later, however, the Burgh-mote

[1] State Papers, Domestic, Vol. I, No. 35, 1558.
[2] Patent Roll, No. 906, membrane 9, 1559.
[3] 1st Bk. Ord., f. 121.

decreed that 'whereas Mr. William Lawrens hath the east diches of the castell at will onlie and not for any terme certeyne and refuseth to have turves digged there for the buttes of the Cytie, yt ys agreed now that yf he suffer turves to be digged there for the same buttes at all tymes needefull and also a paire of buttes to be made and mayntened in the saied diches for children that then he shall have and enioye the same as heretofore he hath done And that if he shall at any tyme henceforth refuse so to doo and suffer then yt shall and may be at all tymes after suche refusall lawfull to the maior with the more parte of his brethren to let the same dyches to any other.'[1]

The east ditches to which reference has been made were those lying immediately outside the Castle walls on the eastern side and adjoining Bewmonds, which was an enclosed space stretching eastwards down the slope towards Gold or Southgate Street. There were ditches or moats on all four sides of the Castle, but though there is evidence that in earlier times they were filled with water from springs in the hill to the west of the City, it is obvious from the leases granted in Elizabethan times that they were then dry and used as pasture. The Castle itself, dating from late Norman times, covered an area of about 5 acres. Forming a sort of semi-bastion, with a maximum width of 80 yards from east to west and a length of 280 yards from north to south, it projected beyond the City walls in the south-west angle of the defences. Milner, writing in 1798, gives a description and a sketch of the Castle, and states that his ideas of it were gathered from a sketch made by Speed in 1615, from personal observation of the ruins and of excavations made in his time, and from 'certain hints which occur in ancient writers concerning it'. All that now stands is the Great Hall which has been associated with many important events in the nation's history; the remainder was demolished after its capture by Oliver Cromwell in 1645.

The condition of the Castle in Elizabeth's reign is well revealed in a survey made in 1579. In January of that year Sir

[1] Idem, f. 196.

Richard Norton, Walter Sandys and James Wright delivered to Lord Burghley, Lord Treasurer of England, the report of the investigations which they had made as commissioners appointed by Her Majesty's Court of the Exchequer for that purpose. It appears from this report that the Mayor and Commonalty had previously sent a petition to Lord Burghley asking for some relief from the financial burden which the custody of the Castle entailed. The commissioners' findings may be summarized as follows:

(*a*) The ditches and rampart on the west side of the Castle, covering about 3 acres, were found to be overgrown with moss and small bushes. They yielded an annual rent to the City of 20*s.* which was thought to be reasonable.

(*b*) Within the Castle itself there was the Castle Green of 1½ acres which was let to the keeper of the Great Hall for 10*s.* a year on condition that he kept the Hall clean and ready for the Assizes and Sessions of the County. The commissioners thought this an excessive rent, and made a special note of the 'olde walls and ruinous rooms' which they found surrounding the Green.

(*c*) The ditch on the east side of the Castle, facing Southgate Street, was similar in its overgrown condition to that on the west; it contained about 1½ acres and was let for 5*s.* a year. They thought this should be increased to 10*s.*

(*d*) The commissioners had a conference with the Mayor and his brethren who pointed out that they had spent £14 and other odd sums on repairing the middle roof of the Great Hall, although the letters patent which gave them custody of the Castle did not require them to do so. They added that no other custodian would have been so careful in carrying out such repairs and that in time the Assizes and Sessions of the Shire would assuredly have been transferred elsewhere to the great prejudice and hindrance of the citizens.

(*e*) The commissioners inspected the Great Hall and after consulting workmen and others found that Her Majesty had at considerable cost repaired the south aisle, but that if the north aisle were not speedily repaired, being at this time 'very ruinous and gretelie decaied', the whole structure would shortly collapse and thus the repairs already undertaken by Her Majesty and the City would be of no avail.

(f) The commissioners concluded by supporting the City's petition that the Lord Treasurer should grant financial aid.

From time immemorial watch and ward had been kept in the City and every townsman had to do his share. Each aldermanry supplied a certain number of householders for the nightly watch and to them was handed over the 'great horn', with which they roused the citizens in case of danger. This task was generally disliked, and there are recorded instances of persons evading it and being fined for refusing the 'great horn of the watch'. The selection of suitable persons, both men and women, for this duty was in the hands of the Aldermen, who, at times, had evidently made their choice in an unfair and arbitrary manner, for in 1423, after vigorous protests especially from the poorer section of the population, the Burgh-mote decided that a new system should be adopted.[1] Henceforth, starting at Newbridge in the lower part of the High Street, the tenants of six consecutive houses were taken for the watch on one night, the next six for the following night, until street by street the whole City had borne the burden equally. As regards the details of the defensive forces of the City in Elizabethan times, other than watch and ward, the evidence is unfortunately very fragmentary. It is known that the large cities and boroughs had their companies of men-at-arms and, no doubt, members of these volunteered for duty in time of threatened invasion as, for example, at the time of the Spanish Armada when Portsmouth was garrisoned by Hampshire men who were found arms and uniform and victualled themselves on eightpence a day. From the *English Mercurie*, published at Whitehall, 23rd July, 1588, for the prevention of false reports, it is learnt that 'large bodyes of militia' were 'disposed along the coasts under experienced commanders with proper instructions how to behave'.

[1] *Black Book*, pp. 59–60.

Written in English, on four sheets of paper, there has survived an inventory entitled 'A view of able men, armour and weapons within the citie of Winchester, taken the 26 day of September, 1559'. In this there come first the names of men entered as archers and then others as billmen. At the end is a summary of able men showing 18 archers, 45 billmen and 2 gunners, making a total of 65 able men. Presumably these were men whose arms were provided by the City, for there follows another list of men, containing 73 names, together with a strange assortment of weapons and armour which they could muster and which were apparently their own property. These include 'alman rivattes, 42; bowes 30; sheffes of arrows, 29; jackes, 2; sculles, 25; splintes, 35; sallettes, 37; swordes, 45; daggers, 43; billes, 54; polaxes and gleves, 3'. Five of the men in the second list also appear in the first one—Richard Edes, a billman, also had a bow and a sheaf of arrows; Thomas Bran and John White, billmen, also had their own bills; John Chirche, a billman, and Thomas Thorpe, an archer, also had swords and daggers. There were, therefore, should need arise, at least 135 armed men in Winchester in 1559. There was another 'view' taken twelve months later, when the number had risen to 218, but many were without weapons. To overcome this difficulty, an arrangement was made whereby the older and more prominent citizens handed over their weapons and armour to the younger men. It is interesting to compare these numbers with those of Southampton where, in 1570, there were 439 able men supplied with arms and armour, and in 1577, 421 men armed with culivers, pikes, bows and bills.

A closer examination of the Winchester lists of able men shows, as one would expect, that the magistrates and the wealthier citizens were the better armed. They all had 'rivets', together with a number of other pieces of armour and weapons. As examples, William Lawrens, former mayor and member of parliament, had 'alman rivets, one harquebus, one sallett, one longe bowe, one sheffe of arrows, one scull according to the statute', and Richard Bethell, another former mayor, had 'a corselet, one pyke, one harquebus, one sallett, one longe bowe, one sheff of arrows and one scull according to the statute'. The commonest weapon was the 'black bill', which was also required by statute to be kept in readiness. This was a time when the harquebus, an early type of portable gun supported on a tripod or a forked rest, and the culverin, another small fire-arm, were increasingly being used by armed forces but, as shown above, Winchester could produce only two of the former. The long bow was still in use and its practice by young people and able bodied men up to 60 years of age, 'spiritual men and justices excepted', was compulsory. The 'Herbar' (Orams Arbour) was the 'lawful place' for every inhabitant of the City 'to shoote and use shootinge', and failure to comply with the ordinance meant a fine. As late as 1589, more than thirty men were presented before the Court at one session 'for that they had not used nor exercised shootinge in longe bowes by the space of one month last paste contrary to the fourme of the statute', and each one was fined 6s. 8d., which was quite a heavy penalty in those days.

Musters were held twice a year and the scene of these assemblies was the 'Herbar', outside the Westgate, where it was lawful 'to and for the Mayor Bayliffes and Commonalty and other inhabitants of the Cytie to make their musters and other lawfull assemblies'. On this spot, at the times appointed by William Abere, the muster master for the County of Southampton, acting on the instructions of the Lord Lieutenant, the men-at-arms gathered to be inspected by Sir Walter Sandys, captain of the militia, and to perform their march-past to the music supplied by the 'band' which, as at Southampton, consisted of two drummers and one fife player. From the Chamberlains' rolls it is gathered that the expenses of these musters were met by the 'chamber' of the City, that is, from the City's annual revenues. The muster book, giving a complete account of the number of men and weapons on parade, was carried by one Thomas Vanderplank to the Lord Lieutenant, the Marquis of Winchester, at his manor of Abbotstone, near Alresford, and he received fourpence for his labours. On another occasion, Michael Marks took it to the Earl of Sussex, the Portsmouth garrison commander, and he was paid 1s. 6d. The fife player received a similar sum and the drummers 1s. each; twine for the cords of the drums cost 6d.; 'two pounds of match' cost 6d.; and William Abere, the muster master, was rewarded with £2.

The Chamberlains' responsibilities did not end there, however, for they were also called upon to pay for the supper given to Captain Sir Walter Sandys and Mr. Abere at the White Horse Inn after each muster, and for the dinner given to the Marquis of Winchester whenever he came in person to take the muster. Between each of these assemblies the arms had to be cared for and it was decided that 'Gyles Blonden shall have the keepinge of the armes of the Cytie by inventorye and shall dress scoure buckell leather and varnishe the same at all tymes nedefulle during his lyfe and that he have yerelie forty shillings'. In 1597 the Mayor, William Badger, punished a certain John Corshall who 'being commanded by the Maior to fetch the corselet of Mr. William Waller and to bring it and scour it, and for that he did not yet go was committed to ward and the xii^th day being brought before Mr. Maior and his brethren at the counsell house confessed the commandment and his faulte and sayeth he is sorrie for it'.

It is remarkable that neither parish nor civic manuscripts, written in Winchester at the time when preparations were being made to resist invasion by the Spanish Armada, throw any great light on the excitement which must have prevailed in England, and especially in the southern counties, at the time. The Armada appeared in the English Channel on the 19th July, 1588, but for some time previous to this the Queen had called for funds in order to equip forces adequate to resist it. Hampshire was not asked in vain and the county made a generous response. Five citizens of Winchester appear in the list of subscribers, namely, William Badger—£50, William Symonds—£50, William Burton, Edward Cole, William Hodson—£25 each. There is no direct evidence to show whether any of the citizens joined the armed forces on land or sea, though their services were undoubtedly sought. As has been mentioned, it is possible that Winchester men were to be found in the militia which was stationed in and around Portsmouth, but it is unlikely that any were to be found among the sailors of the English fleet, since the Admiral, Lord Howard, had only three small vessels from Portsmouth and none at all from Southampton among his fleet. But there was an attempt to press local men for the navy, for William Bennett, Master of Her Majesty's bake-house for the Navy, sent a letter to the Mayor, Edward Cole, asking him to dispatch certain bakers in the City for service at Portsmouth. The Mayor not only showed 'slack diligence' in providing the bakers, but when a man had actually accepted 'pressed' money he took steps to see he was released. This brought an indignant letter from the master baker who declared that it was a shame to the City that they should have so many women bakers, and that after a while they would fain have to take them to serve the Queen. This letter is one of the few documents among the City's records which give information about those stirring times, but there is a reminder of the part played by the fleet in the shape of a monument in St. Bartholomew's Church, Hyde, to the memory of Edmund Norton, gentleman, of Tisted and Avington, who received a pension of 2s. a day for his good service by sea in 1588.

CHAPTER XIII

The Church

When Elizabeth succeeded her half-sister Mary on the throne in 1588, there was considerable speculation as to how long the new régime would last, and some even predicted its immediate downfall. But from the day of her arrival in London on the 23rd November to the coronation day on the 15th January, Elizabeth deliberately wooed the people of the capital by joining whole-heartedly in their festivities and in revelling with them in the enthusiastic loyalty which they displayed. Her first objective was to show them that she was keenly interested in their welfare, and that her hopes for the future were centred on recovering for the Crown the goodwill which her predecessor had dissipated. The country was no longer to be at the mercy of Spanish or Papal influence; future policy was to be based on its vital needs. 'Elizabeth struck the key-note to a new age when she resolved to identify herself with her people', and it was not long before there were distinct signs of a revolution in national policy.[1] There were also changes impending with regard to religion, but the signs of these were not so easily discernible because they were overshadowed by the foremost political question of the day, namely, the Queen's personal and dynastic security. With the principal fortresses of Portsmouth and Berwick falling into ruin and the country bare of munitions, with an empty treasury and a huge debt owing to foreign creditors, a decisive breach with the Papacy had to

[1] J. B. Black, *The Reign of Elizabeth*, p. 4.

229

be avoided. The wisest policy, therefore, was one of extreme caution until a stable government was established and a religious policy, which would secure the allegiance of the maximum number of her subjects, could be devised.

The difficult situation in which Elizabeth found herself with regard to religious affairs had its roots in the quarrel which her father, Henry VIII, had provoked with the Pope, and in the ensuing controversies which prevailed during the latter part of his reign and in those of Edward VI and Mary, who succeeded him. During these troublesome times one of the most prominent figures was Stephen Gardiner, who had been consecrated to the see of Winchester in 1531, a year after the death of Cardinal Wolsey whom he succeeded as Bishop, and to whom he largely owed his advancement. Gardiner sat in court with Archbishop Cranmer when the latter pronounced the marriage of Henry VIII and Catherine of Aragon null and void in 1533, and later he acknowledged the King as supreme head of the English Church. Although he was prepared to repudiate the Pope's supremacy, he held firmly to the rest of the Roman Catholic doctrines. He witnessed the surrender to the King of all the monastic lands of St. Swithun's Priory by William Kingsmill, the last Prior, and the subsequent institution of the new Chapter, consisting of a Dean and twelve Prebendaries, with Kingsmill himself as the first Dean.

At the accession of Edward VI in 1547, Bishop Gardiner entreated the Lord Protector Somerset to be moderate and cautious, and urged that the period of the minority of the King was not a suitable time for any revolutionary religious movement. But his advice was ignored and for a time he was imprisoned in the Fleet. Shortly afterwards he was ordered to preach before the Court, on St. Peter's Day, 1548, a sermon embodying the views of the Lord Protector and his friends. His discourse, however, revealed that he had no sympathy with the destructive elements developed by the reformers, and next day he found himself a prisoner in the Tower, and a year later, after trial, deposed from his bishopric. He languished in his prison for five years and did not return to Winchester until Mary came to the throne in 1553, when he was reinstated, and twelve months later he officiated at the marriage of the Queen with Philip of Spain in the cathedral.

Within another fifteen months Gardiner was dead. His successor was Dr. John White, a native of Farnham, who had been educated at Winchester College of which he had later become Headmaster and then Warden. It was whilst he held the wardenship that he was committed to the Tower 'for refusing to give in to the irreligious measures of the Duke of Somerset'. He lay there until Mary's accession, when he was raised to the see of Lincoln and three years later, in 1556, translated to Winchester. This move to his native diocese undoubtedly gave him great pleasure, although it cost him £1,000 a year which he had to pay out of the revenue of his see to Cardinal Pole, who 'complained that the temporalities of Canterbury', of which he was Archbishop, 'were so ruined by his predecessor, Cranmer, that he could not live in a manner suitable to his rank'.[1] Bishop White's episcopate was short but eventful. In the first year, 1557, three persons were burnt as heretics at Southwark, which was then in his diocese; the next year, 1558, a gentleman of some standing, Thomas Benbridge, suffered a similar fate at Winchester, while White himself, by his indiscreet utterances in speaking the funeral oration of Queen Mary, incurred the displeasure of the new Queen, Elizabeth; finally, in 1559, he incurred further displeasure by defending the ancient faith with tremendous vigour at a public conference at Westminster Abbey and by threatening to excommunicate Elizabeth. He was again sent to the Tower, and when he refused to take the oath of supremacy he was deprived of his bishopric.

For over a year and a half the bishopric remained vacant, and it was during this period that Elizabeth deposed the Marian bishops and attempted to reconstitute the Church. She had required the clergy to acknowledge her as 'the only supreme governor of this realm as well in all spiritual and

[1] Milner, *History of Winchester*, Vol. I, p. 278.

ecclesiastical things or causes as temporal'. The bishops, with one exception, Kitchen of Llandaff, refused to have anything to do with this oath of supremacy or with the new prayer book, but the lower ranks of the clergy were not so courageous. As a modern historian says, 'the one indubitable fact is that the Marian pastorate in overwhelming numbers passed over into the service of the establishment without a murmur'.[1] The acceptance by the laity naturally followed that of the lower clergy, though it was by no means complete and it varied in different parts of the country. In Winchester there was a comparatively small number of citizens who resisted the law and became recusants, paying the usual fine when ordered to do so; the remainder could most probably be divided into two sections, namely, those who, unmoved by the doctrinal changes imposed upon them but attracted by the use of the English tongue in the Anglican service, continued as a matter of habit and convenience to attend their parish churches, and those, whose conscience being troubled, made a compromise by attending the service which they felt to be heretical and yet remaining at heart faithful to the Roman creed. As for the clergy in Winchester, it has been claimed that 'a greater proportion of the dignitaries of the cathedral and of the masters and fellows of the college made the sacrifice', by refusing to take the oath of supremacy, 'than of any other cathedral or learned society in England'.[2]

When at last the bishopric was filled, the choice fell upon Robert Horne, who had been Dean of Durham but during the persecution of Mary's reign had gone into exile, from which he is reputed to have returned a fiery Puritan. From the day of his arrival in Winchester he had no easy task. In June, 1561, he reported to the Queen's minister, Sir William Cecil, that many churches were destitute of incumbents. Twelve months later, in reply to an inquiry made by Archbishop Parker, he declared that he was still faced with a considerable shortage of clergy, especially in Winchester.[3] Of

[1] Black, p. 17.   [2] Milner, Vol. I, p. 281.
[3] Library, Corpus Christi College, Cambridge, MS., No. 122.

the Marian Dean and twelve prebendaries of the cathedral only six had been willing to take the oath of supremacy; the remainder, along with the headmaster and second master of the college, on account of their refusal had been deprived of their offices. This information was given in the reply to the Archbishop's inquiry of 1562, together with the news that in the City and the Soke only the Rector of All Saints' with St. Thomas's, the Vicar of St. John's and the Rector of Winnall could be numbered among the beneficed clergy, a striking contrast to the normal number of eight or ten as seen before and after this time at the Bishop's visitations of 1555 and 1572. Further evidence of the situation within the City is contained in an ordinance of the Burgh-mote dated 1562, to the effect that 'iiii churches remayne to be servyd within the Cytie that is to saye St. Thomas Saynt Laurens St. Mary kalender and St. Maurice And for the better servinge of these iiii churches the Cytie be dyvided into iiii equall portions of leike valeue by suche men and so manye as to master mayor and the xxiiii[ti] shalbe thought good'.[1] It is difficult to say why a matter of this kind was decided by the municipal authority, but it may be that the decision to retain the four parishes was made by the Bishop, who then asked the Mayor to settle the boundaries of the respective parishes.

There is some doubt as to the date when this ordinance was put into effect, for it was not until eighteen years later, and actually after the death of Bishop Horne, that, for example, the union of the parishes of St. Peter in macellis (in the Shambles) and St. Thomas was ratified. Then in 1580 the Mayor, Bailiffs and Commonalty declared that 'for divers good and lawfull consideracions us thereunto movinge we doo by theise presents as well geve and graunte our full consent assent and agreement unto the union knittinge together and consolidation of the saide parishe churches to contynewe endure and remayne as one parishe for ever'.[2] The redundant parish churches fell into disrepair and joined the large number of decayed religious edifices which were to be

---

[1] 1st Bk. Ord., f. 134. [2] 2nd Ledger Book, f. 247.

found in and around the City. If one can rely on the lists given by Milner, which were for the most part compiled from bishops' registers dating from 1282, there had been in the liberty and soke of Winchester no fewer than ninety-two churches, chapels and convents, including those belonging to the various religious communities.[1] It is possible that in these lists there is a certain amount of duplication, but much corroborative evidence concerning the sites of these churches is to be found in the tarrage rolls, the *Black Book* and the Books of Ordinances, and particularly in the Ledger Books which contain copies of leases of City property.

The concentration of the religious life of the City, other than that of the cathedral, within the four remaining parish churches was not wholly due to the confusion created by Henry VIII and continued by his successors. It was in far greater measure the result of the general decline of the City which had been going on for at least two hundred years. The tarrage roll of 1416 drew attention to the sites of many former churches, the City's petition to Henry VI in 1439 recorded the decay of seventeen parish churches during the preceding fifty years, and finally between 1536 and 1540 there came the dissolution of the abbeys, friaries, convents and hospitals, both within and without the City, so that the Cathedral, St. Mary's College and the Hospital of St. Cross alone remained of the former religious establishments with which Winchester had been so well endowed. It was to the City thus despoiled that the Protestant Bishop Horne came early in Elizabeth's reign, entrusted with the task of securing uniformity of worship amongst clergy and laity. His early reports to the Privy Council were most discouraging, for although there was not so much recusancy in the southern part of the country as in the north, he complained that he had so far failed 'to reduce the inhabitants of the City of Winchester to good uniformity in religion' or 'to have the cures there served so as the common prayer might be frequented, which have not been done since Massing time'.

[1] Milner, Vol. II, Appendix VII.

Two years later he wrote ,'Winchester is most noted in Hampshire either for good example or evil—all that bear authority there, except one or two, are addict to the old superstition and earnest fautors thereof.'

In support of this claim by Bishop Horne that most of those in authority at Winchester were Roman Catholic at heart, there are the two letters sent by the Secretary of the Privy Council on 4th November, 1564, one to the Sheriff of Hampshire asking him to declare 'such particular matters as hee knoweth to be objected againste the Mayour and Baily of Winchester touching matters of Religion', and the other demanding the appearance before the Queen's Privy Council of Robert Hodson, Mayor of Winchester, Richard Birde and John Winnall, Bailiffs, and Richard Burton, a former mayor, to answer such matters as should be objected against them. A week later, on the 11th, the Mayor and the two Bailiffs, but not Richard Burton, appeared to answer for 'their contemptuous behaveour' in not aiding John Bedham of Winchester, who had been appointed by the Sheriff of Hampshire, by virtue of letters from the Lords of the Council, to apprehend the wife of one Harman of Winchester. All three were committed to the Marshalsea prison in Southwark, where debtors and those guilty of contempt of court were usually lodged; but on the 23rd of the same month, 'uppon their submyssions' they were released and order was given that bonds should be taken in the sum of 100 marks ($£66$ 13s. 4d.) apiece to use their utmost diligence in apprehending Anthony Harman of Winchester and, if he should be found, in taking good bonds with sureties of him to appear personally before the Privy Council to answer such matters as at his coming should be declared unto him. It would seem that Robert Hodson and Richard Birde were not without the sympathetic support of their fellow freemen, for in a postscript to the Chamberlains' Accounts for 1564 there is the acquiescence of the eight auditors to the payment of $£6$ to Robert Hodson and $£4$ to Richard Birde to cover their expenses when summoned before the Queen's Council. John Winnall would no doubt have been similarly treated had he not died shortly after his release from prison.

There can be little doubt that at this time great disorder prevailed in the Church, due to opposition from Catholics and Puritans alike. The initial dispute started by the latter concerning the comparatively small matter of the use of vestments gradually widened until eventually the use of organs in churches, of the ring in the marriage ceremony and of the sign of the cross in baptism, kneeling at communion, the excessive number of holy days and 'other dregs of popery' were brought into the field of bitter controversy. Many of the bishops had openly displayed dislike of vestments and at the same time shown sympathy with the Puritans. Prominent among these bishops was Horne of Winchester, of whose episcopate it has been said that it was 'characterized by wholesale destruction all over the diocese, as well as at New College, Oxford, of missals, stained-glass windows and rich architecture'.[1] Milner, representing the Roman Catholic view, is particularly severe on him, stating that his appointment to Winchester was 'a calamity to the City as well as to the bishopric'.[2] Quoting from another source, he accuses him of having been 'a man that could never abide any ancient monuments, acts or deeds, that gave any light of or to godly religion'. 'Not content,' he continues, 'with removing or defacing the roods or crucifixes, with such other images or paintings, it appears that he also destroyed the numerous statues and chapels which adorned the cathedral, though these have been left standing in so many other churches. The venerable chapter-house also and cloisters, part of which was the work of Wykeham, were pulled down in his episcopacy, to the defacing of the City and the weakening of the church itself.'[3]

Although Milner further accuses Horne of showing a 'vindictive and intolerant spirit' towards Bonner, the former Bishop of London who was now in prison within Horne's diocese, which was 'aimed at revenging the blood of the

[1] W. Benham, *Diocesan Histories, Winchester*, p. 173.
[2] Milner, Vol. I, p. 283.   [3] Idem, p. 284.

Protestants put to death in the former reign' of Mary, he does admit that during the twenty years of Horne's episcopate no capital punishment took place in Winchester, or its neighbourhood, on the score of religion.[1,2] It must be recorded to the credit of Bishop Horne that he and his Dean, John Watson, gave £40 and £60 respectively to the City coffer.[3] The total sum of £100, known as the Bishops' Stock, was to be used, by way of loans without interest, to help freemen to revive trading facilities in the City. It was perhaps appropriate that Horne should be succeeded by the Dean who had shared his regard for the welfare of the City. John Watson, Doctor of Medicine, had been educated as a physician, but took orders at the beginning of Elizabeth's reign when many laymen were being ordained to fill the places of the ejected Catholic clergy. He held many benefices, being successively Prebendary of Winchester, Archdeacon of Surrey, Chancellor of St. Paul's, Dean of Winchester, and finally Bishop of the same diocese to which he was consecrated in 1580.

During the past twenty years Puritanism had been steadily growing. It was a protest not only against religious forms which its adherents claimed had no basis in the Scriptures, but also against the 'spirit of greed and materialism that saturated society and corrupted the Church'.[4] There is trustworthy evidence of several bishops indulging in simoniacal practices and of the Queen and her courtiers showing scant respect for the sanctity of church property. A letter from the Warden and Fellows of Winchester College to the Queen, dated 13th March, 1581, throws a curious light upon the state of the Church.[5] It states that at her request they have given a lease for forty years of the parsonage and rectory of Downton, Wiltshire, to Her Majesty, understanding that she means to confer it on Mr. Wylkes, clerk of the Privy Council, in consideration of the service done to the Queen and the realm, but they 'doe most humbly desyre and beseeche that her

[1] Idem, p. 289.   [2] Idem, p. 291.   [3] 1st Bk. Ord., f. 224.
[4] Black, p. 153.
[5] State Papers, Elizabeth, Vol. cliii (quoted by Benham).

Majestie will make stay of the lyke suites to be hereafter tendered' by any person unto Her Highness, and they request her to give letters of assurance on this point, in order 'to discharge them of the hasarde of the decay of their mayntenance, the hurtinge of soe worthye a foundation and the burden of their consciences being sworne to the preservation thereof as far forthe as the authorities of their founder might extende and their oath as dewtifull subiectes maye be measured by her Majesty and the lawes of her Realme in that behalfe provided'.

The next bishop, Thomas Cooper, who followed Watson in 1583, was translated from Lincoln and held the see of Winchester for ten years, during which time the punishment of Catholics began to take a more severe form. Ever since Elizabeth's accession there had been a rounding up of Catholics whenever there was diplomatic tension with Rome or with Spain, and recusancy had been punished by a fine of one shilling per Sunday in accordance with the provision of the Act of Uniformity. But since the publication of the papal bull excommunicating the Queen in 1570, there had been no end to Jesuit intrigues which during the next ten years led to an intensification of the campaign by the government against all Catholics. Recusancy was punished by the infliction of the enormous fine of £20 per month; attendance at mass cost the offender 100 marks or a year's imprisonment; proselytes and proselytizing priests were judged traitors; and in 1585, all 'jesuits, seminary priests and other priests' were ordered to leave the country within forty days. It was during the time of Bishop Cooper that capital punishment was inflicted for the first time in Elizabeth's reign at Winchester, and according to Milner four persons were executed.[1] Elizabeth's government claimed that those who suffered in this way did so 'because they were traitors and sedition-mongers; but the Catholic priests were just as convinced that they were martyrs for their faith. Therein lies the profound pathos of this terrible time'.[2]

[1] Milner, Vol. I, pp. 291–5.   [2] Black, p. 149.

Throughout the whole of the reign there was this confusion between politics and religion, since both the reformation settlement of religion in England and the safety of the State itself were in danger. This is well illustrated by the trial, followed by the sentence of death, of Mary, Queen of Scots, in 1586. News of this event was bound to cause serious repercussions not only throughout this country, but also in Scotland and across the Channel in France and Spain. To explain her action in this matter to her own subjects, Elizabeth sent a proclamation entitled 'for the publishinge and declaringe of the sentence latelie geven against the Queene of Scotts' to all the important cities and towns, with the command that it should be proclaimed publicly, and then returned to the Chancery as quickly as possible. The copy of the proclamation received at Winchester is endorsed thus: 'the xii[th] of december 1586 betwene the howres of fyve and sixe of the clocke of the nighte in the afternoone of the same daie . . . Dorington one of her maiesties messengers did deliver unto the maior and bayliffes of the Citie this proclamacion within written and the writ therunto annexed. And we the saide Maior and bayliffes callinge unto us the Recorder Justices Aldermen and Citizens the xiii[th] of this instant month of December Anno Domini 1586 in the presence of them and of divers others her maiesties faithfull subiectes betwene the howres of nyne and tenne of clocke in the high strete at the market crosse beinge the usuall place for proclayminge her maiesties proclamacions did then and there accordinge to the tenor and effecte of the saide writ and proclamacion solemplie proclayme and openlie publishe the saide proclamacion And the contentes therof as by the saide writ it was to us commaunded.'[1]

The proclamation tells of Mary's complicity in the Babington plot for the destruction of the sovereign and the subversion of the realm, her trial according to law, and the judgment of the thirty-six commissioners. It goes on to declare that the carrying out of the sentence of death is very

[1] 1st Bk. Ord., f. 250.

much against Elizabeth's wishes, but that Parliament, in order to safeguard the country and its people, had insisted upon it. There is no mention of religion in the proclamation, but Mary died on the scaffold asserting that she was a martyr for her religion and not a criminal, and her death brought about an almost unprecedented explosion of wrath throughout Catholic Europe.

At the same time that Bishop Cooper was busily attending to recusants and seminary priests, he was also engaged in controversy against the Puritans who wished to abolish, amongst other things, the episcopate. Elizabeth had dealt hardly with the Puritans, just as she had with the Catholics, when they refused to conform to the usages of the national church. She suppressed the Puritans' religious meetings and treated their pamphlets as seditious. The 'Martin Marprelate' tracts appeared in 1587–88 and were intended, as their title suggests, to 'mar' the bishops. Written in a jocular and ribald manner, they tended to destroy much of the traditional reverence for the episcopate. After a while the secret press on which they were printed was seized, and of the originators one John Penry, a minister, was executed, and another, Job Throgmorton, allowed to go free. Some of the tracts were answered in an equally scurrilous manner, and Bishop Cooper was among those who joined in the controversy. His work, 'Admonition to the People of England', composed with gravity and elaborate argument, brought upon him a storm of furious and coarse invective, one of the rejoinders to him being entitled, 'Have ye any work for the Cooper?'[1]

When Bishop Cooper died in 1594, he was succeeded by the second William of Wykekam, who followed him from Lincoln. Unfortunately he held the office for ten weeks only before he died, but during that time he preached before the Queen and with remarkable courage informed her that, if the possessions of the see of Winchester were plundered as systematically during the next thirty years as they had been during the past thirty years of her reign, there would not

[1] Benham, p. 182.

The Church

remain sufficient income to keep the roof on the cathedral. From a monument in the church at Easton, near Winchester, it is learnt that William's wife was Anthonina, the daughter of William Barlow, Bishop of Chichester, and that she had four sisters, all of whom were married to bishops. These were Anne, wife of Herbert Westfayling, Bishop of Hereford, Frances, wife of Toby Mathew, Bishop of Durham and later Archbishop of York, Margaret, wife of William Overton, Bishop of Coventry and Lichfield, and Elizabeth, who married William Day, Provost of Eton, who followed the second Wykeham at Winchester, but held the bishopric for two years only. Next came Dr. Thomas Bilson who had been educated at Winchester College and New College, Oxford, and became successively Warden of Winchester College, Bishop of Worcester, and in 1597 Bishop of Winchester. He was no stranger, therefore, to the City and it is not surprising to read that shortly after his arrival here it was decided by the Mayor and his brethren that their wives should go to the Bishop's Palace at Wolvesey to welcome Mrs. Bilson and present her, at the City's expense, with a sugar loaf weighing ten pounds.

In the later part of Elizabeth's reign the increased activity of the ecclesiastical commissioners and the excessive fines which many were unable to pay in full led to the apprehension of many recusants. When Bishop Bilson came to Winchester he found an extraordinary state of affairs at the gaol in Winchester Castle where the recusants were imprisoned. In a letter to Sir Robert Cecil, Secretary to the Queen, dated November, 1599, the Bishop described how he had committed a priest named Kenyon to the gaol to be kept in strict confinement.[1] But 'he was rather daily feasted as a guest, than safely kept as a traitor, and was suffered most wilfully to escape upon the very day' that he should have come up for trial. The Bishop discovered that until recently the keeper of the gaol had been a certain Anthony Uvedale, a recusant, whose family for generations past had held the

[1] Hyland, *A Century of Persecution*, Kegan Paul, 1920, pp. 340-5.

manor of Woodcote, near Bramdean, from the Crown, on the service of the keeping of the gaol. Before he died, this Uvedale, 'fearing the danger of the law, and loath that the prisoners for recusancy should come into any man's keeping but at his own appointment, conveyed the inheritance of the gaol with the aforesaid manor of Woodcote unto Anthony Brewning, his daughter's son, a child of seven years, whose father and mother were both recusants', and this, claimed Bishop Bilson, was the true reason why no man was allowed to have the custody of the gaol, except as would show favour to recusants. In conclusion, the Bishop admitted that the maker and executor of the conveyance of inheritance were actually two of his own officers, and he suggested to Cecil that since the child, Anthony Brewning, was a ward, the manor of Woodcote and the custody of the gaol should revert to the Crown until the child came of age. But Cecil apparently took no action although the Bishop wrote to him again in twelve months' time.

There was a long and somewhat tedious inquiry into the escape of the priest, Kenyon, which revealed an almost unbelievable slackness in dealing with the recusant prisoners at Winchester, a state of affairs which is all the more remarkable in view of the increasing rigour of the law in these matters during the later years of Elizabeth's reign.[1] It may be that the bishops who preceded Bilson, two of whom held the see for very short terms, were fully occupied with other matters in what was in those days a very large diocese. Of these activities in connection with episcopal government, concerning which there is plenty of material, some account has already been given, and it is now necessary to give some attention to parochial affairs, though the surviving records of these are not as numerous as one could wish. Of the many small parishes of the City few registers are now available for the period under review. There are those of St. Swithun upon Kingsgate and those of St. Mary Kalender and St. Peter (Colebrook Street), both of which were united with St.

[1] Idem, pp. 340–5.

Maurice. These contain nothing more than entries of baptisms, marriages and burials. But in connection with two of the parish churches in the Soke, namely, St. Peter's (Chesil) and St. John's, there are churchwardens' accounts covering the whole of the latter half of the sixteenth century.

From the accounts of St. Peter's (Chesil) which are rather fragmentary, one learns that in 1573 the utensils belonging to that church comprised 'a communion cupp of silver, a diaper tabel clothe, a cope of silke, ii surplesses, ii service bookes, a cusshyon of velfet, ii silke clothes, a pall of silke, and a silke clothe that hangeth over the altar'. In the four previous years, to carry out the orders of the archbishop, expenditure had been incurred in purchasing 'A nomelly (homily) boke—x^d·; A comynyon boke—vi^d·; A boke for the mynstracion of the Sacrament—iiii^d·; A new Catachissime boke—iii^d·; The Commandments—xi^d·. The churchwardens put on record the payments made for the elements for the Holy Sacrament on the three great festivals of the Catholic Church as follows: Christmas, wine—xii^d·, bread—ii^d·; Easter, wine—xxi^d·, bread—iiii^d·; Whitsuntide, wine—xxi^d·, bread—iiii^d·.' They add a note that the wine was 'malmsie' at two shillings a gallon. The next item of interest concerns John Tempell, a hellier or tiler, who 'the fyrst daye of Julye, 1576, draged the holiwater pott out of the church porche without the consent of the churchwardens'. In 1584 they 'payd for a clothe for the Comunyon tabel, containing iiii elles and a halfe, x^s· 1$\frac{3}{4}$^{d}·, and for makyng thereof, vi^d·', and in 1593 they make an entry, 'to our knowledge wee have no recusants in oure parishe—putting up the bill as to this, iiiid'.

The accounts of St. John's, the neighbouring parish of St. Peter's, are more complete and there is a copy of a continuous series of them between the years 1549 and 1596. The receipts and expenses tell of the changing religious atmosphere in later Tudor times. In 1559, shortly after Elizabeth's accession, 2s. 4d. was paid 'for pullin down the Alters'. But before this, in the Protestant days of Edward VI, who is referred to as 'in earth the supreme head', the church brasses were sold and so were 'a guilded image, iiii peices of alebast, a puter candlestick of 18lbs. weight, and a 100 weight and ½ a 100 weight of parchment books', all for £2 19s. 8d. A little later the church of St. John suffered a heavy loss through the fall in the value of the old silver coinage. There was, in January 1551, £29 10s. 0d. in silver shillings in the church box, and the churchwardens unfortunately allowed it to lie there instead of converting it into gold coin, with the result that it lost half its value. A note, added later, states that there was never since that time so much money in the church box, hinting possibly that the parish in general relieved itself of its base metal at the church's expense. In earlier days, when Mary came to the throne, there began the revival of Roman Catholic usages and money was again laid out on the purchase of books, vestments, a holy water stoup, a holy bread box, candlesticks, a sepulchre cloth and 'paskell and funt tapors'.

After paying for the pulling down of the altars in 1559, the churchwardens were called upon to buy 'a paper of the Ten commandments', and some time afterwards 'a frame for the Comunion table and bookes for the churche'. In 1566 there was an outlay of 13s. 4d. for a Bible, perhaps the same one which twenty years later cost 6s. for binding; the next year there was 'xii^d· for an Omelie Book and vi^d· for a Comunion Book; for making a Bill of Answers to the Articuals, ii^s·, for delivering the same to the Reigester, iiii^d·; and for the Commandments, xii^d·; for ix ells of Holland cloth, xiii^s· vi^d·, for making the surplis, ii^s· vi^d·.' Later, in 1579, the churchwardens had to appear before the commissioners, consisting mainly of clergy, who were appointed to supervise the establishment of the religious settlement in all the cities and towns throughout the realm. They summoned before them the churchwardens and swore them to present all persons who would not conform, by writing the names of all such recusants in a book and seeing that they appeared at the next Quarter Sessions of the peace.

Among other payments were 'xii^d· for a Reigester Book, iiii^d· for reigestering the Burials, Weddins and Christings;

i½ᵈ· for a ½ lb. of candells; xxˢ· for x ells of holland for a surplis and xviᵈ· for making; xxˢ· for church rails; iiˢ· for a table cloth; iiiiˢ· for a nue beere and mending the old one'. In 1569 one reads of an expenditure of 'xᵈ· at the visitation and viᵈ· for charges of the side men, being the first charged at a visitation to the parish, and iiiiˢ· for a Dinner for the Church-wardens and Side men'. It would seem that the Sacrament was administered four times a year at St. John's, for there is an entry, dated 1586,—'xvˢ· iᵈ· for wine and bread for the Communion at Easter, Witsontide, Alhalowtide and Christmas'. The inventory of church goods for 1596 records 'ii table cloths, ii towels, ii quishlings, i carpet, ii palls, ii silk Alter cloths'. As late as 1595, 'Kingale' or 'Church ale' money was received into the church funds; in one year there is an entry—'Received at the Kingale and drinking afore and after and for wheat and malt sold, iiˡⁱ xviiˢ· iᵈ··.'

Kingale was the Whitsuntide festival when ale or money was contributed by the parishioners, and on a given date the churchwardens, having bought more ale with the subscriptions, sold the lot for the benefit of the church funds. The practice had developed into an occasion of unashamed carousing and Bishop Cooper in 1585 had informed his clergy that 'whereas a heathenish and ungodly custom hath bene used before time in many partes of this lande about this season of the yeare to have Church Ales, May games, morish dances, and other vaine pastimes upon the Sabath Dayes, and other dayes appointed for common prayer, which they have pretended to be for the relief of theire Churches, but indede hath bene only a meanes to feed the mindes of the people and specially of the youth with vaine sight which is a strange perswasion among Christians, that they cannot by any other means of contribution repaire theire churches but must first do sacrifice to the Devil with Drunkenes and Dancing and other ungodly wantonnes. These are therefore to charge all Ministers and Churchwardens and other like Officers that they suffer not any such Church Ales, Morish dances or Riflings within theire parishes'.

In addition, there are many entries over a period of more than fifty years dealing with the church clock and the church bells. The first clock at St. John's was provided about 1560 by public subscription. In that year 4s. was paid to set the clock going on the 'Great Bell', and in the previous year £9 2s. 1d. was collected 'towardes makeing the clock and chimes'. It was agreed that Edward Churcher should have 4s. yearly paid to him out of the church box, in quarterly payments, for keeping the clock and dressing the bells and doing other necessary duties about the church. Large amounts were from time to time spent on the bells; in 1575 after £5 10s. 0d. had been 'gathered for the bells', there was paid out £7 for the 'Nue casting of the Great Bell', and over £4 for 'expenses attending casting the first bell'. A year or two later nearly £10 was spent on 'expenses attending casting the forth bell', while £2 was received out of the parishes of St. John and St. Peter (Chesil) towards the bells, and a further 22s. in money and corn 'out of the country', together with £2 15s. 0d. from 'the sale of old mettle'. In 1596 there is a list of 'subscribers for keeping the Clock and Chimes by the Year' which includes twenty-five names. The amounts vary from fourpence to two shillings and reach a total of £1 3s. 1d. In the same year £2 15s. 9d. was collected and paid to Gilbert Hill to keep the clock in order and ring the eight and four o'clock bell, which was presumably the curfew bell. On many occasions small sums were paid out to the bellringers to enable them to quench their thirst after their strenuous task; one such entry in 1591 reads—'iiis· for Drink, ringing for the Queen'. Later on in these churchwardens' accounts, under the date 1605, there is an amusing and somewhat ambiguous entry which runs thus: 'paid iiis· to the Ringers at the Triomphe when the Parlement House should have been blown up'.

But two years before the bells of St. John's rang out to celebrate the timely discovery of Guy Fawkes and his fellow-conspirators, Queen Elizabeth had died, leaving to her successors the task of solving the ecclesiastical difficulties which, in spite of her efforts, had made themselves more and more distinctly felt as her reign progressed. Of the religious strife which had prevailed throughout the greater part of the sixteenth century, Winchester, chiefly through the activities of her bishops, had seen a good deal, and though the majority of the citizens were content to accept Elizabeth's ecclesiastical system, there were undoubtedly a few who would not allow their convictions to be curbed by motives of political expediency.

CHAPTER XIV

Conclusion

In the foregoing chapters an attempt has been made to give the reader various glimpses of the scene prevailing in Winchester during the latter half of the sixteenth century. This has been done by viewing the general situation analytically and from several angles and yet, at the same time, not losing sight of the City as a living unit liable to be influenced by winds of change from many directions. There now arises the further task of summarizing all that it has been possible to reveal. Consideration must be given to the extent to which conditions in Winchester conformed to the general pattern throughout the country and, by comparison with similar towns and cities, attention must be paid to the features which made this ancient cathedral city somewhat different in its outlook and development.

When Elizabeth I came to the throne Winchester was already a very old town, the site having been in continuous occupation for at least fifteen hundred years. In Norman and early medieval times it must have had, as the acreage and the street plan within its walls indicate, a population approaching 8,000, and this number had now, for reasons previously stated, dwindled to less than half that total. It was a town which was decaying in some ways and was apparently not sharing in the increased prosperity brought about by Elizabeth's careful government. London, with a population nearing 300,000, was comparatively more outstanding than it is today; the next three cities, York, Norwich and Bristol, all of which had previously been rivalled by Winchester, had slightly more or less than 20,000, while Southampton, which had lost its Italian trade and complained that it suffered as a port from competition from London, was even in worse plight than Winchester.[1] Lincoln, like Winchester, a cathedral city and county town in the midst of a rural area, had experienced a similar decline in population over the same period. The number of families there, however, was never more than three-quarters of the number in Winchester.[2] A similar story could be told of the other old cathedral cities which had no staple or flourishing industry to sustain them. But in other parts of the country the outlook was more promising. Whereas the once important woollen trade had almost disappeared in Winchester, the small woollen towns of Devonshire were going ahead, and the west country as a whole was prosperous with its chief city, Exeter, now surpassing Winchester. Similarly the West Riding towns, later to become famous centres of the clothing trade, were emerging from their lowly status, and the small Midland towns were showing signs of increasing activity and development.

The Elizabethan period has been regarded as a time of tremendous and varied activity, when the national spirit rose to a very high point and when the earlier medieval urban society was disappearing before the advance of fresh ideas concerning industrial and commercial organization. It has been considered a transition period. Though this may be true of the nation as a whole, and though some parts of the country may supply striking evidence to support this view, the records of Winchester do not seem to indicate that this city was keeping in step with any general advance. For most of its inhabitants the city walls or the suburbs were the limits of their world, those who came from beyond these limits were foreigners, and there is very little to show that important national events, such as, for example, the defeat of the Spanish Armada, made any great impact on the lives of

[1] A. L. Rowse, *The England of Elizabeth.*
[2] J. W. F. Hill, *Tudor and Stewart Lincoln.*

the citizens. The minutes of the meetings of the Mayor and his brethren do suggest, however, that the ruling oligarchy had lost none of its vigour and had, in fact, assumed a greater sense of responsibility, particularly in handling the increased revenue derived from former monastic and other properties, and in dealing with the increasing poverty and unemployment. It is unfortunate that there has not survived any other writing or commentary on municipal affairs which can be compared with the valuable chronicles of John Hooker, the Elizabethan town-clerk and historian of Exeter.[1]

Winchester was still a close-knit and self-contained community; it was semi-autonomous with its own corporate life and its own special interests. The liberties which it enjoyed had been obtained by royal charter and its powers were exercised by the grace of the Queen. Probably the most important feature of its history at this time was the continuity of medieval custom which could be seen in the routine of administration, particularly in connection with the election of its officers, the maintenance of public order and morals, sanitation, water supply and paving, the controlling of the price, sale and quality of food, and the assessment of rates and the collection of taxes. The freemen of the City, from whom the chief officers were chosen, were conservative in outlook and zealous upholders of tradition. The citizens bought and sold and went about their affairs in much the same way as their ancestors had done, for neither society nor institutions had altered to any great degree. The one exception was, of course, the alteration in the religious establishment, but even this does not seem to have been of more than minor importance to the average citizen who adapted himself to the changed conditions without undue friction. As for the royal decrees affecting trade and other matters, the magistrates, remembering the City's dependence on royal favour, put them into effect with the same zeal with which they administered the municipal ordinances.

This period was not one of marked change or development

[1] W. T. MacCaffrey, *Exeter—the growth of an English county town.*

as far as Winchester was concerned. The City was still the ecclesiastical centre of a very large diocese as well as the assize town for a considerable portion of central southern England. It had its own Quarter Sessions together with the very convenient Pie Powder court. Moreover it was centrally placed within the county of Southampton (Hampshire) of which it was the recognized county town and the largest market. These were factors of which Winchester was always ready to take advantage and, therefore, this was rather a time when efforts were being made to preserve the City's dignity and prestige and to prevent any further decline in wealth, trade or population. The granting of the royal charter of 1587, which embodied all those privileges gained in the past five hundred years, had undoubtedly renewed the burgesses' confidence, so that placing its reliance in its astute Recorder, Thomas Fleming (later Lord Chief Justice), in its famous High Steward, Sir Francis Walsingham, and in its wealthy patron, the Marquis of Winchester, the City was hoping to overcome its immediate difficulties and find some way of acquiring greater prosperity and importance.

Index

Index

Index

Brethren (bretherne), Mayor's, 13, 37, 43, 45, 60, 62, 66, 71, 76, 85, 96, 102, 103, 104, 105, 107, 108, 109, 110, 111, 112, 116, 120, 121, 123, 135, 138, 157, 168, 182, 186, 187, 189, 190, 194, 197, 206, 213, 214, 216, 217, 221, 222, 223, 241, 250

brewers, 184, 185, 193
  incorporation of, 185-8
  wages of, 202, 203
brewing, 173, 193
Brewning, Anthony, 242
Brexstone, Cuthbert, 108
  Richard, 110
  Stephen, 110
  William, 41, 44, 107, 108, 174, 178
bricklayer, 131, 201
Brinstan, Saint, 25
Bristol, 30, 93, 119, 248
broadcloth, 54, 126, 130
Brode, Thomas, 41
Brooker, John, 160, 161
brooks, 24, 151, 175, 195, 204, 205, 209, 212
Brothers, Stephen, 111
Browne, George, 41, 81
  Hewe, 42
  John, 168
  Steven, 41, 145, 158, 160
Browninge, Richard, 42
Bryan, Thomas, 107
Bub's Cross, 103
Buckholt, 176
Buckhurst, Lord (see Sackville)
Budde, William, 71, 77, 186
bulks, 60, 195
Bull, Richard, mayor, 36, 37
bull-baiting, 62, 216
burel, cloth, 199
Burghley, Lord, 143, 223
Burgh-mote, 12, 13, 17, 34-46, 53, 64, 66, 70, 73, 74, 78, 79, 88, 89, 92, 95, 144, 154, 155, 167, 182, 183, 186, 187, 188, 189, 191, 192, 196, 204, 209, 212, 220, 221, 224, 233
burglary at Guildhall, 71, 113-16
Burte, Lewin, alien, 141

Burton, Dionese, 109
  Richard, 41, 44, 45, 171, 172, 235
  Thomas, 163
  William, 28, 227
bushel, Winchester, 197
  imperial, 197
butchers, 75, 79, 184, 195, 198, 206, 216; wages of, 202
butter, 79, 216
buttery, master of, 120
butts, 130, 222
Bye, John, 87
Byketon, John de, 24
Byrde (Burd, Bird), Anthony, 22, 41, 64, 81, 214
  (Birde), Richard, 41, 43, 79, 95, 97, 139, 160, 235
  Thomas, 40

Cage, city, 216
cakes, 130
Cambridge, town, 19, 210
  university, 148, 210
candles, 196
Canterbury, Archbishop, 143, 231
  city, 212
Caplin, John, 95, 96, 98, 101
  Steven, 96
  William, 169
capon, 61, 198
capper, wages of, 202
carpenters, 184, 201
carrion (carreyne), dead, 43, 206
carvers, wages of, 201
Castle (Winchester), 13, 15, 27, 126, 219, 221-4, 241
  constableship, 221
  ditches, 27, 127, 221, 222, 223
  great hall, 222, 223
  green, 130, 146, 221, 223
Cathedral (St. Swithun's Priory), 19, 21, 24, 27, 30, 54, 65, 71, 106, 107, 219, 230, 232, 235, 240
  close, 26, 151
Catherine of Aragon, 230
Catholics, Roman, 139, 235, 236, 238, 240
cattle, 216

Index

Index

Index

harquebus, 225, 226
Harvie, Richard, 35, 174
Haselbie, Andrew, 173
hatmaker, wages, 202
Hawkehaye, Domus Havoc, 28
Haywood, Henry, 178
Health, 13, 112, 204–18
'Heaven', 23
'Hell', 22
hellyer (helier), (tiler), 184, 201, 243
Heneage, Sir Thomas, High Steward, 93
Henry I, King, 197
Henry II, King, 11, 48, 183
Henry III, King, 94, 156
Henry IV, King, 35
Henry V, King, 87
Henry VI, King, 31, 81, 154, 234
Henry VII, King, 197, 198, 211
Henry VIII, King, 25, 35, 49, 57, 63, 80, 98, 136, 146, 200, 204, 230, 234
Herber, see Arbour
Herbert, J. A., City of Winchester, Calendar of Charters, 48
Hermit's Tower, 20, 28
Heycroft, Christopher, 115
Hibbard, John, 41
hides, 54, 195
    duty on, 134
Higgins, Richard, 122
High School, 26
High Steward, 49, 51, 92–4, 97, 99, 117, 251
Highways, see Streets
Hill, Gilbert, 246
    J. W. F., Tudor and Stewart Lincoln, 16, 249
Hilson, widow, 110
Hobbes, John, 163
Hodson, Robert, 40, 100, 235
    Thomas, 41, 44, 145
    William, 64, 68, 70, 227
hogs, see pigs
hog sty, see pig sty
Holmede, John, 114
Hooker, John, 250
horn, great, 224

Horne, Robert, Bishop of Winchester, 96, 114, 232, 233, 234, 236, 237
horses, 216
hosiers, see tailors; wages, 202
Hospital (or House), Christ's (Peter Symonds'), 22, 121, 122, 124, 139
    St. John's, 20, 22, 25, 40, 45, 54, 57, 59, 61, 67, 80, 214, 217
    St. Cross, 234
Howard, Lord, Admiral, 228
Howston, Leonard, 42
Hue and cry, 103
Humber, Richard, 111
Huntingdon, Earl of, 99
Hursley, Vicar of, 105
Hyde, 19, 28
Hyde Abbey, see Abbey
Hyland, A Century of Persecution, 241, 242

Impositions, 134
Incorporations of craftsmen and traders, 13, 54, 185–92
Influenza, see plague
Ingleby manor, 122
Inkpenn, Roger, 26
Inn, 85, 187, 196, 198, 215
    Bell, 22, 197
    Chequer, 21
    Eagle (hotel), 29
    George, 20, 126, 127, 128
    Hart, 23
    King's Head, 22, 128
    New, 20
    Star, 22
    Swan, 29, 108
    Tabard, 21
    White Horse, 20, 227
Innkeepers, 63, 79, 186, 187, 193, 194, 215
'ipocrise' (hippocras), 130
Ipswich, High Stewardship, 93
isett, 39
Itchen Abbas, 177

Jackson, Robert, 108
James I, King, 70, 89, 91

Index

Index

Index

Pole, Cardinal, 231
poll-tax return (1377), 30
pond, town, 129, 216, 220
pontage, 54
Poor, relief of, 111, 112, 144, 146–52, 217
Pope, 230
Population, Winchester, 16, 29–33, 248
 Bristol, 30
 London, 30
 Southampton, 30
 York, 30
Porke, Francis, 120
Portsmouth, 48, 147, 180, 211, 224, 227, 228, 229
post-horses, 103
Potinger, John, 16, 41, 81, 90, 139, 175
Potter, Thomas, 177
poultry, 198
pound, see pinfold
Powlet, Christian, 141
Pratte, John, 160
Pratts, Agnes, 109
Prebendary, 230, 233, 237
presentments, 82, 172–5
Priory, St. Swithun's, see Cathedral
prists (priests), 185
 seminary, 72, 105, 238, 240
Proceedings of the Corporation, A, 67, 102, 218, B, 124, 218
proclamation, royal, 72, 104, 112, 197, 239
Protestants, 234, 237
Prothero, G. W., Statutes and Constitutional Documents, 136, 139
Provost, 56, 73
Pulley, Thomas, 186
pump, common town, 23, 120, 127, 209
Puritanism, 237
Puritans, 232, 236, 240

Quarelles, 44
quietus est, 76

Rabbits, 178, 179

rack (tenter), 199
Raleigh, Sir Walter, 218
rate, poor, see relief of poor
Recorder, 37, 52, 60, 67, 71, 72, 86–9, 90, 92, 95, 96, 98, 102, 108, 111, 112, 121, 135, 141, 153, 179, 218, 239, 251
 fee of, 88, 131
 London, 89
 see Fleming, Thomas
recusants, 72, 105, 112, 232, 234, 238, 240, 241, 242, 243, 244
Redhatt, 23
Reding, citizen, 107
Reform Act (1867), 95
registrar, bishop's, 70
 for horses, hay, leather, etc., 92
regrating, 153, 198
Religion, 229–47
Religious houses, 26, 30, 33, 80, 126
 dissolution of, 234
rent, fee farm, 17, 33, 76
 ground, 17–29, 79
 house, 117, 125–9, 130, 152, 217
replication, day of, 170
Richmond corner, 27
Richmond, court at, 143
rippier, wages, 202
River (Itchen), 15, 145, 175, 199, 204, 206
Roberts, Richard, 163
Rokesbury, Nicholas, 173
Rolls, account, chamberlains', 12, 33, 36, 60, 67, 117, 124–32, 154, 220, 226, 235
 court, 12, 155, 157, 160, 161, 162, 169, 171
 subsidy, 12, 140
 tarrage, 12, 16–33
 taxation, 137
Roman, times, 15
 ground level, 219
Romsey, 176
Rose Lion, 181
Rouen, 211
Rowles, Thomas, 176
Rowse, A. L., The England of Elizabeth, 249

263

Index

Index

Index

Thomas, J. H., *Town Government in XVIth century*, 16, 210
Thorpe, Launcelot, 23, 91, 108
  Thomas, 41, 84, 125, 225
Throgmorton, Job, 240
Tichborne, village, 119
  Sir Benjamin, 218
tin, duty on, 134
tinkers, 148
tipler (typler), 173, 193, 194
Tipper, John, 174
Tisted, 228; manor, 119
Titchfield, 176, 180
Titow, J. Z., *Economic History Review, XIV.2.1961*, 16
Tiverton, 110
tolls, 54, 133, 183
Tower, of London, 230, 231
Town Clerk, 16, 21, 24, 53, 77, 81, 89–91, 103, 114, 115, 116, 118, 123, 124, 131, 139, 141, 188, 190, 193
town pump, *see* pump
Trade, 182–203
Treasurer, Lord, 139, 223, 224
trespass, 160–7, 170, 177
trespass on the case, 160
Trinity Marsh (West Ham), 122
trumpeters, Queens', 120
Trussell, John, 25, 35; 'Origin of Cities', 218
Trustle, Christian, 175
Tucker, Dionese, 180
  Thomas, 110
tucker, wages, 202
turner's ware, 216
Twenty-four, 37, 38, 42, 44, 45, 52, 53, 58, 61, 65, 66, 67, 69, 73, 77, 86, 87, 88, 91, 102, 125, 146, 188, 214, 233
Twyford, 127, 128, 130
Twyne, John, 156
Tyrone's rebellion, 93, 102
tything, 103

Ulnage of cloth, 33, 117, 126, 130
uniform, *see* livery

Usages, ancient, of Winchester, 36, 83, 156
Uvedale, Anthony, 241, 242

Vagrancy, 147–51
Vanderplank, Thomas, 226
Vanderplant, Adam, 141
Valoer, John, 35
velvets, 183
Venables, Richard, 111
venire facias, 170
vessel, *see* City Plate
vestments, 236
Vibert, James, 156, 173, 178
Vincent, Robert, 174
visits, royal, 118–20

Wager his law, 165, 166, 167, 170
wages, of artificers, labourers, etc., 201–3
Walis, William, 41
Waller, William, 227
Wallingford, 48
Wallop, Richard, 88
walls, city, 54, 82, 130, 131, 152, 219, 220, 248, 249
Walsingham, Sir Francis, 49, 51, 92, 93, 97, 99, 119, 131, 143, 251
Ward, Anthony, 110
Warnford, recusant, 105
  village, 119
Warneford, Mary, 174
  Richard, 126
Warr, Lord de la, 129
Warren, Antony, 178
  William, 180
washing place, 130, 131, 175, 206, 209
watch, and ward, 83, 215, 224
Waters, Jane, 109
Waterson, James, 41, 145, 169
weavers (weyvers), 184, 185, 199, 202
  incorporation of, 191–2
weights and measures, 54, 197–8
wells, 209
West, Lady Mary, 139, 174
Westfayling, Herbert, Bishop of Hereford, 241